CHANGING
EDUCATION FOR
DIVERSITY

CHANGING EDUCATION

Series Editors:
Professor Andy Hargreaves, Ontario Institute for Studies in Education
Professor Ivor Goodson, University of Western Ontario

This authoritative series addresses the key issues raised by the unprecedented levels of educational change now facing schools and societies throughout the world.

The different directions of change can seem conflicting and are often contested. Decentralized systems of school self-management are accompanied by centralized systems of curriculum and assessment control. Moves to develop more authentic assessments are paralleled by the tightened imposition of standardized tests. Curriculum integration is being advocated in some places, more specialization and subject departmentalization in other.

These complex and contradictory cross-currents pose real challenges to theoretical and practical interpretation in many fields of education and constitute an important and intriguing agenda for educational change. *Changing Education* brings together leading international scholars who address these vital issues with authority and accessibility in areas where they are noted specialists. The series will commission books from all parts of the world in an attempt to cover the global and interlinked nature of current changes.

Published titles:

David Corson: *Changing Education for Diversity*
Joe L. Kincheloe and Shirley R. Steinberg: *Changing Multiculturalism*
Colin Lankshear: *Changing Literacies*
Louise Stoll and Dean Fink: *Changing our Schools*

Titles in preparation include:

Gill Helsby: *Changing Teachers' Work*
Kenneth Leithwood, Doris Jantzi and Rosanne Steinbach: *Changing Leadership for Changing Times*
Bob Lingard: *Changing Educational Policy*
Carrie Paechter: *Changing School Subjects*
Peter Tomlinson: *Changing Approaches to Learning and Teaching*

CHANGING EDUCATION FOR DIVERSITY

DAVID CORSON

OPEN UNIVERSITY PRESS
Buckingham · Philadelphia

Open University Press
Celtic Court
22 Ballmoor
Buckingham
MK18 1XW

and

1900 Frost Road, Suite 101
Bristol, PA 19007, USA

First Published 1998

A catalogue record of this book is available from the British Library

ISBN   0 335 19588 1 (hb)   0 335 19587 3 (pb)

Library of Congress Cataloging-in-Publication Data
Corson, David.
    Changing education for diversity / David Corson.
      p.   cm. — (Changing education)
    Includes bibliographical references (p.) and index.
    ISBN 0-335-19588-1 (hb). — ISBN 0-335-19587-3 (pb)
    1. Educational equalization—Cross-cultural studies.
  2. Minorities—Education—Cross-cultural studies.   3. Critical
  pedagogy—Cross-cultural studies.   4. Multicultural education—Cross
  -cultural studies.   I. Title.   II. Series.
  LC213.C67   1998
  370.11′5—dc21   97-34976
                                                                          CIP

Typeset by Type Study, Scarborough
Printed in Great Britain by Biddles Ltd, Guildford and King's Lynn

For Patricia Corson

CONTENTS

SERIES EDITORS' PREFACE

Around the world, schools, and the societies of which they are a part, are confronting the most profound changes, the like of which have not been seen since the last great global movement of economic and educational restructuring more than a century ago. The fundamental forms of public education that were designed for an age of heavy manufacturing and mechanical industry are under challenge and fading fast as we move into a world of high technology, flexible workforces, more diverse school populations, downsized administrations and declining resources.

What is to follow is uncertain and unclear. The different directions of change can seem conflicting and are often contested. Decentralized systems of school self-management are accompanied by centralized systems of curriculum and assessment control. Moves to develop more authentic assessments are paralleled by the tightened imposition of standardized tests. Curriculum integration is being advocated in some places; more specialization and subject departmentalization in others.

These complex and contradictory cross-currents pose real challenges to theoretical and practical interpretation in many fields of education, and constitute an important and intriguing agenda for educational change and for this series, which is intended to meet a deep-seated need among researchers and practitioners. International, social and technological changes require a profound and rapid response from the educational community. By establishing and interpreting the nature and scope of educational change, *Changing Education for Diversity* will make a significant contribution to meeting this challenge.

David Corson's work has spanned many years and many cultures in a career dedicated to understanding, addressing and advancing issues of cultural and linguistic diversity within schools and society. This book crystallizes his work in a conceptually powerful, yet readable and accessible way so that educators everywhere will be able to see how they deal with issues of diversity, with fresh eyes.

Running through David Corson's illuminating text are ideas that he has appropriated and integrated over time to deepen people's understanding of diversity questions: the importance of language and discourse in making people feel included in or excluded from our schools and societies; the fundamental idea of emancipation as something that extends far beyond tolerance or inclusion as a way of enabling formerly oppressed or marginalized cultures to take and express power in society; the sense of social justice that the author makes central to all his explanations of diversity and of schooling itself; and, most recently, the recognition that society is moving into a special historical moment, one we call postmodernity, where powerful and contradictory forces are giving greater prominence to diversity issues in some ways, but marginalizing them even more strongly in others.

Changing Education for Diversity, then, is a book of great conceptual power that educates its readers about diversity issues; exemplifies these issues in rich case studies of the education of aboriginal peoples, immigrant girls, minority language groups and the urban poor; and uses a framework of key ideas that will lead new and experienced teachers and administrators to think much more deeply and critically about what dealing with diversity effectively and in socially just ways really entails. Great cultural and linguistic diversity will be more and more the cultural norm in the highly mobile, postmodern world in which we now live. David Corson's book offers a critical yet practical approach to help people engage justly and effectively with this increasingly inescapable reality.

PREFACE AND ACKNOWLEDGEMENTS

Teachers and schools everywhere in the English-speaking world are asked to give fairer treatment to diverse students and their communities. In response to these demands, practising teachers and school administrators are often at a loss in knowing how to do this, because their training has done little to prepare them for coping with student diversity. Teacher educators are also anxious to provide more on this topic for student teachers, but a single book addressing as many of the current issues as possible has not appeared. This book is written with pre-service and experienced teachers in mind. It can be used in the final year of teacher preparation, in postgraduate courses, and in teacher professional development and in-service programmes.

The questions the book addresses are simple ones: how can schools become more welcoming places for students from diverse backgrounds? How can they respond to student diversity and still provide high quality education for all? What is the range of issues that teachers and administrators need to think about in providing for students from diverse backgrounds?

While these questions are simple, the answers to them are not easy, and this book-length treatment only begins to provide those answers. Every teaching context is a different one for shaping responses to the needs of students who come from diverse backgrounds. Every child is different, even those whose cultural backgrounds might wrongly suggest that they have a uniformity of outlook, or a need for uniform treatment in education. Accordingly this book provides examples of reforms in education for diversity for teachers and administrators to learn from, not to copy.

Outline of this book's contents

Chapter 1 introduces some key theoretical and applied ideas that underpin the other chapters. These include the idea of postmodernity, which offers a way of understanding the present condition of society in English-speaking countries; the idea of social justice that is necessary for giving fair treatment to people from diverse backgrounds living within the postmodern condition; the idea of critical realism, which provides a conception of discovery for understanding and interpreting the human condition; and the idea of 'critical policy making' which offers schools a way to begin the process of reforming education for diversity. In this first chapter, all these ideas are worked into a discussion that links the use of discourse with the exercise of power at every point.

Chapter 2 describes a school that combined the work of teachers, administrators, parents and the local community over a long period, and did so successfully to further the interests of various communities. That school's success in reforming itself shows how far schools can really go in changing themselves to meet diversity. It seems a good example of critical policy making at work, so I use it to illustrate the idea of critical policy making introduced in Chapter 1. It also seems a good example of 'community-based education' at work. This chapter introduces that concept too and couples it with a discusson of Freire's educational thought. Also outlined is a transformational model of school reform that seems relevant to schooling for diversity of all kinds.

Chapter 3's discussion of aboriginal education is highly relevant even to countries that have no aboriginal populations and to schools that have no aboriginal students. This chapter presents reforms in the education of the Amerindian, First Nations, and Inuit peoples of North America, the Polynesian peoples of the Pacific, the Aboriginal peoples of Australia, and the Sámi of Scandinavia and Russia. These many sites for changes in aboriginal education give insights into all the areas of education for diversity that are being reformed or could be reformed. In fact, if all the many kinds of education for diversity could be placed on a continuum, ranging from those most deserving of radical reform through to those needing only minor changes, aboriginal education would sit at the radical extreme end of the continuum. *It provides the model from which reforms to all other types of education for diversity can be argued.*

Chapter 4 collates the little that we know at present about reforming the education of immigrant girls. Although serious and multiple disadvantages do affect girls from different cultures, this double effect receives only spasmodic attention in the educational literature. The chapter opens with a survey of broad differences in school achievement between girls and boys, as revealed in recent research in English-speaking countries. It links this discussion with the different rewards that girls and boys tend to get from schools, which link in turn to unequal discursive and power arrangements in schools that affect immigrant girls unfairly. The chapter then collates the research into the special problems that first generation immigrant girls can have. This research comes from several high immigrant countries. I argue from that evidence towards more worthwhile policies and fairer school practices.

Chapter 5 argues for a very different accommodation to the needs of inner city students. It begins with important equity factors, like race, class, culture, and gender, that affect different groups differently, especially in societies where ideas like 'a level playing field' and 'no special interest groups' are part of the rhetoric that sustains inequalities. The chapter's four major sections then follow. The first two raise many of the central issues for teachers in urban schools. They cover matters of bias and discrimination, and the importance of arranging schools so that all children receive guaranteed access to academic meaning systems. The last two sections suggest reforms to policy and practice that link equity issues with high quality education. These sections offer ways to value sociocultural differences and to give all students entry to the school's culture of literacy.

Chapter 6's first section looks at the education of immigrant and refugee language-minority children up to middle childhood. It concentrates on bilingual education, because most forms of bilingual education are aimed at younger children. The second section concentrates on ESL (English as a second language) education because this is the more common provision for immigrant children at secondary or high school levels. The third section looks at the education of linguistic minorities, like the Gaelic peoples of Britain, the rapidly growing Hispanic population of the United States, and the francophones of Canada. These minorities live permanently inside the borders of English-speaking countries, but they identify with cultures and languages that are different from the majority of the population. All these sections stress the point that 'talking about text' is the key practical activity of schooling. In contrast, the chapter ends with a final section on the education of Deaf signing students, a language minority who 'talk about text' in another way.

Chapter 7 argues for two further things that we need to have to make the educational world safe for diverse groups. The first is a regular supply of well trained and widely educated young teachers, who can challenge, change, and reform schools as a direct result of the high quality curriculum provided in their teacher education. The second is a critically informed knowledge base for teachers to work from: the sort of knowledge that beginning and experienced teachers can draw upon and apply, to bring about the reform of education for diversity. In brief, this final chapter discusses ways of providing new teachers with a good supply of critical knowledge about their professional work and it suggests the things those teachers might do to make better use of it.

Special features of the book

In writing this book, I have worked to create a clear, jargon-free writing style that invites careful reading. To help me in this, I have asked a number of students and colleagues to read the manuscript and to comment on its accessibility for readers. While the ideas that the book advances are far from easy, it is difficult to present them more accessibly than I have while still retaining their force and sense. All the ideas are well within the range of the ideas that present-day teachers can assimilate and relate to their work. I have also kept theoretical ideas to a minimum and linked them with practical issues in every case. In addition, the book makes only minimal use of the rather controversial terms 'minority' or 'minorities' except in two types of context. First, when citing the ideas of other writers who have used these words in their work, I follow their lead. Second, I follow the established practice of using 'language minority' or 'language minorities' to refer to groups who use languages other than the majority language used in a language community.

The book is filled with examples of reforms that students of education everywhere can learn from. It would be quite wrong to say that these examples are limited in their relevance to the countries and contexts that produced them. This is because education for diversity, regardless of where it is practised in the English-speaking world, faces most of the same broad problems and many of the same structural constraints. Those who are active in reforming the new international world of education know only too well that they have much to learn from the experiences of other countries. I believe that the examples offered in this book can be drawn upon to give powerful educational insights, especially if they are read with the good-will of an open mind, and then applied with originality, ingenuity, and imagination to new educational settings.

The reader will find extensive referencing to the book's up-to-date, international, and cross-cultural bibliography. In this book, references can appear in one of two places: in the main text, or in the endnotes. I have combined these two styles of notes and references to help with its readability. On the one hand, the book uses ordinary notes that are assembled numerically by chapters at the end of the book. These have three purposes: first, to cross-reference important points within the book, showing page numbers where that is useful; second, to provide extra information in certain places where the inclusion of that information in the regular chapters might be distracting for readers; and third, to provide multiple bibliographical references, using the Harvard system, when those multiple references might be distracting for readers if they were left in the text. On the other hand, I have also used the Harvard referencing system in the actual text of chapters to refer to single authors or works, especially where that information seemed necessary for quick access to other points, or to the Reference section itself.

Finally the 'discussion starter' questions at the end of each chapter will be useful for students of education who are reviewing their work after reading parts of the book. They will also be useful to university or college teachers using the book as a text. These questions highlight key points and also aim to stimulate informed discussion among pre-service and experienced teachers.

Acknowledgements

My thanks for their help in various ways with the development of this book: to graduate assistants Mary Harris, Tiu Strauss, and Hiroko Yokota; to research officers, Michelle Goldberg and Sylvie Lemay; to students and colleagues, who read and commented on the manuscript, Nina Bascia, Carol Beynon, Mark Fettes, Jim Ryan, and Sonia James-Wilson; to support and technology staff who kept me on track, Marilyn Borg, Tony Gallina, Patrick Hopewell, Martin Loeffler, and Rita O'Brien; and to Tim Corson for producing the final manuscript and the index.

one

REFORMING EDUCATION FOR DIVERSITY: LEAVENING POWER WITH SOCIAL JUSTICE

Education for diversity refers to any formal teaching and learning opportunities provided for groups of students who differ in some educationally relevant way from the majority of students attending a society's schools. For my purposes in this book, I am narrowing that definition slightly so that it applies only to students who differ on some one or more dimension of ethnicity, class, race, gender or language.[1] The key question in all this, as later discussion reveals, is whether the differences that exist between educationally diverse students and the majority of students in a given setting *are* educationally relevant. If they are relevant, then some different type of educational provision is warranted.

Reforms to education for diversity are now receiving world-wide attention partly because of the great population shifts that occurred over the past two or three generations. These population shifts highlight issues that formerly went unnoticed, even in countries that always had significantly large diverse groups. In some places, these shifts have provoked intolerance and even violence in communities that saw themselves as culturally stable or homogeneous. At the same time, a more welcome result of these great population movements is the recent development of a climate of international opinion advocating the more open and accepting treatment of people of diversity. This acceptance is winning the support of legislation binding on all countries who are signatories to international agreements.[2]

In many places important reforms are beginning: in the education of girls from immigrant cultures; in the education of indigenous cultural groups; in the education of the urban poor; in the education of immigrant and refugee language minorities; in the education of other linguistic minorities; and in the education of the signing Deaf. Using an international and cross-cultural scope, this book surveys these critical changes in education. It presents policies and practices that already work in real schools, and from which the world of education can learn.

To address these topics, I combine two central traditions in social science inquiry: concern for the postmodern condition of the present-day world, and concern for the practical reforms that can come from critical realism. I suggest how these traditions can combine in a fruitful collision of ideas and practices that are emancipatory for diverse groups, but which respond at the same time to the challenges of education within the postmodern condition.

In this opening chapter, I introduce some key theoretical and applied ideas that underpin the rest of the book: the idea of postmodernity as a way of understanding the present condition of society within English-speaking countries; the idea of social justice which seems necessary for giving fair treatment to people from diverse backgrounds now living in the postmodern condition; the idea of critical realism which offers a conception of discovery for understanding and interpreting the human condition; and the idea of critical policy making which provides schools with a way to begin the process of reforming education for diversity. All these ideas are inserted into a discussion that links the use of discourse with the exercise of power at every point.

Diverse voices in the postmodern world

Postmodernity is neither an intellectual movement nor a philosophy. It is a condition of society said to characterize the age that contemporary social institutions are part of. Postmodernity is often portrayed as having two distinct but balancing tendencies: an almost universal trend away from things like centralization, mass production, specialization, and mass consumption, including the standardized school systems that used to be the norm almost everywhere; and an almost universal trend towards the development of flexible technologies that are developed and used in smaller and more diverse units, including a rapid increase in diversity among schools and greater devolution of educational control.[3]

In this new world, many more voices are being raised, including the voices of those who were once dispossessed; these voices are bringing a surprisingly different range of messages to policy makers and practitioners alike. These messages express human values that were once silenced by dominant ideologies and belief systems. Yet, in responding to these new voices now appearing at local levels, powerful forces beyond the local are still ignoring the messages that they raise. This is especially true of education, and it is true of education for diversity in particular. Even the trend towards devolving control to local schools has led to injustices on a grand scale in many countries.[4]

Part of the problem, as I suggest later in this book, is that postmodern education almost everywhere in the English-speaking world is set firmly within capitalist social relations. Seen on so grand a scale, this tight coupling of capitalism with all aspects of social life is a relatively recent development. This is because the pure free-market economic arrangements, that are so essential to capitalism, were limited in their effects as long as capitalism was kept a little separate from government:

> For forty years after the early 1930s the intellectual supporters of pure free-market economics were an isolated minority, apart from business-men whose perspective always makes it difficult to recognize the best interests of their system as a whole, in proportion as it concentrates their minds on the best interests of their particular firm or industry.
>
> (Hobsbawm 1989: 334)

All this has changed in recent decades. Even government itself has been cap-tured in many places by free-market views that are far less restrained than those that formerly applied.[5] Many present-day politicians, and the intellec-tuals who advise them, tend to believe that for governments to succeed the whole world is best viewed as a business and best interpreted in business terms. As a result, citizens living in societies where this ideology is dominant are forced to live their lives within the ideology, whether they want to or not. This is because public policy and the world itself are saturated by the ideology.

In this limited and limiting world-view, the dominant metaphor is that all human beings inhabit a marketplace where the quality of something is decided according to the price it can fetch, rather than according to any intrinsic and real qualities it might have. This trend is having a harmful impact on human social relations themselves, especially on the bonds that exist between people. These bonds are valued more often by the standards of economic transactions than by the more lasting ties of culture or class. In turn, the unfortunate effect of all this is to project a respect for 'sameness' onto the social world, rather than a respect for the actual 'diversity' that the social world contains.

In spite of appearances to the contrary, then, these capitalist social relations are the most assimilationary cultural forces that the world has ever seen. This means that any diversity in provisions that the new diverse voices are winning is being taken away by the pressure towards assimilation that capitalism creates. In addition this paradox occurs because capitalist social relations are also prospering under the new freedoms and the open message systems that are part of the postmodern condition. What does all this mean for education?

On the one hand, in this new world of postmodernity, human diversity is being recognized at last. On the other hand, people's *real* sociocultural identities have little value in the marketplace of that new world. As a consequence, wherever the values and interests of schools are linked tightly into that marketplace, students and teachers from diverse backgrounds find that their interests are still missing from education. Students still feel anonymous and distant from the school's goals. Furthermore, they feel powerless in the face of this anonymity, and the remoteness from the school of their families and communities worsens these feelings of alienation. So rather than a route to freedom and self-fulfilment, the world of the school is still a place of daunting obstacles for people who are different from the majority of students in some way. Fortunately schools in many places are beginning at last to wrestle with these issues.

Teachers and critical realism

In this book, I present critical realism as a form of discovery and action that can help teachers and schools find a way through these much needed changes. The ideas presented here complement the ideas of writers like Hargreaves (1996). He asks policy makers and researchers to pay more attention to the multiple voices raised by teachers and students, and so get a better understanding of why 'one size fits all' reform is unworkable. But expanding on this idea, my further point is that teachers, policy makers, and researchers need to pay much more attention to the multiple voices raised by any of those communities with a stake in the practice and aims of schools. The evidence is growing that the simple participation of teachers and administrators, on its own, in administration is not necessarily helpful when a school tries to address issues to do with education for diversity (Lipman 1997).

Critical realism is a process of discovery that identifies the actual structures that restrict human action.[6] In other words, it tries to identify things that can be changed, or removed, or supported, to help free up human action. Although these structures have no existence separate from the activities that they govern and from people's reports of them, we can still understand the way structures work. We can do this by examining people's reports about things that they value and about things that oppress them. These things can range from the oppressive social practices that disadvantage females and diverse sociocultural groups, to the valued cultural beliefs that promote cohesion and a sense of identity among the members of closely knit communities.

Structures are things that we can reconstruct. Teachers do it all the time when they arrange their classrooms in one way rather than another, to suit their students' needs. School administrators do similar things to meet wider needs. We can change or remove structures or we can strengthen them by the things that we say and do in local settings. In fact, the very hope of emancipating ourselves from oppressive structures depends on this being so. In other words, if structures could not be changed, human emancipation would not be possible. Emancipation, for me, means freeing oneself from oppressive influences. It is certainly something that we can help others to do, or better still arrange conditions in which they can free themselves from unwanted structures. In setting the scene for later discussions about changing education for diversity, this chapter links the positive use of emancipatory power with the pursuit of social justice as a social practice worth pursuing.

Education and its discourses of power

For most everyday human purposes, power is exerted through verbal channels: language is the vehicle for identifying, manipulating and changing power relations between people. In this section, I point to the ways that education and the discourse practices that it authorizes can routinely repress, dominate, and disempower diverse groups whose practices differ from the norms that it establishes. I begin with some of the links between discourse and power, focusing on education which often gives power to its own favoured norms of discourse, and so creates discrimination and injustice for the many who favour other discourses.

Discourse in this book refers to the full range of meaning-filled events and practices that we encounter in life. For me, discourse covers all the sign systems, including those that are not usually regarded as part of natural language itself: 'To be able to think is to be a skilled user of these sign systems, that is, to be capable of managing them correctly' (Harré and Gillett 1994: 49). Foucault's views on the links between power and discourse have become influential: rather than a privilege that an individual person possesses, power is a network of relations constantly in tension and ever present in discursive activity. It is exercised through the production, accumulation, and functioning of various discourses. Discourse here is really the object of human conflict, so that the study of power is best located at the point where the wishes of the powerful are played out in real and effective practices. For Foucault, the development of particular forms of language meets the needs of the powerful and it depends upon a particular exercise of power through discourse practices.[7]

Even concepts that are at the heart of this book, like different 'ethnic groups', 'languages' and 'cultures' are constructed through the use of discourse in social situations. This means that these are only approximate descriptions of the lived realities and identities of people. In other words, people struggle over the way these expressions are used to refer to themselves: they resist their use, they embrace their use, or they modify their use. When we apply these labels to real people in situations where important issues are at stake, we always have to confirm that the people themselves agree that these expressions can be used to refer to them. In other words, for us as individuals, identity is a personal possession that we choose for ourselves, not something that we receive at the hands of others. Nevertheless people do make assumptions about other people's identities all the time, using whatever evidence is available to them.

Cultural background and identity

Although a person's cultural background and language are very personal possessions, there are obvious similarities between people in these areas. Social distance (or closeness) between people is maintained by many things: by aspects of social structure; by the opportunities for interaction that people have; by constraints on behaviour; and by many other sociocultural processes and factors. All these things help change the meaning and the value of a person's presentation of self when he or she moves from context to context. In any context, social structure interacts with people's social behaviour and their social location, to add or subtract shades of meaning or significance. So what people say, and the way in which it is said, is heavily influenced by factors outside the individual. For others, our identity is socially constructed, and it changes as we move from place to place.

Our perceptions of ourselves and of our identities also change from place to place, as the discourses we encounter give us different messages. This is an important factor in the way that power works. People have images of themselves and of their roles that make them conform, in their behaviour, to influences in their social environment. Gramsci (1966) highlights the non-coercive aspect of power, comparing it with the more obvious coercive forms of power. His concept of 'hegemony' describes how people agree to do things under the pressure of invisible cultural power. In modern societies, power is based on wideranging agreements of this kind. This non-coercive power penetrates consciousness itself, so that the dominated become accomplices in their own domination.

Clearly there is always pressure on us to shape our identities to the context we are in. Furthermore this kind of hegemony is reinforced from both sides of the power relationship: in their behaviour in any given context, the less powerful tend to adhere to the norms created by powerful groups. They do this while not always recognizing that they are being 'voluntarily coerced'.[8] There seem to be psychological pressures, from both sides of the power equation, that help the powerful by converting coercive forms of power into what is seen instead as legitimate authority (Wrong 1979). For example, this process often shows up in sociolinguistic studies. Labov (1972a) found that stigmatized features of speech are judged most harshly by the same people whose speech most exhibits those features. This is hegemony at work, and it allows formal organizations like schools to feel more legitimate when they stigmatize features of speech or other aspects of people's identities.

In fact, this working out of hegemony is nowhere more evident than in the restrictive cultural environments that most schools create for children from diverse backgrounds. Cummins (1996) sees these schools as places where children who are different in some educationally relevant way are unable to 'negotiate their own identities'. They begin to lose their identity as human beings, before they ever gain it. For him, real change in the education of culturally diverse students means a shift from coercive to collaborative relations of power. Teachers need to redefine their role and the types of structures at work in schools. These are the things that determine the micro-interactions that go on between educators, students, and communities. However, they are never neutral. Either they contribute to the disempowerment of culturally diverse students and their communities; or they enable teachers, students, and communities to challenge the operation of unwanted power structures.

Most teachers probably do their best to promote fairness, and they give the impression that they recognize diverse identities. Yet the professional roles that they fill, as members of a social institution, tend to put great limits on the actions of teachers, often against their will. This is also hegemony at work. Like any social institution that has a long history, education is intolerant of any form of diversity that it has never recognized. Formal education is able to give free rein to this intolerance, even while it hides the relations that underlie its power and passes on a reality that can be highly partisan.

Challenging bias in educational discourse

When it is in our interests to do so, people can easily rationalize and call this reasoning. We can distort through language and call this creative and original description. We can also repress others through language and call this 'being helpful' (Edelman 1984). But we can also make this process go the other way, and have it take more emancipatory directions. Fairclough (1985; 1995) provides some examples of this that are relevant to the work of schools. He presents four descriptions of young people whose families, schools, and communities see them as misfits. They are thought of as 'incorrigible'; 'defiant'; 'lacking in responsibility'; and 'delinquent'. But Fairclough says these four expressions could be drastically reworded, so that the same young people are seen differently: 'irrepressible' (incorrigible); 'debunking' (defiant); 'refusing to be sucked in by society' (lacking in responsibility); and 'spirited' (delinquent).

Probably neither wording in Fairclough's example really captures reality, since each reality depends on the viewpoint of the speaker. Both wordings are loaded in some way. If these distortions can happen within a single language, how distorted must the 'namings' of English appear to those raised in a very different culture. North American Indian languages, for example, differ in important ways from English. Indian languages use more verbs and verb phrases, while English relies more on the use of nouns and adjectives (Ross 1996). One important thing about verbs is that they suggest that people are not one thing or another forever. In contrast, nouns and adjectives tend to create stereotypes in people's minds. For instance, in an Indian language, a person guilty of some crime could not be labelled as 'a criminal' or 'a recidivist'. Yet in English, people are labelled every day and the labels become naturalized. These labels win acceptance as neutral codes. This happens in our schools as a routine activity when professionals designate some children as 'gifted', 'visible minorities', 'learning disabled' or in a range of other ways.

Teachers often do this kind of labelling when they set out the limits of their working interests. Edelman (1984) notes that professionals in schools often engage in rationalization, distortion, and repression in their discourse. They even see these practices as part of their work, because an important part of it is to define the status of the clients of education: the 'underachiever'; the 'retarded'; the 'discipline problems'; the 'dropout'. By doing this, teachers define their own status in relation to their students. Up to a point, they also justify the work that they do. In fact, they use special terms as labels in an exercise of power that would have much less meaning to it if the terms were used by non-teachers. However, in the hands of the empowered professionals, performing their roles, the terms become tools of power that can shape students' destinies. In this way, schools help to reproduce inequalities between groups and between individuals.

The school and sociocultural reproduction

Schools play a key role in 'social and cultural reproduction'. This phrase is a shorthand way of referring to the process by which the features and attributes of a society or culture are passed on largely intact from one generation to another. Clearly discourse itself is the key to reproducing the conventions of cultures and societies. We learn how to perform even the most simple conventional act, such as giving our names to new acquaintances, by observing how others do it, by using and listening to those others as models, and by noting the reactions of others to our performance and changing our behaviour accordingly. In this process of learning everyday conventional acts, each of us is a teacher as well as a learner. In the signs and symbols that we use, we provide models to others; we also learn from the signs and symbols used by others at different times.

Schools are places where most of a culture's dominant discourses are passed around and passed on. Apple (1982) lists some of the major social functions that schools have: they select and certify a workforce; they maintain group privilege by taking the form and content of the dominant culture and defining it as legitimate knowledge to be passed on; they help re-create a dominant culture; they legitimize new knowledge, new classes, and strata of social personnel. In short, for Apple, schools allocate people and legitimize knowledge, or legitimize people and allocate knowledge. As a result, formal education looks after the interests of some more privileged social groups better than it looks after the interests of some other sociocultural groups.

A central thinker in this area is the French anthropologist, Bourdieu, whose work helps us understand several aspects of education for diversity. He sees the culture of the school as a creation of the dominant culture, whose practices are reinvented and perpetuated through education. As part of this reproduction process, some cultural conventions acquire a special status. The owners of these things acquire status as well. When these valued conventions and traditions are passed on to their offspring, the social advantages are passed on with them. Bourdieu is interested in this handing on of valued social attributes, and the handing on of social and cultural power that goes with it.

To help explain the links between education and reproduction, he presents 'culture' metaphorically as an 'economic system'. His phrase 'cultural capital' describes the advantages that people acquire as a part of their life experiences, their peer group contacts, and their family backgrounds.[9] He lists some of these things: 'good taste', 'style', certain kinds of knowledge, abilities, varieties of language, and presentation of self. I return to this idea of 'cultural capital' at many places in this book. It has become an influential idea in educational debate, because the cultural capital that schools place value on is so often quite different from the cultural capital that is valued by people in their own communities and other social spaces.

In fact, the kind of cultural capital valued in schools is not equally available to children from different backgrounds. Diverse groups have their own highly valued sets of cultural capital and these can be quite different from the capital valued in schools. In spite of this, schools still operate as if all children had equal access to the capital valued in education. As a result, schools reproduce arrangements that are favourable to some and unfavourable to other groups, by basing their assessments of success on children's possession of this cultural capital, although it is unequally available. Moreover the value of the school's form of cultural capital passed to the next generation is reinforced yet again, unless schools begin to value other forms of capital. In this book, I suggest many other forms of cultural capital that schools need to acknowledge and give more value to.

Those whose cultural capital is not valued by schools find that their capital is simply *left out* of the reproduction process. Over time, it begins to fade, and to that extent the sociocultural group begins to lose its cohesion, its solidarity, and its identity, unless its members have other avenues for passing on their capital, outside of formal education. At the same time, people still believe that schools are neutral in the way they do all this. Because of the way hegemony works, the members of marginal groups accept that this is 'the way things must be' in education. If their children do not succeed in schools, people come to believe that their children's failure results from their natural inability: their lack of giftedness. They come to believe that the educational selection process is a fair one that is based on objective educational criteria. How does this happen?

Four points stand out in Bourdieu's discussion of the role of schools in reproduction. These points link schools with parents and pupils themselves:[10]

- knowing the lower success rate of children from marginalized backgrounds, and reading the discourses of schools themselves, these students adjust their expectations downwards and these lower expectations become part of the way they look at the world
- when students from marginalized backgrounds do experience success in schooling, their parents often make choices on their behalf that keep them away from the same kinds of opportunities that similarly endowed children from dominant backgrounds are urged to grasp
- schools recognize those who play the game of schooling and who acknowledge the legitimacy of schools in offering that recognition, which means that the slanted criteria schools use to judge success are supported because students and parents agree to submit to those criteria
- school qualifications lose their value if too many people gain access to them, so schools begin to place more value on other factors, especially the cultural capital prized and possessed by dominant groups, such as style, presentation of self, and use of high status language.

In summary, then, the school passes on training and information which can be fully received only by those who have had the culturally appropriate training that the school itself does not give. Again, all groups do have cultural capital of their own, but it is not always the same kind of capital that is recognized and valued in education. When we move from one cultural context to another, things that count as high status cultural capital change. Culturally different children begin to feel lost in a school where the dominant culture permeates everything. On the other hand, this is why it is easy for teachers also to feel out of place, when they venture into new communities and try to interact with the local people themselves.

Against this background, it is hard to escape the conclusion that the power of formal education is socially unjust in ways that are often taken-for-granted, not only by the professionals who staff schools, but also by the parents who send their children to schools. At this point, I want to look more closely at the idea of social justice, and at the kind of social justice issues that teachers and administrators working with diverse groups are beginning to think about.

Education and social justice

Much of the cultural capital valued in schools is only partly available to children who come from class, gender, or cultural backgrounds that differ from the school-recognized norm. But for most of the time, schools still operate as if all children had ready access to that norm. This disadvantages many students from marginalized backgrounds, and the conception of social justice adopted in this book addresses that point. This conception suggests that the 'group interests' of students who come from non-dominant backgrounds deserve differential treatment in educational policies and practices.[11]

The individual and the group in social justice[12]

Traditional views of social justice see the individual person as the starting point for building a just society. Some thinkers in the past looked for universal standards of right and wrong that could apply to every individual.[13] At the same time, other thinkers saw the search for social justice as a way of maximizing the welfare of people in general, without specific concern for people from non-dominant backgrounds.[14] In this view, if the community as a whole was better off, then it did not matter so much if sections of the community were not as well off. Here individual rights were protected, but everyone's individual entitlements were not seen as equal. Building on these views, a more modern approach has evolved. This sees social justice as a set of agreements that rational people reach under conditions that do not allow for bargaining power to be translated into advantage.[15]

But there is still a major problem for non-dominant groups with this more modern approach. In practice it can still leave those people from the dominant culture, who are making decisions, in ignorance about the things they are deciding, because they are not familiar with the collective interests of people from non-dominant backgrounds. In other words, these dominant people are trying to work out in advance, from their own interests as dominant individuals, what arrangements would be chosen by other people whose interests may not be readily understood by anyone who is not from the relevant class, gender, race or culture. Of course this point is very relevant to present-day schools, which are filled with students from diverse backgrounds, but where teachers and administrators are rarely in a position to understand the real interests of the diverse communities they serve.

Going beyond an 'individualist' approach to social justice, the 'discourse ethic' suggested by Habermas (1979) is a more 'collectivist' approach. This gives weight to the justice needs and interests of groups of people who are distinctive in some way. But it also gives weight to the rights of individuals. Habermas says that social justice is found in a discursive agreement reached freely and openly between the participants who have interests at stake in a given setting, because only they will know the issues, values, and interests relevant to a fair decision in that setting.

For example, in this approach most decisions about the use of minority languages in a multilingual society would need to be made at local level. Only broad norms about language use can be decided at system level. Accordingly the following steps might be used to decide the status of minority languages in a school system:

- *at whole system level* (for a country, state, or province): a use of open dialogue to decide any norms that could work as principles and increase the scope for optional use of any single minority language
- *at district level*: a use of open dialogue to decide more 'context-bound' norms that give status to minority languages, following the norms already identified at system level and also making use of any local grounds for compatibility or trade-off
- *at school, department or grade level*: a use (as often as necessary) of open dialogue within increasingly devolved settings, with agreements on compatible claims and, where necessary, compromises over incompatible claims.

Here any sets of interests that prove incompatible are resolved through compromise. As a result, people's minority language interests are accommodated in two ways: compatible interests provide the material for building norms; and incompatible interests become the basis of compromises in an informed consensus. In other words, people's reasons and accounts are consulted and taken into consideration at every level.[16]

This approach to social justice does not ask what *the* just society would be. Instead it seeks as many conceptions of justice as there are distinct possible conditions of society or subsets of society or culture. Every situation is a new setting for beginning the search for social justice. Looking at social justice in this way allows us to see the potential role that individual schools and classrooms have in creating a more just society, not only for individuals but especially for groups of people who are different in some way. All this means that Habermas's approach to social justice is very relevant to my theme in this book. At various points, I return to the idea that school decisions about fair practices and fair policies need to be taken as close as possible to the actual setting where those practices and policies have their impact.

The importance of acquired human interests

This more collectivist approach to social justice looks after needs that are not biologically given or naturally present in all people. In contrast, earlier theories looked for basic human rights, welfare needs, or primary goods that can be reduced to biological needs that all humans have. Habermas, on the other hand, is trying to allow for 'new' possibilities in social relations.[17] For him, human interests are not just opportunities for individual benefit and advancement. There are other human interests and these are not equally present in individuals, in men and women, in the members of every class, or in the members of every cultural group.

These human interests often turn out to be incompatible across class, culture, or gender groups.[18] Nevertheless by using something like the approach to social justice that Habermas has developed, we can bring these incompatibilities out into the open. In this way, any potential for compatibility can be identified, and, if necessary, a negotiated compromise can be reached for dealing with incompatibilities. I should stress, however, that this is little more than what powerful sectional groups within dominant cultures have been receiving from one another for centuries. When powerful groups seek different social arrangements, for example for their own different religious sects or professional bodies, they agree to compromise in the interests of all. Unfortunately non-dominant groups have usually been denied this sort of treatment, because of biases that I discuss later in this book. Below and in Chapter 2, I offer 'critical policy making' as a method for schools to use in doing all this.

These needs as human interests are more like the needs that minority cultural and class groups develop: the need to have their sociocultural values recognized; the need to live within social arrangements that are not hostile to those values; the need to have their languages or their language varieties valued and supported, and their discourse norms recognized.[19] This more collectivist account of social justice seems relevant to the history and the actual situation of Canada, which offers a model in this area for other countries.

Social justice ideas in one country[20]

This book is written for an international readership and draws on research and examples from many countries. While I live in Canada, I am not a Canadian by birth. I have lived for many years in three other countries (Australia, England, and New Zealand) and spent long periods in many more places. As a result, I know that there is much that Canada can learn from the rest of the world. But with that personal background, perhaps I can make the claim with some objectivity that Canada does offer an approach to social justice that other countries might learn from. While Canada is sadly lacking in the enabling structures to make it all work, it already has the legislation, the attitudes, and the national mindset rather firmly in place. How has it reached this point?

Canada's progress to a more collectivist view of social justice begins with its signing of the United Nations Declaration of Human Rights in 1948 (Ungerleider 1992). From here onwards, it followed a largely accidental course towards becoming a more just society. Canada's policy of official bilingualism was developed in response to obvious inequalities between the country's francophones and anglophones. The unintended effect of that policy was to help create a climate in Canada of mutual respect among all ethnic groups. Following that policy, Canada took steps to change other legislation that discriminated against minority language groups. Other policies on immigration, citizenship, and multiculturalism built a social justice infrastructure into Canadian society that heavily influences educational policy.

Not surprisingly philosophers and social theorists in Canada have ideas on social justice and power that tend more towards the collectivist. For example, Coulombe (1993) warns that to preserve the Canadian federation means redefining the meaning of citizenship. This includes redefining the place of diverse communities in a liberal society, in order to take into account shared communal interests, especially those to do with language and culture. Abella also discusses the features of diversity that exist in Canada. To address these features, she calls for policies of integration rather than assimilation:

> An integrated community is one whose members feel that their unique participation is both desired and desirable; an assimilated one denies participation to those who seek to assert the relevance of their differences.
>
> (Abella 1991: 358–9)

Even liberal accounts of social justice in Canada have tried to insert the collectivist ethic. Although this seems inconsistent with the traditional view in liberalism that individual rights must have priority in public affairs, the effort continues. Charles Taylor (1992), for instance, believes that a society with strong collectivist goals can still be liberal if it can respect diversity, especially diversity that includes those who may not share its common goals. For him, the political search by Québec for recognition of its distinctness as a society within Canada is a collective goal that can even be allowed to override individual rights under certain circumstances. He believes that the integrity of cultures has an important place when people make judgements about the nature of 'the good life': 'rigidities of procedural liberalism may rapidly become impractical in tomorrow's world' (Taylor 1992: 61).[21]

As critics of liberalism observe 'what defines liberalism is its disregard for the context of choice, for the way that choices are situated in cultural communities' (Kymlicka 1989: 206). This usually means opposition by liberals to minority rights. To address this weakness, Will Kymlicka tries to rework liberalism, as it is usually interpreted. He tries to address its failure to respond to people's strong intuitions about the importance of cultural membership. In conclusion, he argues that membership of a cultural community has to be a relevant criterion for distributing the benefits and burdens even in a liberal theory of justice.

Putting individual and group views of social justice together

While teachers always try to see their students as individuals, even individual identity itself comes from group membership. This is because a culture is not just a convenience made available by chance to the individuals who acquire it. It is the very means by which individuals are socialized and from which they develop their identity. Consequently, in searching for social justice in education, there is little that can be done for the individual's identity that does not begin with the group at the same time. For children coming to school, culture is never left behind at the school gate.

At the same time, individualist ideas on social justice are very relevant too, not least in schools. As soon as teachers ask questions about learning, knowledge, and understanding, these individualist views become important because good education is always concerned with individual students, as well as with groups. Students have rights of access to a curriculum that empowers them for later life, including appropriate teaching methods, and fair forms of assessment. These basic rights come from individualist accounts: natural rights, welfare, fairness, future happiness, protection of future options, etc. So a view of social justice that includes group needs could never be completely collectivist. In laying stress on it here, I am trying to swing the pendulum back, away from the individualism that still dominates educational practice, and towards greater recognition of collective identity.

Dealing with all this can test the skills and patience of teachers and school administrators. Education for diversity is not something that is easily done well. It demands a use of power that is not only active and purposeful, but also informed, sensitive, and emancipatory. Obviously not all uses of power are harmful: power has both a negative and a positive moment. The challenge in bringing about change is to use power to separate wanted from unwanted structures, and then through classroom or administrative action to replace unwanted with wanted practices: to replace a negative exercise of power with a positive one. To help make all this work, the next section suggests that 'emancipatory leadership' is a good way for teachers and administrators to exercise power in contexts of diversity.

Emancipatory leadership for teachers and administrators

This style of leadership has many features. For schools in communities of great diversity, emancipatory leadership seems a useful complement to other approaches to school leadership, like 'instructional leadership' and 'transformational leadership'. These also have their advantages and their place, but their limitations too. Chapter 2 describes an administrator and a school's staff who practised a more emancipatory approach to leadership in a school that serves a diverse population. Some of the features of emancipatory leaders, that go beyond the instructional and the transformational, are very relevant to the critical policy making discussed in the next section:

- emancipatory leaders know when they are out of their depth in complex sociocultural areas: they acknowledge the greater expertise of community members or colleagues in certain situations linked to concerns for diversity, and they act accordingly
- emancipatory leaders try to make their own presence a matter of small importance to the context of debate and decision making: they withdraw from centre stage by deliberately limiting themselves to making consultative contributions to debate, and by offering their opinions last, rather than first
- emancipatory leaders remove the effects of their own power from the process of decision making: they make it clear that they will accept any decision that is the outcome of a democratic consensus, and that they will try as much as possible to do so without voicing their reservations or acting on any negative feelings they might have
- emancipatory leaders agree to leave the implementation of any decision in the hands of those chosen for that task by the group.

Administrators concerned to make decision making as democratic as possible use this emancipatory form of leadership for many group-based decision-making activities. For example, it is consistent with much of the administrative work that goes on in contexts of professional collegiality and equality. This form of leadership asks for a lot of goodwill in an administrator. But the rewards that come from free and open participation under these conditions, and the reflected goodwill that others show, certainly make it worthwhile.

At the same time, emancipatory leadership is not really suited to routine administrative action. There are many routine decisions that administrators in schools need to take quickly and on their own authority. People often find it oppressive if valuable time is spent debating things of little importance, especially when this means that critical issues are being overlooked. So administrators also need an agreement from their colleagues about areas where they can feel free to take unilateral decisions and where they can expect to be supported in those decisions. Still 'emancipatory leadership' and 'critical policy making' seem good ways to reach that sort of agreement too.

Critical policy making in schools

The approach to critical policy making presented here brings together two of the more influential approaches to discovery in the social sciences. The one already introduced comes from Habermas. The other is Bhaskar's critical realist 'conception of discovery' (Bhaskar 1986).[22] The ideas themselves are similar and also very simple.

Briefly, Bhaskar shows that people's reasons and accounts are the most basic evidence available to us for deciding anything about the social world, because they tell us the things that are in people's minds about that world. His approach to (policy) discovery follows from this:

- human reasons and accounts are basic social scientific evidence
- by consulting the reasons and accounts of people, decision makers learn about the values, beliefs, interests, ideologies, and material entities that are important structures in the lives of those people
- people's reasons and accounts offer evidence about what their beliefs, etc. are, and also about what they believe about those beliefs, etc.
- by using people's reasons and accounts as the starting point, we can begin to work out the reality of influential structures in people's lives: the things that they value, and the things that oppress them
- action to keep wanted structures, or to replace unwanted with wanted structures (emancipation), can then be taken.

This summary suggests that the first step in changing anything is to consult the reasons and accounts of participants who have interests at stake. Clearly this sort of consultative process is very like the discourse ethic that I sketched above from Habermas, so Bhaskar's ideas inform the rest of this book too. Both approaches involve devolving real decision-making power to the people whose interests are at stake: those who are really in touch with the structural factors that oppress them, or with the structures that they value.

Several stages for critical policy making at school level follow directly from these ideas. I introduce these here, and in the next section.[23]

1 Identifying the real problem(s)

Critical policy making begins when people identify a regularity or an irregularity of some kind in their school. Those responsible for the change process then try to state this 'effect' clearly as a problem.[24] Next they allow their statement of the problem to be criticized by a wide range of participants with an interest at stake in the problem, or by their representatives. If this confirms that the problem is a real one for participants, the problem then becomes the starting point for policymaking.

2 Trial policies: the views of stakeholders

In critical and open dialogue, participants work out a trial solution as a response to the problem, aimed at replacing the unwanted problem with a wanted policy.

3 Testing policies against the views of participants

Participants in the change process test the effectiveness of their solution. Using critical dialogue, they undertake small scale research of several types: for example, they observe the trial policy in action and get feedback on it; or they look for alternative solutions, including devolving decision making to some smaller unit in the school.

4 Policy implementation and evaluation

The policy making ends when the policy solution meets the needs and interests of relevant participants; or should the policy not meet people's expressed needs and interests, it is modified or rejected.

These four stages offer an ideal framework only.[25] Much more could be said about creating specific forms of interaction within the various stages, especially in intercultural settings.[26] But as an ideal framework for use in schools, the outcome of Bhaskar's critical realism would be rigorously democratic, like the outcome of Habermas's 'discourse ethic'. In fact, if schools followed either approach to decision making, both of these basic tenets of democracy would be met:

- everyone's point of view and interpretation of the world would be consulted
- everyone's interests would be taken into account when shaping the dominant narratives through which the distributions of power, position, and privilege were accounted for and justified.

If all this is as democratic as I suggest, how can these ideas be worked out in actual practice?

Stages in critical policy making

Putting these stages to work in a context of diversity needs more fleshing out than I have given so far. Chapter 2 shows how teachers and administrators in a school went through the following stages when reforming a multi-ethnic school.

Identifying the real problem(s)

The problem situation

The interests, attitudes, values, and wishes of people with a stake in the policy area provide the basic evidence for critical policy makers. To get access to that evidence, the circle of decision makers in a school widens to include people fully in touch with all those things. The actual influence that these 'outsiders' have is also strengthened. The school taps the special expertise of these people, using it to broaden their understanding of the problem situation, and to add insights about the range of possible solutions. This means consulting the needs and identifying the interests of relevant teachers, students, parents, community members, and also policy makers working in the wider system.

The role of expert knowledge

Evidence from studies of expertise confirms the value in solving a problem of being 'an expert' (Glaser and Chi 1988). Clearly experts and novices contrast with one another in their problem-solving ability. The greater success that experts have comes from their coherent understanding of what counts as relevant knowledge. This contrasts with the fragmented grasp that novices have. But in a school that tries to serve diverse communities, the professionals are often the novices. The expertise needed extends well beyond the professional knowledge that teachers and administrators acquire as part of their regular work. It requires the depth of insight into the local community and its cultures that experts in those cultures possess.

Skills relating that local knowledge to the work of teachers and administrators can come in other ways too. Study in fields like anthropology, applied ethics, and sociolinguistics are a valuable form of professional development. Sometimes it is even mandated, as happened in a celebrated legal challenge in the United States (Labov 1982). However, when parents and others are brought into a school to provide local knowledge, they are often ready to accept the authority of the professionals on face value alone. In this situation, where community involvement increases, teachers and administrators working with parents have more than usual demands placed on their expertise. They try to become as expert as possible, or at least make it their business to know where to find real expertise.

The problem(s)

After becoming expert in the field of the problem, a group assembles a set of key points from their study of the problem situation. Each point represents a fact of some kind, or an informed assumption, or even an important community or staff attitude relevant to the problem situation. From a discussion around these points, key problems start to emerge. However, different people see similar problems in different ways, and they want to state the problems in their own way. When this happens, it is important to treat these as different problems, at least until the group reaches consensus about the way they are stated. If there is no consensus, then they probably are different problems that do need to be treated differently.

Clearly the language in which a problem is framed is central. Again, if people cannot agree on the framing of a problem in language, then there are probably more problems than just one to address. Different people often see different interests at stake in a problem situation, and so have different perspectives on it. So it is important that the statement of any problem is unambiguous, because if it means different things to different members of the policy group, then it will have no consistent meaning for other people trying to understand the policy.

A decision-making group often allots some priority to the problems that they deal with. Again conflict is likely, because people from diverse backgrounds often have trouble reaching unanimity when ranking complex problems. But a critical approach to policy making actually invites this kind of disagreement, because conflict is the essence of the critical approach. People rarely solve conflicts by trying to adjudicate between alternative value systems that produce very different conceptions of a problem or its solution. Different group interests are not rival claims; they are incompatible claims that need some sort of compromise which comes about when people of goodwill negotiate on the basis of an agreed norm. This suggests two types of problems: compatible and incompatible ones.

Incompatible problems are met through an informed consensus, where the decision makers compromise in pursuit of their greater goals by agreeing to solve one another's incompatible problems as best they can.[27] Often there are fewer incompatible problems in formal decision-making settings than people expect. Decision makers of goodwill, who are concerned about social justice, can become skilled in adopting other people's problems as their own. They do this by trying to see the world from the different points of view of those others. However, when people from very different cultures are involved, it can be a mistake to think that we can fully understand other people's points of view. In other words, it is not helpful to see compatibility where it does not exist, just for the sake of 'consensus'.

Compatible problems provide the material for drawing up norms that can be referred to again and again when dealing with new problems. The overarching problem of providing the best education possible for all children in the school is the most important source of policy norms. A policy group identifies the things needed to address that overarching problem, and these things become norms for referring back to when making other decisions. Critical policy makers build a context for discussion where everyone can participate in deciding norms without the intrusion of unreasonable power factors. In other words, teachers and administrators adopt the very different leadership role that I discussed above: emancipatory leadership.

Trial policies: the views of stakeholders

Policy guidelines
Policy guidelines are solutions to policy problems. Sometimes each guideline offers a single solution to a problem, but more often it takes many different guidelines to solve a complex problem. Sometimes a set of guidelines helps solve a range of problems.

The value of these tentative guidelines depends on how readily they can be tested as solutions against the real world of the school's problems. This means that they are stated very clearly, like the statement of the initial problems themselves. In other words, the language used in the guidelines is not vague, high sounding but empty, or overly restricted in meaning to some privileged group. The guidelines can be put through the tests of the next stage only if they are understood in much the same way by everyone who meets them. The people with a stake in the policy area put the guidelines through a critical inspection, to make them sensible, and to ensure that they do replace unwanted with wanted forms of policy determination.

Controllable change: stages in policy guidelines

Often guidelines for change move forward too fast. When reform activities move quickly towards a major restructuring of a school, it is important that the organization is not permanently damaged by hasty implementation. To avoid this, policy makers evaluate the implementation process in some way at every suitable stage. For dealing with complex problems, solutions can be in the form of guidelines set out in linked stages. Each of these stages are then tested in some way against the reasons and accounts of all those likely to be affected by the policy. Some stages involve small scale research to be carried out before later stages can be reached, or even before later stages can be identified. The policy guidelines set out the nature of this research and its purpose, because this activity itself is part of the solution to the school's problems.

Testing policies against the views of participants

Testing policies by trial applications
Again the critical responses of people to the trials are the key to this stage. If the trials are carefully conducted, perhaps within a single department or age level of the school, this allows small adjustments that improve the policy. Alternatively the trials might lead to wholesale rejection of the policy guidelines, sending policy makers back to reconsider their problem. They might modify the guidelines, or devolve the solving of the problem down to a unit that is more relevant to it, such as a school department, an individual grade, or a single class. But this is not the same as shelving the problem.

Constructive action of some kind needs to follow. Otherwise the use of 'trial applications' can be seen as an administrative device to stall the reform. For example, pilot programmes can often just delay genuine change while creating an impression of reform (Popkewitz 1982). But if decision makers can assure people that they are really searching for solutions to critical problems, and if they continually bring people up to date, then there should be less room for doubt that real reform is on the way.

Testing policies by research
Small scale and large scale research methods are useful for supplementing trial applications of a policy's guidelines. However, as methods, they too are subject to critical error elimination, because they may not reveal what policy makers think they reveal, or they may not reveal all that policy makers need to know. For example, a survey of community opinion based on questionnaires can be an unreliable guide in deciding an important policy point. This is because the survey's results could be overturned by later evidence that might come perhaps from focus groups taken as samples from the same community. In areas of education for diversity where much is at stake, decision makers accept research findings in the same way as courts accept the verdict of a jury: that verdict can be quashed or revised in the light of later evidence. Like a jury's verdict, a policy is always open to further criticism.

Policy implementation and evaluation
The final stage in policy research is the statement of the 'official' policy itself. Yet even this policy will still be tentative because the social context in a school dealing with great diversity is a dynamic one. Problems come and go as the sociocultural and political setting of the school changes, and the solutions offered to one set of problems cannot logically be applied to new problems that arise from a changed context. Also the priority of various parts of the policy will change, perhaps as a result of critical challenges by people who find that they do have an interest in the problem field. All these changes

in perception and in context are aspects of organizational conflict that critical policy makers welcome and build into their planning.

What the above section describes in outline is really an evolutionary approach to planning that allows teachers and administrators to work closely with community members from diverse backgrounds.[28] This seems to work best in schools with complex sociocultural problems, especially schools in inner urban settings or in remote communities. Schools in these settings can experience rapid changes in many areas. A policy responsive to the school's dynamic, social, cultural, and political context should partly 'self-destruct' about once a year. This happens in response to changes in staffing, funding, community involvement, first and second language needs, horizontal and vertical policy changes from within the wider system, and new knowledge from relevant research.

Conclusion: raising some questions

In this opening chapter, I have linked the ideas of postmodernity, social justice, and critical realism in an attempt to outline the far from easy problems that confront those wanting to reform education for diversity. In the later pages of the chapter, I also advanced critical policy making as an approach that offers schools a practical way of embarking on the reform of education for diversity. Up to this point, in describing the critical policy making stages, I have not yet dealt with three important questions:

- Why would school administrators and teachers, who are already empowered by the conventions of their work, want to surrender a good deal of that power by embracing critical policy making and the 'emancipatory leadership' that goes with it?
- Why is participatory decision making so valuable a part of changing education for diversity?
- How would the process contribute to the emancipation of students from marginalized backgrounds of diversity in real schools?

These are intriguing questions. While they are very relevant to points in this chapter, I postpone addressing them until a little later. I do this at the end of Chapter 2, after describing a school that put many of this chapter's recommendations into practice.

Discussion starters

1 What characteristics distinguish the postmodern world from what went before it? Could you give concrete examples of these characteristics from your own experience, to help illustrate your points?

2 Do you think that the situation for children from diverse backgrounds is better in today's world than it has been in recent history? Why? Can you identify changes that have occurred or that should occur?

3 How much say should parents and community members have over the organization and curriculum of schools? How much say do they have at present? Do the parents of children from diverse backgrounds differ from other parents in any respect? Can you specify those differences and give examples?

4 What does 'hegemony' mean? How can the idea of 'hegemony' be useful for understanding the way that schools manage to do the things that they do? Can teachers' professional behaviour itself be affected by this non-coercive force?

5 How far can schools go in accommodating the cultural capital of diverse groups? Are some schools better placed to do this than others? What might the risks be to a school if it recognizes the cultural capital of diverse groups and also tries to change itself in response to it?

6 Whose cultural capital are schools recognizing if they do not recognize the cultural capital of diverse groups? Can you be specific about this cultural capital and about who benefits from this and who loses?

7 Do you agree that both individual and group needs and interests should be taken into account in deciding the fair distribution of benefits and burdens in society? Why or why not? Do teachers have a special role to play or responsibility in making this process work?

8 What is 'emancipatory leadership'? Could teachers use this leadership style in their own classroom management and pedagogy? Would you feel more comfortable, or less comfortable, if you worked in a school where emancipatory leadership was regularly practised? What advantages and disadvantages might it bring? Are there situations in your own experience where this style of leadership is used? What are they?

9 Considering the two features of democratic decision making on p. 18, how democratic can schools really be in their decision making? Can you give specific examples of changes that could be made? How could teachers be more democratic in the way they treat students, inside and outside classrooms? What limits would you want to place on the process of 'critical policy making' outlined in this chapter?

two

BUILDING COMMUNITY-BASED EDUCATION THROUGH CRITICAL POLICY MAKING

Regardless of the school's best efforts in educating for diversity, policies and practices that stop at the school gate are unlikely to have much impact in areas that really matter. This is because children's lives and experiences outside school shape and affect their activities and performances inside school. Policies of real reform in educating for diversity involve the school's community in its work, not only to communicate the work of the school to parents, but also to draw on the community's knowledge, expertise, and cultural practices to shape the work that schools do and make it relevant to the lived experience of children from diverse backgrounds.

In doing this, it is sometimes necessary for schools to reduce the influence that other agencies outside the local community have over the school's operations. Towards the end of this chapter, I discuss ways in which the power of educational bureaucracies over schools is declining in many places to allow communities more say in what happens in their own schools. It is clear from studies of reform in diverse contexts that community involvement is often frustrated when people from diverse backgrounds find that all the major decisions are made by remote officials, who do not share the culture of the place, and might not care very much about it.

Later sections in this chapter describe a school that combined the work of teachers, administrators, parents and the local community over a long period, and did so successfully. That school's success in reforming itself shows how far schools can go in changing themselves to meet the needs of children from diverse backgrounds. Again it is not a model to be copied, but it is a case study to be learned from. Also it seems a very good example of 'community-based education' at work, so I introduce that idea here. I couple it with a discussion of Paulo Freire's educational thought, and follow it with discussion of a transformational model of school reform that seems relevant to schooling for diversity of all kinds.

Community-based education

'Community-based education' is different from 'community education'. Daigle (1997) sees 'community-based education' as a form of social action within a community framework that extends beyond schools as institutions. It allows community members to become self-oriented participants in the creation of the learning environment that the school offers. This dynamic form of development contrasts with the less dynamic demands that 'community education' often makes. Although the point of community education is sometimes to question taken-for-granted structures that oppress people, it usually leaves these structures in place. Nevertheless, as I suggest in Chapter 5, community education is also needed sometimes to educate local people about impending changes, as part of the process of reforming education for diversity.

Community-based education begins with people and their immediate reality. Above all, it allows them to become meaningfully involved in shaping their own futures through the school and other agencies in their community.[1] In fact, meaningful school reform often depends on this kind of participation, in which people renegotiate and reconstruct the ways in which a school relates to its community's interests. Usually community education is less concerned with changing formal structures and more concerned with studying them (Husen and Postlethwaite 1994). In contrast, community-based education tries to put into practice many of the reforming educational ideas of Freire (1972), who urged people to become self-aware and active political subjects. He especially wanted to enable learners to become active participants in shaping their own education.

Freire's generative themes

In my teaching life, I have been much influenced by Freire's educational philosophy. In 1972, I began an adult literacy programme, for an Australian State, which was one of the country's first such programmes (Corson 1977). Freire's *Pedagogy of the Oppressed* was given to me then by a friend. In fact, it was the only text on adult literacy available to me at that time. Although Freire's ideas were difficult to reapply from the slums and rural villages of Brazil and Chile to the affluent and very different Australian context, his work became a guiding philosophy for me. His ideas have been influential in my thinking and teaching ever since.

Freire's pedagogy gives priority to the use of dialogue as the essential accompaniment to literacy education. In this way, he sees literacy work not only as a way of giving voice to the oppressed, but also as a way of making them the controlling agents in their own lives. He asks adult literacy students, and other people of little power, to talk about 'generative themes' that they choose for themselves from their own experiences. These themes are based on things in their lives that trouble or delight them. Later, the actual words that adult literacy students begin to read and write are chosen from the words that crop up in their generative themes.[2]

Freire's reasoning here is that no curriculum is neutral, especially one that is selected by people remote from the circumstances of learners themselves. A dialogic teaching approach gives the learners more control over their own curriculum. It allows them to become the teachers of their own experience and culture, who choose and direct the themes that provide their own courses of study. Their literacy teachers are then able to use these themes as a basis for the literacy work that they do with students, who are motivated and interested by the relevance of the curriculum to their lives.[3] When used over time, the pedagogy is certainly empowering for oppressed groups of people.

At the same time, Freire's pedagogy always leaves room for a teacher or leader of some kind, who then acts as the empowered and empowering facilitator. My idea of 'emancipatory leadership' goes a little further, although it is quite consistent with Freire's philosophy. I am more concerned to see the 'empowered ones' withdraw functionally from the setting under certain conditions, especially from a setting that involves people whose culture the 'empowered ones' might not really understand, or cannot understand. Real community-based education then becomes possible.

Community-based education and language revival

Community-based education is much more suited to changing education for diversity than simple community education. It certainly seems relevant to the needs and interests of diverse communities who want to emancipate themselves from pressures to conform to unwanted, dominant, cultural structures. But community-based education, aimed at making schools more organic to their local culture, is still a new idea for mainstream education in many places. Consequently it may be useful to look at ways in which community-based education can be used for another purpose.

There is a history of this sort of work in community efforts to promote minority language revival in many countries. In Britain, for example, community-based education with this sort of focus has a long tradition, especially in the former Inner London Education Authority (ILEA). When this sort of community consultation occurs, professionals begin to see the local community and its needs with very different eyes, as one British administrator noted:

> For the past twenty years we have been sitting in County Hall identify-
> ing the views of the Asian community. In the last two years we've gone
> out to talk to them, and found they had completely different views from
> those we perceived.
>
> (Tomlinson 1984: 93)

Fishman (1990) outlines some strategies from several places that have
helped to focus local community interest on reviving ancestral languages.
Above all, to reverse language decline and promote minority language interests, Fishman stresses the need for good neighbourhood organization.
Clearly community-based education can offer this sort of social support,
while also encouraging self-help for families. All this can come from a range
of activities that are begun by the school, or through its specialist services:

- providing home visits by social workers who are minority language
  speakers
- organizing parent groups and bilingual language exchange centres, which
  often become self-sufficient in place of formal support systems
- having experienced parents teach other parents, not just the art of parent-
  ing but the place of that art within their own culture
- bringing the activities of the school and the activities of the family closer
  together, especially through childcare or playgroup arrangements that
  offer contact with adult specialists in tutoring, computers, dance, drama,
  writing, library research, athletics, and after-school jobs.

In Fishman's view, all the community activities mentioned in the last point
have taken over the traditional role of the family as the major partner with
the school. While these are areas of community education, they are also
intense settings for language use, for the communication of cultural attitudes, and for the revival of linguistic, cultural, managerial, and political
skills.

The empowerment of local people from diverse backgrounds comes about
when community members make contact with the school through and
around extension activities like those above, and are then drawn into the
running and support of the school itself. To make this start to happen, there
are three main things that teachers and schools have to do:

- give the process all the time it needs
- do some careful school-based planning to make the process work
- nurture the process by building commitment to it among other school
  staff.

In response and over time, the local community takes on a new role. They
begin to supplement and even displace the professionals from areas that
are more properly the responsibility of people who have the same cultural

interests as the children. The next section focuses more directly on some of the structures, attitudes, and beliefs that change when we change education for diversity.

A transformational framework for community-based education

Changing education to take account of diversity is a transformational act of great complexity. Because schools have existed in their present form for so long, people tend to take them for granted. In other words, for most people the way schools are at the moment is the way schools should be. This means that even where a school and its community are willing to consider gradual but radical change, people are often unable to conceive of doing things very differently. To help address this problem, Daigle (1997) decided to look at communities that had already been through their own radical changes successfully.

The focus of Daigle's study was North American aboriginal communities who have transformed their school systems. Her interest was in the things that the schools actually changed and the processes that they used to do it. She designed the following conceptual framework for her study. In this framework, the vertical axis (the italicized items) takes its categories from an earlier study.[4] These categories are areas that need special reform measures when changing a school from the mainstream pattern to a more community-based institution. The arrows indicate the direction in which the transformation process should move:

governance approach	external structures	>	community-based internal structures
programme/methods/ goals/structures	consensus/integration	>	conflict/transformation
philosophy of education	homogeneity	>	liberating
school culture	assimilation/ dominant culture	>	bicultural/integration and preservation of aboriginal culture
language	non-recognition of the minority language(s)	>	minority language preservation and revitalization
social, economic and political development	dependent on external structures	>	growth of self-reliance and self-sufficiency
retention rates of minority students	low	>	higher
community as a resource	exclusionary	>	inclusionary

organization	top-down	> bottom-up
	formal	> informal
	programmed	> process based
	institution centred	> locality centred
	reactive	> proactive

(after Daigle 1997)

These transformational categories are clear already in Daigle's outline above, without much further discussion. To exemplify them, the rest of this chapter sets out in detail how one school went about reforming itself to follow the direction of all the arrows in the above framework.

Critical policy making and emancipatory leadership in settings of diversity

This section shows how the two key ideas of critical policy making and emancipatory leadership can work in practice. Richmond Road is a school that put ideas similar to these to work. The school's enrolment was partly aboriginal children and partly immigrant students. In later chapters, I refer back to this discussion at various points, because the model offers ideas for reforming all types of education for diversity, at every level of schooling.

By engaging critically with the cultural interests and values of its local community, Richmond Road school anticipated the national reforms in New Zealand by many years.[5] As a result, the school's history offers a model for other schools in the country to learn from. The key policy issue for the school to address was how to provide an organization integrating a curriculum, pedagogy, and evaluation system that recognized the different cultural values of its highly pluralist local community. To increase the alternatives available to children from diverse backgrounds, the school tried to celebrate group collective identities and to lay constant stress on fairness for everyone, especially for those of little power:

> What has resulted at Richmond Road is an approach to multicultural education that recognizes the identities and claims of groups *as groups* and attempts to represent and legitimate their collective identities . . . in its delivery of education. In so doing, the school has sought to reconstitute the school environment to the *real* educational advantage of minority children.

(May 1994: 62)

Because this school provides a model for schooling of this type, it has already been the focus of international attention.[6]

In the early 1990s, Richmond Road School already had a well functioning pluralist curriculum and organizational structure. Dating back many
years, a Maori educational leader was able to communicate to the staff his
vision of what a multi-ethnic school for students and teachers should be. He
was helped in this by a strong sense of his own Polynesian identity which
gave him the provisional authority of having more authentic knowledge in
this key area.[7] The process that he adopted closely resembles the approach
to critical policy making outlined in Chapter 1. His restructuring activities
preceded the development of this critical policy making approach. However,
it is clear from May's account (1994) that the principal's approach to
restructuring the school, from his earliest efforts, drew on his own skills as
a person committed to critical and emancipatory reform. He based his
reforms on problem identification, and on the negotiation, consultation, and
error elimination needed to find workable policy solutions.

The restructuring process in outline

In 1990, Richmond Road had 270 students of whom 21 per cent were
Samoan, 20 per cent were European New Zealanders, 18 per cent were
Maori, 34 per cent were the children of other Polynesian immigrant peoples,
and 7 per cent were Fijian Indian and others. In providing for this diversity
in the student body, the key to the principal's reform was to establish new
and very different organizational structures at Richmond Road. Cazden
(1989) describes organizational structures and patterns of interaction
among staff, children, and the community, which were clearly effective in
meeting the values of the cultural majority as well as the range of cultural
communities that the school draws its pupils from.

Even after a change of principal, the school continued to show its ability
to be a 'self-sustaining system' by taking on the task of critical reform and
improvement needed to keep a worthwhile system operating. Cazden
describes how Richmond Road was different:

> In contrast to the isolation of teachers in single-cell classroom schools,
> Richmond Road teachers work in a setting of intense collectivity. Chil-
> dren and staff interact in complex organizational 'systems', as they are
> always referred to: vertical/family groupings of children; non-hierarchi-
> cal relationships among the staff; curriculum materials that are created
> by teacher teams at the school and rotate around the school for use by
> all; and monitoring systems for continuous updating of information on
> children's progress.
>
> (Cazden 1989: 150)

For his vertical grouping system, the principal borrowed from the example
of non-graded country schools. Six ropu (vertical groups) operated in shared

or separate spaces: one of them was a Samoan bilingual group, a second a Maori bilingual group, a third a Cook Island Maori bilingual group, and a fourth the ESL language unit for non-English-speaking newcomers to New Zealand. The fifth and sixth ropu were English-speaking only.

Each ropu included children from the entire age range, from 5-year-old new entrants to 11-year-olds. Children stayed in the same ropu for their entire time in the school, working with one home group teacher in frequently changing vertical home groups of 16–20 pupils. Also attached to the school were Maori, Samoan, and Cook Island immersion culture/language pre-schools.[8] The school's three dual-immersion bilingual units received the graduates from these pre-school language nests, if parents agreed. During half of each morning and every other afternoon, the teachers in these units spoke only Maori, Samoan, or Cook Island Maori, and they encouraged the children to do the same.

Paired teaching and peer instruction were common in this school. The provisional authority of the late principal, coming from his specialist cultural and administrative knowledge, was a model for provisional authority among all the school community members. In other words 'whoever has knowledge teaches'. As one of the school's teachers noted:

> Sometimes this would be a teacher; other times it can be a child; other times it can be a parent from the community. I particularly like that. Although we have a principal, assistant principal, senior teachers, and then we ordinary plebs, it has never really worked that way. It's always been a case of who has the greater knowledge.
>
> (Cazden 1989: 152)

As a result, the official hierarchy had much less meaning among the school's people. For example, the school's language leaders or language assistants had no formal professional training, yet they worked as full teachers because of their expertise and the valuable on-the-job training they had received. Also, the school's caretaker[9] was involved in the educational work as a valued colleague, supporting children and staff, respected by parents, and a friend to all the children. Parents too contributed their special knowledge and 'the front door was always open'. The school became organic to its cultural community.

The stress on communal activity for the students was extended in other directions too: Bonds were forged at various levels. The vertical grouping of the ropu allowed cooperative curriculum and resource development by the teachers. Working in five curriculum groups that cut across the ropu teaching teams, teachers collaborated in making 'focus resources' for school-wide topics. These topics followed a multi-year plan, so that all the different cultural groups were assured of exposure to each topic. Each team made materials at ten reading levels for use in four learning modes; each teacher was responsible for making a number of different items. When ready, teachers presented their materials to colleagues during staff meetings. Then the materials were rotated throughout the school, staying in each ropu for fixed periods. Clearly as well as collaboration, there was efficiency and effectiveness here. Like the school itself, curriculum materials matched the community that the school served, and they targeted the needs of these students.

Richmond Road was also a learning community for adults: they learned about teaching, about other cultures, and about themselves. Community-based education became a practical reality. Professional development moved forward as well. The principal encouraged staff to share and explore their own and each other's cultural and class backgrounds, which were as diverse as the children's. He stressed teacher workshops and conferences, contact with up-to-date theory, worthwhile staff meeting discussions, and critical policy development. By working together themselves, teachers learned about collaborative ways of learning and this offered a sound model for the students. For example, Cazden quotes one staff member: 'I think that's why the children work together here, because they can see us working together' (1989: 150).

Clearly too the competitive nature of regular schooling was missing from this more collectivist environment. It is also evident that the school showed high regard for a range of cultural discourse norms and for the cultural values that support those norms.[10] The school put the self-esteem of the pupils ahead of their academic performance, while expecting to improve that performance as a result. This meant a stress on the students' growing sense of cultural pride, their sense of who they were, and their sense of involvement in a worthwhile school community. Meanwhile the environment for academic development did not suffer as a result. May (1994) offers extensive data confirming that the children's academic progress was as good or better than comparable students elsewhere. He explains the success of the school in delivering a quality 'product':

> Moreover, by concentrating on the process of learning at Richmond Road the 'product', so elusive to ethnic minority children in the normal circumstances of schooling, is also being achieved . . .
>
> The resource-based process model provides a means for fostering the independence of learners. It also allows for the inclusion and affirmation of cultural and language differences in the learning process.
>
> (May 1994: 113–14)

Cazden also set Richmond Road against a United States report on 'effective schools'[11] and saw that report's essential features matched 'amazingly well' at Richmond Road (Cazden 1989: 143):

- shared values, especially about the purpose of the school, what students should learn, and how teachers and students should behave

- a common agenda of activities that provide opportunities for interaction and link students, faculty and administration to the school's traditions
- a distinctive pattern of social relationships that embodies an ethos of caring.

In his study, May (1994) looks at Richmond Road's continuing progress under a new principal and its development of its own 'language policy across the curriculum'. May argues that its development supports the view that a curriculum reform addressing pluralist needs can come about through structural changes within a school. He sees Richmond Road as a 'relational school': it manifested a democratic decision-making framework among staff and an established consultation process with the local community. It did all this in a setting that built upon its pupils' contacts with their own cultures and strengthened those links. Consultative bonds radiated in every direction, connecting individuals, ideas, and groups. In fact, these bonds were valued as the point and purpose of the school's policy and planning.

May's critical ethnography[12] shows that the principal's success came from several things: his ability to cultivate enthusiasm for his restructuring; his democratic approach to deciding on the course of change; and his willingness to give people all the time that they needed to change. I see his approach to school administration as a form of emancipatory leadership. This is still rare in schools in the late 1990s, but it was even less common in the 1970s and 1980s when these reforms began. May also confirms that the principal's plans for change were gradual and carefully managed. He brought about his key structural changes over eight to nine years.

Coming from an oppressed community himself, the principal knew that traditional forms of schooling act in a hegemonic way.[13] They maintain inequalities for children from diverse backgrounds by making them conform to the dominant culture, which children tend to do without having much room for protest inside the controlling structures of schools. He wanted to reduce these pressures to conform and used this idea to develop his strategy. May sets out the principal's policy making strategy. I recount some of that detail below to illustrate similarities between the critical policy making process recommended in this book and the actual practices followed in Richmond Road's development.[14]

Identifying the real problems

The social conditions of community deterioration and dislocation that surrounded the school prompted the reforms. But the principal himself was the catalyst for change by showing his willingness to build the knowledge and ideas of others into his own thinking. Through his own critical openness, he freed the staff to look for issues in the school's problem context. He asked them to raise problems, and to take the lead in discussing them in formal meetings. He consistently asked staff to look for critical alternatives in their practices, to break away from the constraints of monocultural or dominant ways of doing things. While promoting a strong sense of ownership over the curriculum by teachers, he also made sure that everything was decided according to what was best for the children, both as individuals and as members of different cultural groups. This became the overriding normative principle for the school. He also encouraged teachers who were unsympathetic to his vision to leave, and he waited for this to happen before pushing forward with radical changes.

Richmond Road raised expert knowledge to a level that is rare in schools. In one sense this meant capitalizing on external professional expertise by letting it work in the school's interests. But in a more important sense, this meant recognizing the value of the expertise of the staff and the community. To foster staff expertise, the principal used staff development as his key strategy, encouraging staff to see the school's problems from many different theoretical perspectives. The staff library had many subscriptions to high quality, cross-disciplinary journals which were read by all the staff. These were often used as the starting point for the professional development programme, which was built directly into the regular structure and timetable of the school.

Participation in this professional development programme was part of a teacher's duty at this school. Full attendance was expected and sessions often lasted as long as three to four hours. Once meetings identified a relevant problem, they targeted the field of the problem through a stimulus paper read by one or more staff members, or through the distribution of a collection of readings on the topic. In-depth discussion was often followed by a week's break. This allowed wider reading by all staff. It also stimulated new ideas and interest group discussions. Finally, in another full meeting, policy action was proposed and implementation followed. Through this process, the staff became used to adopting a theorized approach to their practice. They developed collaborative expertise at the same time, and worked always to keep communication lines open between themselves.

The school also gave priority to keeping communication lines open with other people who had an interest in the school's development. Early in the history of the reforms, the staff created an open door policy for the community. They worked to reduce the usual gap that stands between parents and teachers by giving parents a sense of their own status and efficacy. They welcomed them into the school and asked them to say what they liked and disliked. To build a sense of community involvement, the school regularly held open house events that celebrated new developments. Staff incorporated the ceremonies and customs of the communities themselves into these events. The school also held regular cultural ceremonies to which community members flocked. As a result, parents felt drawn to contribute to the teaching and other activities.

In their interaction with community members, staff worked hard to develop inclusive and reciprocal relations with all parents, especially with people from non-dominant backgrounds. Through their behaviour, disposition, and speech they tried to show intense respect for human difference and for cultural difference. This atmosphere led to a natural growth in community involvement in policy making. As one parent in May's study observed:

> The philosophy of the school – where decisions are made – is that the community – everybody that's involved with the school – makes a decision. It's the way it's always been as far back as I can remember. And it's not just a handful of people that say 'right we're going to do that'. I mean if the consensus is that we're not going to do it – this is from the community – well we won't do it. And that's it, and that's how it's always been. It seems to work well. Quite often it takes quite a long time to resolve things but that's the best way – don't rush into it, think about it. It might take a couple of months to resolve one particular thing but when it's resolved it's resolved well!
>
> (May 1994: 94)

So we see very clearly in this setting that community interests were consulted, not fobbed off.[15] The community was highly engaged in running things and deciding directions. A good example of this was the creation and organization of each of the three language and culture immersion pre-schools on the premises. These changes were all community driven. Also the more recent development of a fourth pre-school responded to community suggestion and advocacy. In these pre-schools, the buildings were controlled by the school's board of trustees (school council), but the parents controlled their own finances and sorted out their rules. Matching the principal's objective of elevating those with little power, these practices freed the parents to do it all themselves.

For more than a decade, the school involved influential members of the community in matters of governance and gave them real power to direct the school in the community's interests. As a matter of policy, the school encouraged these leaders to mediate in difficulties that arose for children from diverse backgrounds or among community members. This policy included appointing professional and ancillary staff drawn from the local communities, giving them status in the school, and involving them directly in school governance. Later, with these community structures in place, it was easy to consult the interests of parents and community members and to relate them to the interests of students and staff.

To achieve all of this, the principal built commitment to the changes through constant dialogue with participants. He helped people see that conflict and criticism are inevitable and productive. He fostered a sense of self-worth among staff, which encouraged them to withstand the inevitable pressures that radical reforms like these create, even when gradual. The principal's policy of having staff, pupils, and parents formally choose to be in the school, after learning of its differences, also built a sense of commitment and loyalty. This policy extended to choices about enrolling in the different units within the school. For example, the school always fully counselled parents on the role and purpose of the bilingual units, and then gave them the choice of enrolling children there, or in the English-only units. This choice extended to the children as well, who also had the option of using either of their two languages at any given time in bilingual classroom programmes.

Finally, the school showed a critical realist approach to power relations within the wider system. To advance the interests of the school, the staff kept in touch with those power relations and adopted a stance of guarded scepticism towards them. This meant collaborative resistance, as a school, to unwanted outside pressures. At the same time, it meant provoking or anticipating change where necessary. Most usefully, it meant taking strategic advantage of rule changes in the wider system to solve school problems and to further the process of reform. For example, in 1985 the school introduced New Zealand's first inner city Maori bilingual unit, as soon as a change in the government's rules allowed it.

In ranking its problems, the school also adopted a critical realist approach to internal power arrangements and decision making. The decision-making groups used conflict constructively in their problem search. To achieve this, they compromised where necessary by agreeing to solve each group's incompatible problems as best they could. For example, although the larger Samoan community was the first to ask for its own pre-school and bilingual unit, the board of trustees, under the chairmanship of a Samoan parent, acknowledged the right of the smaller Maori community, who are the ancestral people of the country, to have the first pre-school and bilingual unit. But with that development firmly in place, unanimous support for the Samoan developments followed quickly.

Trial policies: the views of stakeholders

The principal moved in careful stages when addressing more complex problems. Even after involving the staff and the community in the decision-making process, he made only small changes and did so gradually. He underlined the fact that there are no quick answers to complex policy problems, but also took pains to convince the community that the school was engaging in genuine reform. He achieved this by carefully demonstrating to the community the success of each stage in his reconstruction, and then by consulting them again, modifying the process, and moving on to the next stage.

To provide opportunities for staff to consider the more professional aspects of the reforms, he organized the school so that formal curriculum teams could consider curriculum problems. Individual teachers were released from class time on different mornings to take part in these policy making sessions where problems were identified and tested against the knowledge and interests of teachers. In these cycles of error elimination, the problem area was crossed and recrossed; the theories of participants were continually tested against the evidence available, including that most important form of evidence, the views and wishes of stakeholders themselves.

In its long history of reform, Richmond Road developed a tradition of using trial applications of its policies, and of evaluating the critical responses of people to the trials. For example, over several years senior teachers trialled and then modelled for others the new family grouping structure, using the features of the ideal family as a model for inclusive and extended relations. Applying emancipatory leadership, the principal gave these senior colleagues full discretion in trialling, adopting, and discarding different arrangements. At the same time, he and the teachers promoted free communication with all the parents of the students that were involved.

When the school found a successful family grouping model, the innovators slowly encouraged interest in their ideas among other staff. They then established other similar units, doing this without the principal's direct involvement. The school eventually followed the model preferred by the trial group, but it still allowed teacher discretion over structural details within individual units, such as timetabling, teacher turnaround in responsibilities, etc. This whole process took five to six years and, as an expected outcome of the reforms, the school allowed the structural changes to flow through into pedagogical changes.

In summary

Through community negotiation and professional education at Richmond Road, the principal reorganized the school's grouping system. He created a flat and more egalitarian management system. By negotiation, he lessened undesirable structural constraints, like those that prevent staff from diverse backgrounds from being hired, or community members from having a strong voice in governance. The school's critical approach to policy development was underpinned by its commitment to a culturally pluralist, integrative, and process approach to education:

> Within this, certain values are considered prerequisite: difference is never equated with deficiency; co-operation is fostered not competition; cultural respect is seen as essential to developing a pluralistic society;

and the school's function is directed towards increasing a child's options rather than changing them.

(May 1994: 162)

In this emancipatory setting, staff from backgrounds of diversity began to model relations of equal status. Racist words and phrases disappeared from the language of the school. The different language varieties used by the children became more valued. The ideology of 'always treating children all the same' came to be seen as a racist value, rather than an expression of justice. In summary, as one immigrant graduate of the school observed:

> Now I guess I'm real proud I went to that school. I learnt a lot from that school. It's where I found my identity, my culture . . . That school is one of the best.

(May 1994: 199)

Conclusion: addressing the unanswered questions

After describing the critical policy-making stages in Chapter 1, I mentioned three important but unanswered questions that I try to answer here:

- Why would school administrators and teachers, who are already empowered by the conventions of their work, want to surrender a good deal of that power by embracing critical policy making and the 'emancipatory leadership' that goes with it?
- Why is participatory decision making so valuable a part of changing education for diversity?
- How would the process contribute to the emancipation of students from marginalized backgrounds of diversity in real schools?

Looking at all three questions, it seems clear to me that in almost every setting of diversity school administrators and teachers are being asked to make policies about complex matters for which they have little training or expertise. Usually because of inadequate preparation in intercultural relations, they have few insights into the interests and values of many of those who are affected by their actions. So instead of running schools effectively, administrators and teachers are often disempowered because of their ignorance of the real effects of what they are doing. As a result, their schools can become islands of alienation in the very communities that they are meant to serve.

Teachers certainly try to cope with sociocultural complexity, but they usually lack the means for developing intercultural and inter-class dialogue. At the same time, administrators in schools catering for students from backgrounds of diversity create settings for human beings that require those same human beings to be moulded into a pattern which usually the administrators themselves have chosen. Drowned in this sociocultural complexity, the professionals are often defeated before they begin, because they are asked to plan in advance, from the interests of their own dominant group, what arrangements would be chosen by other people, whose interests may not be readily understood by anyone who is not from the relevant class, gender or culture.

In contrast, there are schools that are collaboratively managed. These schools use policies that are continually revised and based only on the best available evidence about changing circumstances. Schools like these are more likely to be places of staff and community participation and commitment. This is because community and staff participation is really needed to get at that evidence. Critical policy making uncovers the reality of the structures that surround people, especially in their unique local settings, and we get at that reality by consulting people. Moreover this sort of participation is both an end in itself and a means for producing other ends. When people come together to plan something, there is value for them in the feedback, skill development, social interaction, and knowledge growth that they receive. But more than this, participation usually fosters a commitment in people to the results or product of their participation, if those results seem reasonable to them.

Through the different types of input that community-based participation promotes, the school also tends to escape the trap of having its procedures and styles of operation modelled only on dominant and outdated points of view. These are often filled with error and narrow in range. Consequently critical policy making is a reform activity that rewards a school at many levels. As the Richmond Road example shows, there are also political gains to be made from all this when dealing with wider social formations. What are these gains?

By capitalizing on the collaborative management of its staff and community, a school limits the degree to which wider social systems can constrain action within it. In other words, collaborative management lessens the extent to which wider social formations create the ideological framework that restricts discourses of power and initiative within them. A key example of these external pressures is the link that exists between schools, the economy, and the state (Corson 1995a). This structural factor often constrains planning in senior schools whose staff can often be overconcerned with the perceived demands of employers. Working collaboratively, school policy makers can challenge and mould those same constraining relationships to advance the interests of the community, as well as the school itself. Furthermore, when they are challenged in this way, unjust social formations can also be transformed, perhaps lessening their undesirable impact elsewhere in society at the same time. The model that Richmond Road offered New Zealand education will be influential in that country, even when the school itself is no longer remarkable.

Although I am making claims that are based only on commonsense arguments, there is good evidence to support related claims like the following:[16]

- active parent involvement in decision making brings children from different class or cultural groups closer to their teachers, who usually come from the dominant class and culture
- parents from backgrounds of diversity themselves grow in confidence and develop a sense of their own efficacy which impacts positively on student learning
- harmful stereotypes that teachers often develop about pupils and their families fall away as teachers begin to collaborate with parents
- local communities grow in self-respect and win real political influence at the same time as they take greater responsibility for their schools.

Where the community itself has a major hand in policy making and in the education process itself, the whole programme of schooling is directed towards elevating the status of the community and questioning the role of schooling in that process. How does this happen?

If diverse cultural values influence the organization of schooling, the members of that community become the experts. They are the advisers and real controllers of the education programme; their values shape educational outcomes. Local political mobilization with real purpose can begin to occur. As the Richmond Road example showed, community attitudes there were laid bare and discussed. Local people received formal training as teachers and assistants. Parents participated in the other activities of the school to a greater degree and they acquired skills that were previously not their own. All of these things contributed to the elevation of the local groups. Political consciousness awakened where perhaps once there was none, and the community languages of the groups became available as recognized political voices at the same time as their political will began to assert itself.

In the eyes of the wider public, schools with more autonomy also become more legitimate places. This is a concern that Habermas (1971) addresses in his work. He wants to change the discursive randomness that typifies the loosely coupled and often indifferent management styles of public organizations. He sees the decision-making practices of modern institutions, including many schools in their present form, as a negative influence in the search for human emancipation. He believes that social institutions have a pathological quality about them. They operate with the same damaging results that human neurotic behaviour causes; they are a collective manifestation of the 'repetition compulsion' of individuals; and they act to defend a rigid uniformity of behaviour and to disguise that behaviour in such a way as to remove it from criticism.

To improve things, Habermas asks for a new form of 'institutionalized discourse' in public organizations.[17] This would help them recapture their legitimacy for people in general, their sense of direction, and the motivation of their participants and adherents. He asks for a decision-making setting in which there are no outside constraints stopping participants from assessing evidence and argument, and in which each participant has an equal and open chance of entering into discussion. These proposals resemble the discourse context needed in the emancipatory approach to educating for diversity recommended in this book. People recognize the cultural capital of different groups by beginning with evidence of the structures that they value or which oppress them. We find that evidence in their reasons and accounts: in their expressed views. Not to approach things in this way is to ignore the interests of the very constituencies schools aim to serve. Indeed, acknowledging the rights and interests of those constituencies has been the motif of my discussion in this chapter.

Chapter 3 discusses the paradigm for all approaches to educating for diversity. If you are tempted to skip this chapter on aboriginal education because you think it is not relevant to your own situation, let me stress here its direct relevance and importance. The discussion that follows directly applies even to countries that have no aboriginal population or to schools that have no aboriginal students. The many changes that are proceeding in aboriginal education give insights into all the areas of education for diversity more generally that are being changed or could be changed. *It provides the model from which reforms to all other forms of education for diversity can be argued.*

Discussion starters

1 How does community-based education differ from community education? Are there problems in implementing the one that do not affect the other? How might a school resolve those problems? What kind of actions can individual classroom teachers take in promoting community-based education?
2 Only a few teachers seem to have tried applying Freire's ideas to regular classrooms. How could they be modified and reapplied with school-age students? In literacy classes? In mathematics classes? In arts classes?
3 Look at the arrows in Daigle's transformational framework. What kind of changes might be needed to move a school from the left side of the arrow to the right? How would these changes affect the work of classroom teachers?
4 There are aspects of Daigle's framework that could usefully be reapplied to mainstream schools serving dominant culture students. What are they? How could they be reapplied? What changes to the roles of classroom teachers would result?

5 The Richmond Road school described here is very different from the norm and this could make it less helpful as a model for schools elsewhere. What things, if any, can be learned from the Richmond Road experience for schools and communities that you are familiar with?

6 The original principal at Richmond Road was clearly an authoritative and inspiring person. Would you like to work with someone who had that sort of vision? Why? Would you like to work at Richmond Road as a teacher? Or as its principal? What advantages and rewards would teachers derive from working there? What sacrifices would they have to make?

7 Habermas believes that social institutions have a 'pathological' quality about their management. Explain this statement in your own words. Do you agree that this is a serious problem for societies and for educational institutions in particular? What if anything can be done about it?

three

CHANGING THE EDUCATION
OF ABORIGINAL PEOPLES

This is the obvious place to begin discussing the practical reform of education for diversity, because the injustices and unsuitability of past policies and practices stand out most strikingly when we look at the education of students from aboriginal backgrounds. An alien culture, imposed on aboriginal peoples by invasion and conquest, became institutionalized for them when a system of schooling based solely on that alien culture became their only route to formal education. For me, then, changing aboriginal education provides the model for all reforms in educating for diversity. It is its most visible face. *We can set the necessary changes to all other forms of education for diversity alongside the reform of aboriginal education and justify them using variations on the same grounds.* Chapter 1 set out the grounds for changing education for diversity to make it respond more to the needs and interests of people themselves. Chapter 2 gave an example of this sort of reform, linking it with the need for community-based education. This chapter discusses reforms in the education of the Amerindian, First Nations, and Inuit peoples of North America, the Polynesian peoples of the Pacific, the Aboriginal peoples of Australia, and the Sámi of Scandinavia and Russia.

Aboriginal peoples inhabit nation states on every continent. As well as the differences of race or cultural origin that distinguish them from the dominant populations of their countries, aboriginal peoples also differ in having endured a long history of colonial exploitation and repression, usually involving invasion and conquest. All the cultures and languages of these peoples show the marks of this history of oppression that their people have experienced. In a number of countries, these indigenous cultures and their languages survive on the edges or in the middle of dominant invasion cultures that still threaten to overwhelm them. Only recently have governments in some places introduced formal policies to protect and promote aboriginal cultures and their languages, as outlined in this chapter. Elsewhere, the repression of the past continues through tacit educational policies that are little different in effect from the policies of repression that operated in earlier centuries. In some places, current policies are just as harmful as the worst policies of the past.[1] This happens even though it is clear that indigenous people do have special rights and interests that set them apart from other groups.

Voluntary and involuntary 'minority' communities

Discussing variations among diverse communities in their rates of school success, Ogbu (1987) draws a relevant distinction between 'involuntary' and 'voluntary' minority communities:[2]

> the main factor differentiating the more successful from the less successful minorities appears to be the nature of the history, subordination, and exploitation of the minorities, and the nature of the minorities' own instrumental and expressive responses to their treatment, which enter into the process of their schooling.
>
> (Ogbu 1987: 317)

Involuntary minorities are constrained by social, school and classroom structures that have denied them equal opportunity over many generations. Historically, they have encountered a job ceiling in the world of work, inferior forms of education, and random racism in every sphere of living. Their cultural capital has not been recognized in the institution of education, and their cultural interests have not been consulted by policy makers at system or school levels. In short, the members of these minorities have very good reasons for believing that they do not have an equal chance when compared with members of the dominant cultural group. Although they resist the label 'minorities' (with good reason) aboriginal peoples have been made involuntary minorities in their own lands.

Involuntary minorities also have 'secondary cultural differences' that develop as 'a response to a contact situation, especially a contact situation involving the domination of one group by another' (Ogbu 1987: 322). This domination occurs in a setting from which the involuntary minority cannot withdraw, because the setting is their own home. With no chance of living their lives away from the all-intruding dominant culture, they see the differences that exist between themselves and the majority culture as insurmountable. But the same differences are rooted in aspects of their own identity that must be maintained, because it is the substance of a culture that exists nowhere else.

All this contrasts with the structures that affect voluntary immigrant minorities, like many of those discussed in Chapters 4 and 6. Members of these communities see their own cultural differences as barriers to be overcome in achieving success in employment or lifestyle. They are able to look back on their former homelands as places of fewer opportunities, where education in many cases was even worse than the worst forms of schooling that they experience in their new country. Because their primary cultural differences are so recognizable, it is easier for voluntary minorities to adopt strategies that improve academic success and social adjustment.

The same cannot be said for the world's involuntary minorities. For them emancipatory change has been slow in coming. Chapter 5 looks in part at the involuntary minorities that are very much at the centre of Ogbu's concern: the African Americans who are descendants of slaves.[3] This chapter concentrates on the world's indigenous involuntary minorities.

Early educational developments

The early years of European contact with aboriginal peoples saw some of the worst infringements upon human rights that the world has ever seen. On every continent, there were massacres of these peoples by European invaders. In geographically remote centres, like Newfoundland and Tasmania, the indigenous peoples were hunted to extinction as recently as the nineteenth century. From these terrible beginnings, things could only improve. But even recent contacts between indigenous peoples and their colonizers have been a steady escalation of pressures on the aboriginal peoples to conform to the imposed cultures. Until as late as the 1970s, policy makers everywhere believed that their indigenous peoples were better off assimilating culturally, and learning the languages of the colonizers. This seemed to give them access to the cultural and economic goods of the dominant cultures, while moving them away from their own cultural contexts, which were widely regarded as inferior to those of the invaders.

These views now seem little more than a mixture of ignorance and racism, but their impact on educational policy lingers. For more than a century of compulsory education, aboriginal cultures and languages have been ignored. In mainstream schools, they have been ignored and replaced with those of the dominant majority. Often educational authorities have done more than simply ignore aboriginal cultures and languages. There are many documented accounts of injustices regularly inflicted upon indigenous minorities in an attempt to eradicate their cultures and languages through formal schooling practices. Many of these accounts are quite recent and they make harrowing reading.[4]

Reforms began to appear along with compelling evidence supporting the need to maintain minority languages of all kinds.[5] Because of the close links between language and culture, bicultural education also became a necessary part of efforts to promote bilingual education. Gradually in those countries where social justice had some political priority, policy makers became more receptive to the longstanding demands from aboriginal peoples that their cultures and languages receive more protection, and that bilingual and bicultural forms of education were good ways to do this. However, there were other incentives that also caused policy makers to look more kindly on these proposals.

In some countries, governments were motivated by the thought of reducing the long term costs of social programmes for the indigenous poor. It had long been argued that the loss of their languages and cultures was a major factor in the loss of community self-esteem among indigenous peoples. The loss of social identity and hope by aboriginal peoples, especially in remote settlements and in inner urban areas,[6] is linked to the destabilizing inroads made into their cultures by a culture of capitalism through the mass media. In fact, the decline in indigenous language use worsened in the middle years of the twentieth century, when the spreading mass media pressured aboriginal peoples everywhere to assimilate to outside norms based on the marketplace. Gradually policy makers began to realize that they were missing the real causes of low self-esteem and hopeless poverty if they treated it only with costly social welfare programmes. Based on the evidence, this change in policy seems justified.

As later sections in this chapter show, formerly disempowered communities do begin to rise in esteem, in political influence, and in economic self-sufficiency at the same time as the strengthening of their languages and cultures. Higher educational success rates follow, along with an increase in life chances. These developments offer a clear guide to 'education for diversity' reforms of all kinds.

Developments in the late twentieth century

In 1990, the various policies for bilingual and bicultural education in different countries received international support in the International Labour Office (ILO) convention on indigenous peoples. Articles 27 and 28 concern rights to independent forms of education and general language rights:

Governments shall recognise the right of these peoples to establish their own educational institutions and facilities . . . Children belonging to the peoples concerned shall, wherever practicable, be taught to read and write in their own indigenous language or in the language most commonly used by the group to which they belong.

(International Labour Office 1990: 16)

This convention gave strong encouragement to governments to act more justly in their language policies for indigenous peoples. But developments in some places foreshadowed the ILO convention by many years.

Quite radical reforms have occurred in some parts of the world; also there are interesting contrasts between countries. The five countries examined in this section fall into two categories: Norway and New Zealand are both places where the indigenous people are rather homogeneous in culture and language. In contrast, the indigenous peoples of Canada, Australia, and the United States are very diverse in their cultures and languages. As a result, these three countries are much affected in their policy development by the diversity of aboriginal cultures that they contain.

The Norwegian example: the Sámi[7]

The Sámi are the oldest known population of Scandinavia, dating from pre-historic times. In English, they have been called Laplanders, but their officially accepted name is now Sámi. The largest Sámi population lives in Norway where three Sámi languages are in use. Early missionaries from the fifteenth century insisted that the Sámi drop their own languages for religious purposes and use Finnish, which the missionaries commonly spoke. Later missionaries burned sacred aspects of the indigenous material culture, or sent it off to museums. They also put Sámi shamans to death. What remained of the material culture was destroyed by a German scorched-earth policy in 1944, when every building in the County of Finnmark was systematically destroyed in expectation of a Russian attack.

Like all aboriginal peoples, the Sámi have been victims of strong official assimilation policies, lasting for almost 400 years in their case. Norwegian and other settlers in Sámi areas rarely acquired the Sámi language, and were often offended by its use. Nevertheless the clan cultures remain very distinctive. For other Scandinavians, the Sámi languages are closely associated with reindeer-herding and breeding. But this is only a common but far from exclusive occupation of the Sámi, practised in the nomadic heartland by about 20 per cent of the local clan members, but by only 5 per cent of Sámi in Norway as a whole. So the stereotype of Sámi as Scandinavia's reindeer-herders is far from accurate, especially as recent generations have moved to take full control of all aspects of their lives.

The Norwegian government and education system responded earlier than many others to the research evidence stressing the importance of mother tongue maintenance for minority language peoples. For these children, intensive early exposure in school to the majority language, coupled with school neglect of their first language, results in low achievement in the majority language, a decline in mother tongue proficiency, and academic failure. So early and constant programmes to maintain the languages of minority first-language speakers are needed to avoid widespread school failure, and to help reverse the culture stripping so common in some places.

Following Norway's ratification of the ILO convention on indigenous peoples in 1990, the Norwegian Parliament introduced the Sámi Language Act to strengthen official use of the Sámi languages and to declare Sámi and Norwegian equal languages with equal status. Enforced from 1992, this Act affects three areas (Magga 1995): laws concerning the Sámi Parliament which has been operating since 1989; courts of law themselves; and laws for education. The Act aims to enable the Sámi to safeguard and develop their language, culture, and way of life, and to give equal status to Sámi and Norwegian. To oversee the language's future, a Sámi Language Council has its members appointed by the Sámi Parliament, and advises and reports on all matters affecting the language.

The administrative area for the Sámi languages covers six municipalities in Norway's northernmost counties. Obligations under the Act apply to any public body serving part of these six districts. The new Act provides the following for children living in these Sámi areas:

- all children have the right to receive instruction through the medium of Sámi in all subjects
- until the seventh grade (14-year-olds), parents have the choice on whether their children will receive instruction in or through Sámi
- from seventh grade, the pupils decide this for themselves
- children receiving instruction in or through Sámi are exempted from instruction in one of the two forms of Norwegian
- local education councils may allow children with Sámi as their mother tongue to be taught through the language for all nine compulsory years.

Outside Sámi areas, the following first language provisions apply:

- instruction through Sámi may be given to pupils with a Sámi background
- if there are no fewer than three pupils in one school whose mother tongue is Sámi, they can ask to be taught through the language[8]
- in general any Norwegian child, regardless of background, has the right to be taught Sámi
- Sámi history and culture are included in national curriculum guidelines as topics that all children should be familiar with.

Initial fears that many parents would withdraw their children from Sámi-medium instruction in Sámi districts, and so weaken the language's range of influence, seem unwarranted. Sámi parents are already strongly supporting Sámi-medium education.[9] This is very important: it is the intricate link between successful language planning policies, the development of Sámi identity, and the reduction of social problems in the community that seem most relevant to the often desperate social situations of aboriginal peoples elsewhere.

Insights about social and behavioural issues among aboriginal and other young people from diverse backgrounds come from recent research on Sámi identity in Sámiland. Kvernmo (1993) indicates that the presence or absence of behavioural problems among Sámi young people and the quality of their future lives are closely linked to the relative strength of their cultural identity. Moreover Sámi identity is strengthened by a positive attitude among parents to their own Sámi identity and especially to their Sámi language. Kvernmo sees the use of a Sámi first language at home as the key factor in rebuilding Sámi identity.

A revitalization of Sámi identity and culture followed the creation of modern towns on the ruins of war. Sámi people now prefer to describe themselves as Sámi first, and only as citizens of Norway. A new image of a Sámi person has developed, integrating the modern world into the traditional culture to make the Sámi more self-confident and secure in their identity. Although pressure to sustain identity is now mainly coming from language, and less from traditional activities, pan-Sámi solidarity is also an important expression of identity, as the Sámi develop more formal links across the four countries that they inhabit. The new youth radicalism in the 1990s was a factor promoting cultural unity and identity. Even the wearing of small items of traditional clothing at rock concerts or discotheques, or using a few Sámi words as greetings, are regarded among the young as cultural bonding actions of great importance.

Cultural identity is also sustained by the factional tension within Sámi. Dating back to the nineteenth century, two rival but cooperating factions, the conservative and the radical, began to develop. The radical faction has its roots in the more economically disadvantaged Sámi who inhabit the coastal regions of Finnmark and Troms, people heavily affected by the depression in the 1930s, who became involved in radical, Marxist, and later social democratic political movements. The more conservative faction centres on the relatively affluent and more bourgeois reindeer-herding families. Their privileged economic position is now guaranteed by the reindeer-herding laws that give Sámi sole control of this industry, even though it is now integrated firmly into the Norwegian national economy. This factional divide has a positive dialectical effect in the Sámi Parliament, with the radical wing trying to drive the culture forward politically, while the conservative wing works to sustain the culture's values. The absence of this dialectic among many aboriginal peoples elsewhere may be significant for cultural maintenance and revitalization.

Norwegian compulsory schooling has operated much in its present form for 200 years. As a result, for the Sámi, there is a historically shaped, conservative view of what the school is, and what it can be. Even so, there is growing interest in changing schools to make them more 'organic' to the cultural communities that they serve. Experiments using the Sámi language in primary schools began in 1967. It is now both a medium of instruction in bilingual immersion programmes, and taught as a subject in secondary schools (Balto and Todal 1997). In large towns like Kautokeino and Karasjok, the language is used as the everyday language by almost all Sámi.

The Sámi Education Council has a statutory role to advise Sámi parents, both inside and outside the six districts, who write to them, or who are referred by school boards and other agencies. This advice can cover several things: language and cultural maintenance matters, including inquiries about motivating children to maintain the language and culture; what language and other rights the Sámi possess under law; and how to get school boards to act in recognition of the Act. The council also produces high quality texts for all levels and all subjects of basic schooling, in the three Sámi languages. Some of these are similar to textbooks used in Norwegian-medium schooling, but written for Sámi as a first language. The council also translates some texts from Norwegian for curriculum areas such as mathematics, where direct translations of Norwegian are sufficient. But mainly the council's staff write new texts with Sámi cultural content, to replace existing Norwegian texts written for the national curriculum. Lastly, the council engages in corpus language planning to expand the Sámi vocabularies, so that education can be carried on in those languages at more senior levels.

The Sámi College in Kautokeino provides a variety of courses and programmes in higher education to students drawn from across Scandinavia. Fluency in a Sámi language is a requirement for permanent appointment to staff, because most classes are conducted in Sámi, and Northern Sámi is the language of administration in the college. Staff members conduct research on cultural needs, language planning, and educational innovation. As well as four year programmes of training for basic school teachers, there is also a three year kindergarten teacher training programme.

So far, the Sámi education system is strongest in early childhood education, but all provisions have gone ahead rapidly since the early 1980s. As in other aboriginal settings, the pre-school and kindergarten years provide more flexibility and opportunity for integration of Sámi culture and values. Beginning with its early childhood provisions, the Sámi College offers an example of a culturally and linguistically appropriate form of teacher training. The college uses the minority language as the vehicle of teacher education. It also uses 'the

Sámi way' as its backdrop of living cultural expectations to prepare the Sámi teachers as genuine agents of cultural revival and legitimation.

Although qualified teachers are available throughout the country, only now are teachers-in-training at the Sámi College being taught in Sámi, using Sámi cultural values. Previously all teachers were taught 'the Norwegian way' or 'the Swedish way'. In contrast, the Sámi way tries to see the world with Sámi at the centre, not at the edge. It uses Sámi cultural ideas, values, and literature. The Sámi way is more holistic; there are fewer subject boundaries. Emphasis is laid on oral ways of teaching, especially based on 'living' cultural stories, as parables for teaching values, ethics, and lifestyle. Sámi College teachers-in-training are motivated to incorporate this traditional narrative approach into their teaching, so that Sámi children in future will not have to learn so much from books. In 1994, a new first language methods course for teachers-in-training was introduced into the Sámi College. The course aims to produce fully bilingual school graduates in the Sámi districts, and much bilingual proficiency among Sámi-as-a-second-language students elsewhere.

A new problem is how to extend this Sámi way into teaching Sámi children living outside the six districts. It is hoped that the college will gradually infiltrate teachers trained in this way into the wider school system. Accordingly college staff already feel the need to become activists for this method. This is especially important for the very young, because once they come to expect this in their education, then education at later stages will gradually change to meet that expectation. Later, teachers-in-training graduated from schools of this kind will themselves insist on a greater incorporation of the culture. Sámi parents have to be educated too, so that they see the advantages of all this for their children and expect to receive a more sophisticated cultural product from schooling, along with broader forms of personal development for their children, not just a bland qualification.

The growing influence of modern information technology on the curriculum poses a new problem: how to get Sámi values represented in that technology, when those values are best manifested in face-to-face interaction? To address this problem, the Sámi College has become the only place in Norway where students learn how to produce their own teaching materials and computer software for developing classroom resources. This programme is operating in cooperation with the Sámi Education Council, who have had long experience producing materials. Publishers visit Kautokeino to teach students to produce their own materials, and teachers come from all over Norway to study in this course.

An innovatory form of egalitarian school administration has been trialled in many Norwegian schools since the early 1980s. This practice is relevant to the non-hierarchical way that the Sámi have of relating to one another. In Kautokeino's primary school, the three school leaders have only three year contracts as co-administrators, and then return to teaching posts in the same school. As administrators, all three are equal in status and all have an area of responsibility: one for teachers, one for children, and one for curriculum and pedagogy. Responsibility for plant and facilities rotates, and a budget policy committee handles finances. After three years of trials, the arrangement seemed to be working well, with few problems. Parents appreciated having more than one person with authority to relate to, and the approach makes use of the special skills and strengths of each person as an administrator. Over time, many staff in schools with this form of administration will fill leadership roles, if elected to do so by their colleagues. As a result, no one has the unusual powers of ascribed control in the school setting that principals conventionally have.

For Sámi-as-a-first-language pupils, all subjects are taught in Sámi until the ninth grade (16-year-olds), provided that teachers and texts are available. Norwegian-medium classes are provided where there are gaps in the Sámi-speaking staff. The Sámi-as-a-first-language pupils are entitled to as much Norwegian-as-a-second-language instruction as Norwegian-medium Sámi-as-a-second-language children receive in Sámi. Inside the six districts, Norwegian receives a balanced place in the curriculum. But Norwegian classes in the Sámi heartland are getting smaller each year, as the prestige of knowing Sámi increases. As a result, parents in the Sámi districts are now very willing for their children to learn through Sámi, reversing the tendency among parents to stigmatize the language that is still found in some places. School graduates are genuinely bilingual in Norwegian and Sámi. There is now greater Sámi language use among children than in the early 1980s, including children whose parents are culturally mixed. Even non-Sámi-speaking parents in the six districts prefer to enrol their children in Sámi-medium classes, as the status of Sámi has increased because of the Sámi laws. The next step for aboriginal education in Norway is changing the schools themselves to reflect the culture and its values. However, this is not such an easy step, and it is even more difficult in a country like Canada with its many aboriginal cultures and traditions.

The Canadian experience: the First Nations and the Inuit[10]

It is not easy to speak in general terms about aboriginal education in Canada, or in Australia, or in the United States, because these are all federal countries of great size and many different systems of education. The cultural and linguistic differences between any two distinct aboriginal peoples in Canada can be as great as the cultural and linguistic differences between any two distinct peoples elsewhere. In other words, the actual diversity that exists between Canadian aboriginal peoples defeats the stereotypes that once passed for cultural descriptions.

Aboriginal peoples in Canada are now taking back more and more control of their lives. This follows centuries of domination, including harsh policies of assimilation worked out through residential schools and the transporting of entire communities away from their homelands (Haig-Brown 1988). Often there was wide aboriginal resistance to these earlier expressions of domination; this resistance has now coalesced into visible institutions of great influence. A major demand coming from these institutions is that aboriginal peoples should take control of their educational systems. The landmark paper, *Indian Control of Indian Education* (National Indian Brotherhood 1972), was an early step in this direction. Since then, progress has occurred in all areas of aboriginal control of education, although the many advances have been uneven. Some communities have established an effective change process, while others have had less than happy experiences. Clearly cultural survival is linked to language survival in important ways, and based on the number of their speakers, only two Indian languages, Cree and Ojibway, and the Inuit language, Inuktitut, seem likely to survive for much longer as widely used community languages.

Québec is one province where a pattern of decline in aboriginal languages has been reversed. As a result, Québec's model of cooperation between aboriginal, federal, and provincial authorities seems to offer an important lead to other provinces, especially in the relationships between aboriginal languages and French or English. For example, the Cree Way programme offers full immersion in Cree until fourth grade, when either English or French is introduced for half the curriculum. In fifth grade, the official languages become the medium of instruction, except for courses in Cree and Cree culture. The programme has had a wide impact on the community, with parents and siblings joining adult education classes to improve their Cree proficiency (Feurer 1993). Also in Québec, the Cree School Board's language curriculum allows Cree children to learn in their own language and develop a solid foundation for their identity through constant contact with Cree values. In practice, many difficulties are being challenged in this programme. These include the need to work in two Cree dialects, the need to ensure adequate teacher preparation, Cree lexical development, standardization of written and oral forms, and the need to develop a Cree culture curriculum (Herodier 1992).

High quality bilingual education is available in Canada, mainly in French/English bilingualism. The country also has models using aboriginal languages as vehicle and subject of instruction. But while these models are important, they are also isolated and spread across the country. In general, they get little coordination at provincial or national levels, depending instead on the efforts of local aboriginal peoples themselves. Also, while many aboriginal communities want aboriginal language immersion programmes (Heimbecker 1997), there are few reports of evaluations of language-in-education programmes to improve the quality and range of other programmes across the country. An Aboriginal Language Policy Study (Assembly of First Nations 1988) called for the creation of policies to ensure the survival and revitalization of aboriginal languages across Canada. It mentions the desperate need for more resources and the need to develop a means for sharing information and materials. In fact, Canada has a great need for careful and systematically managed language planning aimed at language revival. Yet at present, the country has no such facility and none is in the planning stages.

At the same time, many aboriginal peoples in Canada are revitalizing their cultures, as aboriginal control of aboriginal schooling becomes common (Battiste and Barman 1995). In spite of this, the languages are often not widely used in education. A survey of policy and programmes shows that about a third of the 458 schools surveyed offer an aboriginal language as a subject. But less than 4 per cent of schools reported using an aboriginal language as a medium of instruction. Most of these were in the Northwest Territories where the Inuit language, Inuktitut, was used in the primary grades with gradual introduction of English in later years (Kirkness and Bowman Selkirk 1992).

Other programmes also provide examples of innovatory bicultural practices. In Saskatchewan, early childhood and youth programmes were developed by the Meadow Lake tribal community, using a bicultural approach that gives students the knowledge and skills needed to work effectively in their own culture and in the dominant North American culture. The project brings together a university and the aboriginal community in a programme that was community initiated and controlled (Pence *et al.* 1992).

Toronto has the largest concentration of aboriginal peoples of any region in North America, including the traditional aboriginal homelands. Like Sydney, Australia, Toronto seems a magnet of opportunities for aboriginal peoples. Many travel vast distances and change their lives dramatically to take up residence in these cities. Many succeed, but always with a sense of loss for their cultures and their way of life. As a result, First Nations Survival Schools operate in many urban areas of Canada. As their name suggests, these schools strive to maintain the values and the practices of First Nation cultures, in inner-city settings where the material culture does not exist. A few do insert an aboriginal language into their curriculum. Others concentrate on common cultural elements because of the variety of First Nations peoples served by the schools. Observers see these schools as examples of a compassionate and productive approach to the education of urban aboriginal youth.[11]

In British Columbia, the Nisga'a nation began a community-based bilingual and bicultural programme in 1975 (McKay and McKay 1987). This soon led to higher school retention rates and a greater degree of biculturalism among graduates. Also, in the same province, Seabird Island Community School offers several unique features. This band-controlled school has a strong policy to involve the community: an open door approach, with many community members working as resource persons. Teachers must learn the community language with the children, although many parents do not speak the language themselves. This school's developments are seen as a fine example of implementing Indian control of Indian education (E. Gardner 1986).

Great changes have also happened in Inuit education since the 1970s, but there is much to be done, even to catch up with Inuit reforms elsewhere. Dorais (1992) compares the greater autonomy and collective rights of Inuit in Greenland with the position of Canada's Inuit. He draws a direct link between this autonomy and the relative strength and development of Inuktitut in Greenland. Because of the long and relatively balanced history of intercultural contacts in Greenland, that country's indigenous system offers a model for aboriginal educational development elsewhere (Stairs 1994). At the same time, the Baffin Divisional Board of Education (1989) offers a good model for the rest of Canada. Its Piniaqtavut programme gives students bilingual skills and biliteracy in Inuktitut and English. It stresses Inuit beliefs and values, using a curriculum model of interaction with members of the culture and constant experiences in the culture's activities. Administrators in the Baffin Island system are working steadily to make their schools more organic to the Inuit culture, especially by bringing communities and schools together in planning and consultation.

Elsewhere, in Northern Québec, Inuit teachers are chosen by the community and trained on site. Teachers gather knowledge for the curriculum and implement programmes, using teacher action research to evaluate early language courses and cognitive learning styles. Here too, the community is deeply involved in debating the role of the school (Stairs 1985). In fact, Inuit community members see the problem of balancing the two cultures, the Inuit and the Euro-Canadian, as a more pressing concern than the acquisition of western-style literacy itself (Stairs 1990). This problem of cultural balance is one that the Maori in New Zealand have already addressed; they are more successful in doing this than many other indigenous peoples.

The New Zealand example: the Maori people

In New Zealand, aboriginal schooling has changed rapidly in many places. This change is in response to the belief of many Maori people that the European-style school system is not suited to sustaining a Polynesian culture. The injustice for oppressed peoples in New Zealand and elsewhere is captured by a Maori educationist who asks:

Have you ever heard Maori people talking about leaving their *Maori-tanga* [Maori culture] at the school gate so that they can come to school to learn their *Pakehatanga* [non-Maori New Zealand culture]? Maori people have learned to behave that way in order to survive. When Maori people have been asked what they want from the education system, they have always answered, 'the best of both worlds: *Maori-tanga* and *Pakehatanga*.' They have not wanted to choose one rather than the other but both. The dualism of Pakeha thinking has made the Maori feel guilty for not preferring one over the other.

(Penetito 1986: 20)

New Zealand uses several approaches to modifying majority culture schools. In 1989, a radical reform of educational administration enabled the devolution of much educational decision making away from national and regional levels and down to new boards of trustees (school councils) that are elected for every school in the country. Each school is required to insert into its formal charter a strong expression of commitment to non-sexist and anti-racist values, and guaranteed support for the educational rights of the Maori, especially a commitment to the Maori language. This is because legal interpretations of historic treaty arrangements in New Zealand give all Maori people the right to an education in Maori, should they demand it.[12]

The requirement that schools operate according to a charter drafted in consultation with community groups aims to give people from backgrounds of diversity much more scope to exercise a fair measure of influence over their children's education. This development encourages the reform of exist-ing schools, to take more account of the diversity within them. Because Maori see language at the heart of their culture, their more urgent reforms involve changes in language policy at national and school levels.

New Zealand has no official national policy for its Maori people and their language, although the Maori language has had official language status since 1987. Maori is spoken with only minor dialectal differences throughout the country, and the culture is relatively homogeneous across the more than 30 tribes that remain in the country. Although Maori students make up 20 per cent of the elementary school population, few have Maori as their first lan-guage. Only a draft discussion language policy has been developed (Waite 1992) and policy makers seem reluctant to give much recognition to this draft policy. Instead, New Zealand's language policies have evolved alongside changes to education policies in general. Gradually many bilingual Maori/English elementary schools and monolingual Maori schools have developed. Maori communities and tribal groups themselves have been quick to take advantage of these changes. In fact, most of the positive developments in Maori education have come from the efforts of the people themselves.

Kohanga reo or language nests
Three developments are most significant. The first is the kohanga reo or language nests pre-school movement, which has occurred with little government sponsorship (Durie 1997). Anyone from any culture is welcome to send pre-school children to kohanga reo. Many Maori children begin in early infancy, and continue in these until they start school.

The kohanga reo aims to recreate the atmosphere of a traditional Maori home. It has no formal structures except opening prayers, regular meal breaks, and occasional ceremonies to greet guests. While the language nest has no structured curriculum and little equipment, there is plenty of singing and movement. The children create their own games but they are able to stay close to adults if they choose to, because there are always lots of adults taking part in activities, interacting with the children, and providing language and culture models. Beginning in the early and mid-1980s, the many hundreds of pre-schools send thousands of their graduates into regular state schools. Many of the children are well on the way to active bilingualism and biculturalism, because they inevitably acquire English and the majority culture outside the language nests, where that culture's dominance is unchallenged.

Bilingual and bicultural schools
The second response to Maori rights was the creation of multi-ethnic schools that incorporate the values of diverse cultures into mainstream educational values. Some of them, like Richmond Road, also have kohanga reo operating on the school's premises (May 1994).[13] In these elementary or primary schools, the Maori language is used as vehicle of instruction for some major part of the school day for anyone who wants a bilingual education in Maori and English.

Chapter 2 described the development of one of these schools. It sees that development as a playing out of the critical policy making and emancipatory leadership advanced as cornerstones of education for diversity in Chapter 1. Although Richmond Road, and similar schools, offer a remarkable model for educating for diversities of every kind, new arrangements in New Zealand go beyond this kind of innovation. They allow separate Maori language and culture state-funded schools. These are becoming an integral part of the national pattern of schooling, spreading rapidly wherever Maori communities exist.

Kura kaupapa Maori: Maori elementary schools
The third development is kura kaupapa Maori or Maori philosophy schools. National reforms in educational policy allowed small groups of people to establish their own state-funded schools and Maori people in many places

seized the chance to do so, because the Maori community itself had long advocated this reform. For the pupils, being Maori in these schools is the norm. The school and classroom environment connect directly with the Maori home and community. Consequently the Maori culture and language are central to teaching, curriculum, assessment, and administration.

This Maori philosophy of schooling aims to exclude interference by non-Maori New Zealanders and the structural influence of non-Maori cultural forces. For example, visitors to these schools are approved in advance by the governing community. The community ensures that any visitors, including government officials, have the interests of Maori at heart. This means that educational researchers, for instance, enter these schools only if they under-take to do research that empowers the community or benefits Maori in some other way. But this is not some form of separatism by Maori, because any children are free to attend these schools, if they want an education shaped by Maori rather than by European values. This exclusion of non-Maori structures links with the Maori need to work out what is basic to Maori cul-ture and to re-create what has been lost of the culture's values through its enforced contact with European culture.

A stress on bonding seems to permeate educational ideas seen as impor-tant in Polynesian cultures: bonding with one another, with the culture, and with the environment. This holistic and cooperative relationship with the universe runs throughout the Maori view of language and learning. The aim is the achievement of excellence and mastery of one's total self and the physi-cal environment through a balanced curriculum. Maori ways of thinking and responding to experience are more concerned with the whole than with the part. Ideally then, the curriculum is holistic, with weak boundaries between fields of knowledge and a near absence of frames (after Bernstein 1975): frames which prevent people from learning in their own way, in their own time, at their own pace, and throughout life.

All this means that many regular school practices are changed. School subject boundaries reduce or disappear; anyone who has knowledge teaches; schools are open outside normal hours; and teachers fill a facilitative rather than an instructional role. Organizational and learning styles stress extended family or group involvement, with students given opportunities to learn alongside people with skills, interacting with experts, and not merely (or perhaps not at all) with a textbook. Classrooms and schools have an atmosphere that encourages a sense of belonging, a family feeling of physi-cal closeness, where each student is given personal attention, praise, encour-agement, and the daily experience of success and accomplishment.

High regard is also paid to student differences in learning approaches. In this way the self-esteem and sense of cultural belonging of students is given high regard too. Learning is a cooperative exercise, with children, teachers, parents, and community all involved. Oral language interaction, adult to child and child to child, is the central pedagogy of the Maori school. The older children assist and care for their younger relatives in and out of school. Competitive individualism and individual gain are secondary to collaboration, cooperation, and group benefit. This relative absence of competition limits the forms of evaluation that are desirable: great care is taken to avoid embarrassment in moments of student failure and to discourage conceit in success.

At the same time, these schools are concerned to teach a modern, up-to-date, and relevant curriculum following national guidelines set by the state, whose outcome is the graduation of fully bilingual and bicultural students (Hingangaroa Smith 1995). Similarly patterned secondary schools will follow, and perhaps more Maori language and culture universities too, on a more equal footing with other universities in the country. Like the Maori schools themselves, these will be controlled and run by Maori themselves (Durie 1997). All these developments have been watched very closely by aboriginal peoples elsewhere, not least by Australia's Aboriginal policy makers.

The Australian Aboriginal peoples

Like Canada, Australia's Aboriginal education policies need to address many very different indigenous cultures. Similarly there are huge distances that have to be dealt with in implementing educational reforms. But Australia's approach lessens the problem of the federal nature of both countries by having a single national coordinating body to oversee language policy developments. The National Languages and Literacy Institute of Australia (NLLIA) does this work. Although the more significant developments there are mainly to do with language policy, an underlying trend in Australian social policy for more than a generation has been towards granting more formal recognition and cultural rights to the country's Aboriginal peoples (S. Harris and Devlin 1997).

Much of the groundwork for the NLLIA's work was laid by the National Aboriginal Languages Program (NALP). In the first four years of this programme, more than 90 languages benefited from funding. A formal review of the NALP was very positive about the programme's overall benefits and its role in redressing the serious neglect of these languages. Its achievements included the following: raising awareness among teachers about the problems of Aboriginal first language speakers; increasing the self-esteem of Aboriginal language speakers; winning greater public recognition for Aboriginal languages; and improving student retention rates among Aborigines themselves (AACLAME 1990). The Support for Aboriginal Languages in Schools policy has carried on this work.

In Australia, as in Canada, there is no federal legislation giving official language status to aboriginal languages. This makes it more difficult for the Australian government to protect and develop the aboriginal languages and their cultures in their home territories. Consequently school policies are rather piecemeal in this area, and they vary greatly from state to state and even from district to district. The widest programme of bilingual education is in the Northern Territory where 22 schools offer 17 aboriginal languages to about 4,000 school-age children (S. Harris and Devlin 1997).

Initial literacy in the language itself was the cornerstone of aboriginal education in the Northern Territory. Promising developments came in the 1990s as more qualified Aboriginal bilingual/bicultural teachers became available. Beginning in 1973, the Northern Territory bilingual programme insisted that Aboriginal languages should be taught only by Aboriginal people. This led to a team-teaching tradition. Each community had to decide on a local language for the school to use, and a fluent Aboriginal person worked alongside a teacher of English. This produced informal on-site Aboriginal teacher education that was much needed in remote areas. Later, more formal teacher education programmes began. But by the 1990s, Aboriginal groups became dissatisfied with this old approach to bilingual education. A new approach developed called 'two-way schooling'. The main difference lies in 'who controls the educational process':

> Bilingual education, despite its Aboriginal-centred components, was ultimately managed by Whites, whereas two-way schooling is under Aboriginal control. All these changes were accompanied by a decentralization of leadership.
>
> (S. Harris and Devlin 1997)

While Australia's investment in its National Language Policy was symbolically important, the process of restoring the linguistic rights of Aboriginal peoples through education has been patchy and ill coordinated. Walsh, for example, assesses Australia's response to the decline of traditional languages: 'Bilingual education is one possible solution to this legitimate concern. Regrettably there has been too little and most of it too late' (Walsh 1991: 47–8). There are notable successes, like 'the outstandingly successful [Kriol/English] programme at Barunga school' (J. Harris 1991: 202). But where Aboriginal first language schools do exist, mainly in parts of Northern Australia, the languages are used exclusively in the primary grades. Progressive transition to English is the goal.[14] There are few attempts to revive the languages and the cultures through education.

Many believe that change is not happening because policy makers are unaware of what Aboriginal Australians really want from their education. One account of what Aboriginal people want from education, based on the assembled views of practising Aboriginal educators, includes the following five points:[15]

- attention to the harmony and unity of Aboriginal life: individual achievement which ignores the meaningfulness of the Aboriginal group is not wanted
- preserving continuity with the past, the land and the people: progress is good only if it bolsters Aboriginal identity
- placing value on doing things in response to the total physical and social environment
- personal independence, with no coercion and manipulation: unconditional acceptance of everyone
- interference by White educators is the problem, not the solution.

The most that is being done to address aspirations of this kind, even at local levels, seems to be in the Northern Territory, where the Aboriginal vote is large and relatively significant. Where it is occurring, 'Aboriginalization' has the following features:[16]

- a majority of Aboriginal staff in any school serving an Aboriginal community
- an Aboriginal principal
- a controlling Aboriginal parent body
- Aboriginal priorities in the curriculum
- community-based teacher education
- less centralized bureaucratic control
- minimum levels of non-Aboriginal cultural capital (as much as is needed to make schools work).

For Aboriginal people themselves, getting Aboriginal control over Aboriginal schooling is more important even than academic matters. In addition, there is also strong support from other Australians for extending Aboriginal control of schools. But structural factors are still getting in the way:

> These gains are constantly vulnerable to changes in government, and consequent policy changes, and a still-pervasive non-Aboriginal involvement in Aboriginal 'self' determination. An example is the fluctuating number of non-Aboriginal staff in schools . . . Another example is the continuing behind-the-scenes influence of non-Aboriginal administrators over Aboriginal people in positions of educational leadership. In other words, the 'Aboriginal industry' is alive and well for non-Aboriginal people.
>
> (S. Harris and Devlin 1997)

While the NLLIA does internationally noted work, in many areas of language policy at least, it is undermined in the area of Aboriginal education because its mandate is to provide for indigenous languages at the same time as meeting all its other non-Aboriginal language functions. This understates that important function and takes it out of the hands of people with a real stake in the languages and the cultures that they identify with. Also the NLLIA is handicapped by its remoteness in Canberra and by the narrowness of the goals set for it in relation to Aboriginal languages by the Ministry of Employment, Education and Training (National Languages and Literacy Institute of Australia 1993).

Based on these developments so far, and the size and cultural complexity of the country, Australia's future achievements may never approach the potential for unity of aboriginal purpose that the Sámi Education Council is realizing in Norway. Earlier the NALP tried to link its support for the strongest Aboriginal languages with support for the most neglected. But there has been a rapid and alarming decline in Aboriginal language retention, and, with the languages, a decline in aboriginal cultural identification. While a few languages are described as healthy, most of the surviving languages are weakening or dying (Dixon 1989) and the cultures are disappearing with them. Clearly the trend towards Aboriginalization of schools, appearing in the 1990s, could not arrive soon enough.

The American experience: American Indian, Alaska Native, and Native Hawaiian

Diverse indigenous peoples also inhabit the United States. As well as the many Indian peoples, there are the aboriginal peoples of Alaska, who comprise 20 Alaskan language groups, and the Polynesian people of Hawaii.[17] Several federally funded programmes with their origins in the civil rights movement of the 1960s stimulated greater aboriginal control and involvement in education in various parts of the United States. The passage of the Indian Education Act in 1972 allowed greater devolution of decision making to America's 2 million aboriginal people. Although many communities have taken advantage of this and brought changes to their own educational provisions, the situation for most others is as bad as ever.

American Indians have the highest school dropout rate of any group in the country. The rate is around 50 per cent, and Indian females are dropping out at even higher rates than males. Those pushed out of school in this way go on to live their lives in grinding poverty (Deyhle and Swisher 1997). Yet even those who do succeed in schools find that school success rarely leads to a better life, unless they keep close links with their Indian traditions. The evidence is clear that the most successful Amerindian students have a strong sense of aboriginal identity, maintained in traditional Indian homes where the Indian language is spoken. In fact, these students tend to succeed even where schools do not have a culturally responsive curriculum. As with the

Sámi in Norway,[18] a strong sense of ethnic identity, linked with language maintenance, supports Indian success in school, and improves quality of life generally. However, it is not easy for most Indian communities to maintain their languages.

The shift towards English has become relentless in most communities. At the same time, government action to reverse language decline is sluggish at best (McCarty 1997a). As in many areas of American social policy, the excellent insights into how things should be reformed offered by research far exceed the reforms that are actually taking place. For example, there is much research looking at practices of 'cultural congruence' for schools, but it is little applied.[19] Below I summarize some of the highlights from the many research studies, especially those that offer insights for aboriginal conditions more generally. The earliest and perhaps most influential of these studies comes from a generation ago.

Cultural variations in discourse norms
On the Warm Springs reservation in Oregon, Philips looked at children from several tribes of Native American children, both early and late in their junior school careers.[20] She found that Warm Springs Indian children learned socially appropriate norms for paying attention and regulating talk encounters in home and community that were different from those learned by Anglo-American middle class children. These norms were also different from the norms for classroom interaction, but they were not taken into account in any way in the development of the curriculum. She argues that this incompatibility made it difficult for the culturally different children to understand verbal messages conveyed through the school's Anglo middle class ways of organizing classroom interaction.

Philips offers evidence that Indian children often misunderstand teacher talk: they talk much less in official classroom interaction and respond less often to direct teacher questions; their responses to teacher questions are more often seen as inappropriate by the teacher; and the children's questions suggest uncertainty about their own comprehension. The Indian children show attention in different ways, and are often seen as inattentive, even when they are attending. At the same time, they do pay less attention than other children and are often interacting with their classmates, although they do not initiate work-oriented talk as often as others, or interrupt others to get the floor as much. Also their talk is more evenly distributed among Indian students, regardless of academic ability.

All of these features matched the patterns of communication in the adult Warm Springs Indian communities. This means that they were culturally appropriate things for the children to do, yet the school at the time missed the significance of this for their education. Later in this chapter, I discuss the relevance of different discourse norms for school and classroom practices.

Clearly classrooms are key situations in the lives of all children. They are places where future life chances are distributed.[21]

This idea of key situation comes from the work of American researchers. While living in complex stratified societies, people have certain key gate-keeping encounters that are crucial for entering occupations, for admission to advanced education, and for receiving official services.[22] Because of cultural differences in discourse styles and strategies, some are favoured in these key settings, but others are denied the same ready access to social opportunities. This is really an aspect of Bourdieu's cultural capital: some social groups bring different forms of cultural capital that are not highly valued in these key situations, and this can easily disadvantage them. At the same time, the different dispositions that different groups have for judging the world of others places them at a disadvantage in a world of key situations defined according to another group's dispositions. Formal education is rich in key situations of this kind. Researchers in Hawaii, for example, have studied key situations like 'group reading narration'.

Many native Hawaiian children do not do very well in Hawaiian schools, especially children who are not from the middle class and who are not inside the majority culture. Vogt *et al.* (1987) studied the socialization of these Polynesian children at home and compared it with their lives at school. The researchers tried to identify better instructional practices, methods of classroom organization, and techniques for motivation. Several successful strategies seemed more compatible with the children's lived culture outside the school.

The researchers reduced the high rates of teacher praise given to individuals, and replaced it with more indirect methods of praise, or with praise directed at the group as a whole. They stressed a search for meaning in reading lessons, rather than drilling in skills, and they introduced vertical grouping of children to create settings where advanced students could help less advanced students. By structuring reading lessons in this way, lasting reading achievement scores resulted. The context created was more consistent with communicative contexts created by Polynesian adults for their children, where there is less parental intervention and where children learn in groups that rarely give praise to individuals.[23]

This change replaced the regular pattern for reading group teaching based on the teacher isolating individual students. As a result, students seemed to be liberated by the changes. They began to contribute more freely in a speech style that was familiar to them. Teachers in turn began to adapt their own responses to the more natural styles of the children. These classroom changes also made teachers see the aboriginal children differently. They dropped stereotypes about the children lacking motivation or being hard to manage. Gradually these new participation structures became part of the regular language curriculum.

The evidence from Cherokee, Sioux, Warm Springs, Athabaskan, Odawa, and Hawaiian children suggests that their apparent lack of responsiveness in classrooms is context specific.[24] In other words, it appears in different ways in key situations. For example, all these groups of aboriginal children respond less well in certain activities: when they are singled out as individuals before the group in a formal way; when they have to raise their hands to indicate willingness to answer; and when their responses are assessed publicly. Nevertheless there are great differences between these and other aboriginal groups in norms of behaviour, so great in fact that there is a real risk of stereotyping aboriginal students by forgetting that they are very different from one another, both as groups and as individuals. I return to this point in a later section.[25]

At the same time, aboriginal children from almost anywhere in the world do have one thing in common: the broadly different processes of childrearing and socialization that they experience often lead to interactive patterns that are inconsistent in certain settings with the practices of traditional schools. So how can schools serving aboriginal communities begin to respond to these differences? One way is to create entirely separate schools where aboriginal interactive patterns are the norm, rather than the exception.

Indian focus schools

As in other places, aboriginal communities in the United States have a record of success in running their own schools. These include schools administered by the Chickasaw, Choctaw, Cherokee and Navajo nations. One in particular, Rough Rock Navajo demonstration school, has offered a model of aboriginal control over aboriginal education for all of North America. McCarty (1989) describes Rough Rock as the first aboriginal school with its own locally elected board, and the first to make systematic use of the aboriginal language and culture. These changes were followed by a number of distinct improvements:

- higher retention rates
- higher levels of cultural maintenance
- higher levels of bicultural competence
- more involvement from the wider community in the educational effort
- substantial improvements in oral English and in reading.

The example offered by Rough Rock school has been taken up elsewhere, notably in another rural Navajo school district. Rock Point is a community school which began its own process of parental involvement and community control (Holm and Holm 1990).

At Rock Point, the local language and culture is the basis of the curriculum. The school board members are drawn from the community itself and try to represent the interests of the community as a whole, even when this works against short term gains. To earn legitimacy for its own management, the board insisted on high financial and ethical standards right from its earliest meetings. As a result, outside agencies were so impressed with the management that they found it hard to believe at first that the board itself was really running the school.

The Rock Point staff themselves derived a sense of empowerment from the changes. They grew in confidence when it became clear from the stream of visitors attracted to the school that they were seen as competent. Gradually their belief in their own expertise grew, because the quality of their vision of what good Navajo education should be like was so clearly respected by these outsiders.

The Rock Point parents found themselves freed from the pressures to conform to the dominant culture. Their first language became the language of the school, giving them real access to the instructional and governance process, and open access to board meetings. A Parent Evaluation Committee studied the school's operations, three or four times a year, and reported to the board and the staff on its findings. Parents were also the first resource drawn upon as consultants on curriculum content, and the school regularly hired them as instructors and support staff. Parent conferences were held twice yearly for each class. For these meetings, parents observed classes in the mornings and met with teachers in the afternoon, usually with their own children present. This led to a high level of parental participation in the parent–teacher conferences: by the early 1980s it had reached more than 85 per cent.

Finally the Navajo students themselves were empowered by their social and academic success, by their sense of progressive mastery of the curriculum, and by the value that Rock Point placed on their Navajo identity. The introduction of bilingual education, of local control, and of Navajo teachers was accompanied by a marked increase in student self-confidence and student achievement (Holm and Holm 1995). By changing its structures and practices, the school gradually became more organic to its local community.

Changing aboriginal school and classroom structures

The most authentic research on aboriginal education is done by aboriginal researchers themselves.[26] One of these is Daigle, a Cree woman from Northern Ontario, whose transformational model of school change was presented in Chapter 2. She studied community-based education in three North American First Nations communities, including Rough Rock. These Navajo, Nisga'a, and Cree communities have taken real control of their local schools.

In preparation for her work, Daigle (1997) identified a thread of problem factors that reappears in the research on aboriginal schools. These are key structural pressures that seem to affect the education of most aboriginal children in majority culture schools:

- lack of communication between school, parents, and home community
- cultural discontinuities between school and home community
- loss of communal belonging by aboriginal students
- lack of specific curriculum and pedagogical methods to suit learning styles
- loss of language and cultural identity
- low self-esteem
- low retention rates.

Most teachers of classes that have students from diverse backgrounds in them would recognize factors like the ones in this list. But is it possible for teachers on their own to do very much about these things? Do the structures in traditional school systems get in the way of genuine reform? Usually to get reform going within an existing system, teachers rely on the support of champions from their own ranks, especially people who are prepared to rock the boat by advocating reform. At the same time, teachers also depend heavily on critical and sympathetic leadership from those who manage schools.

Above all, policies for reform need to be structurally linked to the aboriginal communities themselves whose children are affected by what happens in schools. In this way, the change process becomes one of community-based education, where local cultural groups shape school outcomes more in line with their own values, and less in line with the values of geographically or historically remote members of the dominant culture. Chapter 2's discussion of Richmond Road school takes up this theme, which is relevant to all forms of education for diversity. Through negotiation and community education over many years, the principal there reorganized the school's grouping system. He edged it from a horizontal to a vertical arrangement, from mixed to similar language and culture home groups, and from a hierarchical to a flat and more egalitarian management system.

Changing unwanted structural factors, like those that prevent staff from backgrounds of diversity from being hired, or community members from having a voice in governance, means changing people's beliefs about the worth of those practices. Moreover the evidence is clear on these two points: culturally different children are better served by teachers who share the same cultural background (Osborne 1991); and a voice for culturally different groups in school governance makes for better schools (Corson 1993a).

Yet even these changes are not enough if the structures of the school still force all staff to conform to dominant professional values in an uncritical way. Sometimes efforts by culturally different teachers themselves to promote culturally sensitive interactions are frustrated when other teachers prefer to do things the school's way, so that they can fit into wider promotion and seniority structures. This pressure to conform to the dominant culture's structures can even make these teachers inflexible about their own values. Sometimes they become overly hard on aboriginal children, trying to make them highly successful in both cultures, but alienating them from schooling at the same time.

Just changing the culture of some of the teachers is not enough on its own though. The structures of many schools, including the values that were once accepted without criticism, are changing to give real cultural alternatives a chance of working. The principal at Richmond Road found that some teachers needed to leave the school before the reforms could take place. He also found that everyone needed lots of time, if reform was going to happen. But once this kind of gradual change occurs, changes in classroom practices can be tried and evaluated by setting them against the cultural needs of the students so that they begin to feel more at home in both the dominant and their own culture.

Changes in classroom practices

Like any students, aboriginal students begin to succeed in schools when they are comfortable about the classroom context itself. Again having a culturally similar teacher in the classroom to work with, or at least one in the school to relate to, is helpful in reducing the sense of distance that children from backgrounds of diversity feel in schools. In addition, Philips mentions the 'total irrelevance of the curriculum content' to the lives of the Indian children in her Warm Springs study (1983: 132). She found that the children were unresponsive to materials that presupposed a cultural background that was different from their own. Furthermore the absence of Indian teachers who could make these strange materials more relevant made matters worse. But there are also styles of control and interaction which some teachers use to make children feel more comfortable. Cazden (1988) distinguishes between two styles which she calls 'personalization' and 'privatization'.

Teacher control and interaction styles

'Privatization' is a strategy for minimizing 'face threatening situations'. This works when teachers avoid calling on children for public and competitive displays of what they do not know, and instead correct them individually, where necessary, and in private. Many see the relevance of this teacher style to Native American children (Eriks-Brophy and Crago 1994). However, privatization also seems a good teaching practice for use with children from culturally different backgrounds elsewhere. Perhaps the education of children everywhere would benefit if privatization were more widely used, because the practice of correcting students in public, to make a teaching point for the rest of the class, can easily strike at their self-esteem, no matter how carefully teachers handle it.

In contrast, the strategy of personalization is aimed less at eliminating face threatening situations as reducing their negative effect. By using simple courtesies in their interactions with students, like those that adults use in polite relations with one another, teachers can handle even the most difficult disciplinary or instructional tasks well. Cazden suggests the use of affectionate forms of address, diminutives, and, in particular, phrases that show respect for the rights and dignity of the children. When used well, this personalized style also reveals a teacher's awareness of the world of the children, their families, and their homes. At the same time, teachers can add any non-verbal expressions of respect and courtesy that they know are welcome in interactions between adults and children in the different culture.

Cazden also believes that teachers bring about more effective change when they focus on classroom situations, rather than directly on cultural differences. For example, skilled teachers of young children are good at providing 'individualization of instruction' in the new entrant classroom. In this approach, the teacher moves from one child to another dealing quickly with learning problems. But this approach can lead to a negative form of differential treatment,[27] if children are not used to one-to-one interactions with adults outside the home and are threatened by them. Young Polynesian children, for example, are used to interacting with adults informally, but sometimes they are more relaxed working with an adult in a group rather than in an individual setting.

In small group learning contexts, teachers can still personalize their teaching while extending students' conversations as well by using the resources of several speakers. Cazden (1990) also recommends the use of 'wait-time'. When a teacher waits for three seconds or more before responding to a student's utterance, the student speaks longer and in more detail and this allows the teacher to reply at length. In choosing a topic for talk with very young children, Cazden suggests three types of topics:

- those specific to the local culture
- those specific to individual children
- those that are familiar to the teacher and the child.

In fact, shared experiences provide the best basis for interaction with children at any age and from any culture. Clearly the nature of these 'experiences' will change across cultural settings: the culture of the child has to be in the mind of the teacher, and the nature of the experiences that can be shared changes as children grow older (Corson 1988a). Teachers working with the very young need to know about past events in the children's lives and they need to have shared some concrete experiences with the children for them to talk about together and so expand their learning. Teachers working with older students try to get inside the more abstract ideas in their students' minds that represent their developing theories about the world. Once informed in this way, teachers use this shared experience as a basis for interaction.

Giving fair classroom treatment to aboriginal children can be a delicate balancing act for teachers from the dominant culture. Some suggest that teachers who are successful with culturally different students 'may be those who achieve a balance of rights by trading control over participation structure dimensions' and that less effective teachers may be those who try 'to maintain conventional classroom participation structures, only to pay a price in student disaffection and loss of control over lesson content' (Au and Mason 1983: 165). Philips (1983) also draws similar conclusions about teaching methods more generally. Although the approaches in the next couple of paragraphs might not work in all aboriginal classrooms, they do suggest a process of thinking that is valuable in making classrooms more compatible with the diverse backgrounds of children.

Oral language activities: talking about text[28]
There is wide agreement that oral language activities, promoting purposeful and motivated dialogue, are a priority for classroom work with aboriginal students. Crago (1992) recommends much greater use of cooperative learning approaches for Inuit students because peer-oriented talk is an important part of first language learning in the Inuit culture. She also warns that the kind of cooperative approaches found in textbooks needs modifying to accommodate the exact cultural repertoire of the students. Ryan (1994) suggests strategies for older aboriginal students to use for exploring and critiquing aspects of language-in-use. These include opportunities to work alongside a significant and experienced other person on a complex task, where the novice can use, practise, and develop the language of schooling by weaving everyday concepts and language into the academic discourses of secondary education.[29] He also stresses small group work with peers and teachers where real conversation is possible. Sullivan *et al.* (1991) recommend greater use of oral language for a range of First Nations children (Algonquin, Cree, Mik'maq, and Mohawk). They suggest that students do more work in groups when they are writing in English, because this allows a negotiated process of discovery that helps them work through the pressure to conform that comes from only meeting English as a language of control. Richardson (1994) makes similar suggestions, but also recommends that teachers avoid making aboriginal students present their work in public at the front of the class. He also wants to see more parents and elders involved in classwork.

Control

The participant structures favoured by aboriginal students in most studies are better represented in some teaching approaches than in others. Scollon and Scollon (1981) see the critical factor for Athabaskan children as the extent to which all participants assume a mutual right to make their own sense of the interaction. This kind of interaction needs freedom from pressures of time, participant crowding, and impersonal media. It also needs an agreement that participants will not try to focus the situation in a one-sided way: this means a very different role for teachers, and it is one in which few traditionally trained teachers would feel relaxed. Maori and Hawaiian Polynesian children and Warm Springs Indian children are also more comfortable when they have more control over the interaction. This means that certain forms of class assessment could be a source of real problems. The group project format seems a suitable assessment tool, and Philips suggests that this could be used more widely, and even for younger age groups. On the other hand, maybe the very ideology of 'assessing and evaluating' personal strengths and weaknesses is an unwanted structure for people from some cultures?

Assessment and evaluation[30]

Should teachers more often question the relevance of our constant search for evidence of student performance? Perhaps schools could modify their practices a little, even while maintaining high standards. Culturally different people often see this interest in assessment and evaluation as a strange interest at best, and as a culturally offensive obsession at worst. But there are other ways to monitor pupil performance that might be more subtle, and also more culturally sensitive.

For example, a more ethnographic approach to bilingual assessment, where teachers observe language in use rather than try to measure it, could have wider uses in assessing other curriculum skills (Corson 1990). Also peer tutoring, followed by peer feedback in the presence of the teacher, seems to suit the learning styles of many children. At the same time, schools do need to extend children's performances into new areas. As aboriginal children mature, they can be eased into new patterns of interaction. For example, teachers can introduce activities that develop leadership skills by asking children to speak on a matter that interests all the children, or by asking them to take an individual role as part of a group goal, as in a team debate. Nevertheless there is a darker side to assessing students from culturally different backgrounds that is still very much with us.

Evidence confirms that teachers and other professionals make incorrect assessments of aboriginal students' abilities because of cultural and language differences. This happens more often when two factors are at work: when the distance between the teachers' culture and the children's is greater; and when the norms for tests are based on samples that are culturally and linguistically distant from the students being assessed. Studies show that assessment approaches for North American majority culture children do not suit language-impaired Inuit children at all, and other widely recommended and used ability measures are highly biased against Inuit children.[31]

It is not only standardized tests that are loaded against aboriginal students. The context of dominant culture schooling itself is often discontinuous with the discursive practices, the cultural knowledge, and the definitions of personal success that many aboriginal children find valued in their own communities. In turn this leads to routine misassessments. Again in response, rather than insisting that aboriginal children conform to schools, schools are adapting themselves to aboriginal children by changing the monocultural definitions of success that they make for their students. However, the result of different definitions of success is still clear in aboriginal achievement rates in urban settings. Measures of student achievement by 'race' in the Toronto Board of Education find aboriginal students are by far the highest risk group at secondary level, with nearly half not getting enough academic credits to graduate, compared with only a quarter of 'white' students (Yau *et al.* 1993). A factor in this is the high aboriginal dropout rate in Ontario, but even this is not well reflected in the above figures because dropout numbers greatly increase outside urban areas (Mackay and Myles 1989).

School systems often depend on IQ tests for student placements and other decisions. Some recommend developing a new, valid, and reliable test of intelligence for aboriginal students as a way of ending the injustice of wrongly classifying some as mentally deficient (Common and Frost 1988). But there is growing agreement that it is time to stop using IQ tests with aboriginal students. To replace them, some suggest that aboriginal educators develop their own ways of assessing 'intelligence'.[32] Instead Crago (1990) calls for more culturally congruent methods of testing, using these approaches:

- sampling a child's talk from naturalistic situations with other children
- using formats that involve comprehension and repetition
- using speakers of the local community's language drawn from that community.

I would want to combine these suggestions by drawing on the different views of different aboriginal peoples themselves. This approach would use culturally congruent activities, cultural values, and community languages as the way of deciding what counts as achievement in those activities, values, and languages. A very different concept of ability would develop in each cultural setting, perhaps just as reliable in its own way as conceptions drawn from the dominant culture.

Finally, perhaps the very idea of 'intelligence' that lies behind so much dominant-culture testing is becoming obsolete. It is hard to see so culturally relative a concept being translated from culture to culture with much consistency. Although the idea that there are 'multiple intelligences' seems a good one (H. Gardner 1983), the associated idea that these intelligences can be adequately named and described in the language of a single culture is not so good. This seems more and more the case as our realization grows that 'intelligence' is really an expression of people's 'skill in handling discourses within meaning systems of different kinds'. The practice of this ability is something that is highly contextual; it varies across cultures and settings like many other things that we are discovering. Even literacy itself means different things to different peoples in different cultural contexts.

Literacy

The kind of stress that schools put on literacy can be a problem for children from cultural groups who do not value literacy in quite the same way that English-speaking cultures do. Even in European cultures, the use of literacy was once an oral and group activity. Now our uses of literacy have moved away from those older activities. But the same uses continue in many other cultures. In important ways these cultures are certainly literate, but they value literacy in different ways.[33] Often aboriginal peoples, for instance, put literacy to quite different uses from those valued in schools (S. Harris and Devlin 1997). This means that the common school practice of keeping most literacy events inside the private and silent domains of libraries, or in classrooms where no talking is often the rule, can set literacy apart from the values and world-views of many aboriginal people.

Although modern forms of literacy are probably valued by all aboriginal peoples, they are sometimes uncomfortable with some of the things that the school asks students to do while they are acquiring literacy. Because the different ways that literacy is acquired and used vary across cultures and social groups, these 'ways of taking' literacy are often different from those valued in formal education. Heath (1986b) suggests three undesirable ways in which members of different groups sometimes accommodate to the overly formal literacy requirement in schools:

- they may learn to read and write only with excessive effort
- they may come to believe that written uses of language are unrelated to oral uses, and so give literacy a marginal cultural position
- they may reject literacy as not relevant to the ways in which people make sense of their world.

In Chapter 5, I recommend 'critical literacy' as a way of changing school practices to serve the interests of children from class and cultural backgrounds of diversity. This approach to literacy is rooted in the real world needs of students themselves. It tries to allow students to become critical and autonomous citizens who are in control of their lives.

For many aboriginal groups, school forms of literacy can simply get in the way of the things that they have learned to value and appreciate most about their own cultures: things like oral interaction, sharing, community, ligatures, collective action, and collaboration. Philips suggests that the people in her Warm Springs study were reluctant to share what they knew in written form with non-Indians, because of the loss of control over the cultural knowledge that might result. This is certainly a common fear among people whose cultural secrets are private to the group. But there is another explanation for this reluctance to embrace school literacy.

Real differences in cultural values exist between societies that are historically literate and those that are not. This means that for some voluntary and involuntary minority peoples, school-type literacy activities threaten to replace other things that are more wanted and valued. By this I mean activities and customs that fill places in the lives of culturally different peoples that literacy fills in other people's lives. In fact, many other things are much more valuable to some peoples than literacy, especially the bonding things that keep their culture together. Accordingly, if culturally different children are to take up literacy successfully, the way that schools introduce and develop it may need to complement rather than threaten established lifestyles that rightly have a very high value for them.

Classroom cultural compatibility and cultural values
Teachers trying to empower culturally different children are beginning to think more about the compatibility between children's home culture and the teaching styles used in classrooms. As mentioned, some schools in New Zealand, Canada, Australia and the United States are already monocultural, which means that they are naturally congruent with the relevant aboriginal culture. Nevertheless few schools catering for aboriginal children are able to take this path, because of the pluralist mix of students that they contain. Fortunately there are other ways to increase classroom cultural compatibility, so that teachers do not need to displace the majority values from the classroom.

Classroom cultural compatibility is an aim of the Kamehameha programme for Polynesian children in Hawaii. Jordan (1985) says that achieving a comfortable environment does not mean reproducing the home culture in the class, because that would disadvantage children from other cultures in the same class. Instead her aim is to translate relevant values into the classroom by using teaching methods that accommodate the values. For Jordan there are two key things to do here:

- find cultural features in the naturally occurring contexts outside schools that link with educationally relevant forms of student behaviour inside schools
- rearrange classroom practices accordingly.

Others would go further than this, especially when the culturally different students are actually the majority in a classroom. In Australia, S. Harris (1990) recommends 'culture domain separation' in bilingual curriculum organization for Aboriginal peoples. This means teaching all the subjects of the regular curriculum in English, and using the aboriginal language only for subject matter that reflects indigenous knowledge and world-views. Perhaps this approach will become more common, as dominant world-views make more contact with different world-views in contexts of cultural equality. People are certainly raising more questions about the possibility of authentic intercultural communication, especially in the more complex areas of the school curriculum where cultures can show the greatest degree of contrast and even incompatibility[34] These areas include the study of *cultural values*, which is part of the subject matter of regular school subjects like the social sciences, citizenship, religious education and the arts.

Some commentators want to see language and curriculum content firmly rooted in traditional cultural values. For Stairs (1991) a teacher of aboriginal students is a cultural broker who mediates between the aboriginal and the non-aboriginal cultures. However, present practices fall well short of this. For example, in north-western Ontario, 27 per cent of provincial schools, all with large aboriginal enrolments, have no native cultural component in their curricula, much less any recognition of traditional cultural values in their teaching and evaluation methods (Brady 1991). Part of the difficulty for teachers themselves, of course, is knowing what a cultural value is and recognizing different values, where they do exist. A cultural value is an attitude or an interest that people in a group cherish for its own sake, or perhaps cherish in an instrumental way as something essential for maintaining the group itself. It shows up in people's discourse norms and in other public forms of behaviour.

Sometimes cultural values are similar across different cultures and show up in similar behavioural norms. There are many similarities across different aboriginal cultures in their values about learning and schooling, even though the cultures are not linked in any historical sense. Sullivan *et al.* (1991) outline the similar experiences that they had with differences in cultural values while working with Algonquin, Cree, Mik'maq and Mohawk bands. They conclude that the European teacher's way of structuring classrooms often clashes with the aboriginal ways of knowing. Many aboriginal students see ideas and things much more holistically. The idea of narrowing and fragmenting a field of vision often seems strange and alien. Yet academic disciplines and school subjects constantly ask students to narrow and fragment their fields of vision in this way. For example, when school subjects address a single topic like 'the mind', they take the topic out of the socio-cultural context that gives it its meaning.

A strong emphasis on cultural bonding is an important educational value for many aboriginal cultures: bonding with one another, with the culture, and with the environment. These cultures lay stress on building bonds between people, on oral discussion to widen fields of vision, and on seeing links between ideas that may seem unrelated to outsiders. So again, a teaching approach that uses regular oral interaction, adult to child and child to child, is preferred by many aboriginal communities. The key here is to make learning cooperative and interactive, rather than competitive and isolated. Competitive forms of assessment and public evaluations are often out of place in aboriginal education. If competitive evaluation is necessary, its public effects need to be softened. Other teaching strategies reported as successful include group problem solving activities at the elementary level. At the secondary level, even individual assignments are more useful than the 'demonstrating questioning' approach that teachers often favour.[35] However, while this approach can work against the interests of older, culturally different children, other forms of bias are more general, institutional, and systemic.

Stereotypes and discursive bias in textbooks and classrooms

A continuing problem exists in the discursive bias of teachers and the systemic, negative stereotyping of aboriginal peoples that schools historically engaged in.[36] For example, in North America many teachers show a positive bias towards children described as European or Oriental, but a negative bias towards children described as native Indian (Myles and Ratzlaff 1988). Part of the problem is that teachers are still ill informed about the diversity of the aboriginalities and cultures that they are asked to deal with. Without a good, basic understanding of aboriginal cultures, educators will not become competent in presenting aboriginal issues fairly and without stereotypes. Yet the effects of biased teacher behaviour on the identities of aboriginal children themselves can be easily seen. Stereotypical views produce conflicts for aboriginal children in deciding between who they are and who they wish to be. This contributes to later patterns of low self-esteem among many adolescent aboriginal children.[37]

Bias in textbooks is a widespread form of institutional discrimination. Books often contain errors, omissions, and stereotypes about aboriginal peoples and their cultures. Although recent decades have seen improvements in eliminating bias and stereotypes from textbooks, certain negative biases continue to appear, including texts with incorrect information about aboriginal lifestyles, history, and their cultures generally. In Ontario, for example, the structure, vocabulary, illustrations, and content of textbooks approved by the Ministry of Education still contain explicit bias, in spite of claims to the contrary (Moore 1992). For aboriginal children, the biases in textbooks need not be blatant for them to be used in highly discriminatory and miseducative ways, especially with the very young:

> The problem is not one of simple imbalance or misportrayal, distortion or archetypal 'false consciousness' . . . [aboriginal] children are inserted pragmatically into these possible worlds – worlds in which middle class children imitate animals, ducks say 'please' and 'thank you,' and princes rescue blond princesses. Occasionally, these children attempt to interject statements of their cultural backgrounds and histories into the texts of schooling. When this occurs, it requires that they admit to their identity in the public domain of schooling . . . What is missing is any systemic attempt to build on and capitalize on the discourses of Aboriginality in the classroom.
>
> (Luke *et al.* 1995: 229)

In the Australian study summarized above, we see how textbooks are used rather innocently with first grade Aboriginal children, but in such a way as to mark out their cultural difference, at the same time as they silence it. The impact of this kind of teaching, which is taken-for-granted everywhere in English-speaking countries with children from all backgrounds, is devastating for aboriginal children's sense of identity and inclusion. Moreover the social justice implications of this are clear, even in a non-totalitarian society like Canada where discrimination against the culturally different is more often seen as the result of ignorance than intention. Stereotypes, biases, and omissions are created and reinforced by the powerful authority figures that teachers are. They are circulated within the high status social institutions that schools are, and then go directly into the discursive practices of society as a whole. They create the backdrop of meanings and assumptions against which aboriginal people have to live their lives. Tragically they create structural injustices that the victims themselves have little chance of resisting.[38]

Professional education in critical language awareness for teachers and teachers-in-training is one urgent reform that I discuss more fully in Chapter 5. Dealing with textual bias, and with bias in their own language, asks teachers to develop a level of language sophistication that most people do not get naturally from their upbringing, or from ordinary forms of education. As part of teacher education, critical language awareness can address many topics: promoting social awareness of discourse; critical awareness of variety; and practice in readiness for changing and reforming public forms of discourse (Corson 1993a). Perhaps a starting point for teachers is to become more critically aware of what stereotypes are, and how they work in practice.[39]

Differences in discourse norms

There is now much evidence about the different discourse norms that culturally different people acquire from their socialization. As suggested already, these norms reflect different cultural values. Chapter 5 mentions research in the United States that looks at the discourse norms of some African American children, and there are differences between peoples everywhere in the discourse norms that different sociocultural groups use. Teachers often misinterpret the norms when they meet them, because they are unaware of the different ways of interacting that culturally different children might have. Sometimes teachers see aboriginal children as unresponsive or disruptive if they are unwilling to look at them during interaction. Sometimes too they label aboriginal children wrongly as slow learners if they have different norms for answering and asking questions.

In reality, what some see as a lack of responsiveness from aboriginal children in classrooms is often very context specific. In other words, it appears in 'key classroom situations'.[40] As mentioned already, aboriginal children often respond less willingly in certain activities: when they are singled out as individuals before the group in a formal context; when they have to raise their hands to show that they want to answer a question; and when their own responses are assessed publicly. But these patterns do not come from some acute shyness in formal contexts with people from another culture. Rather they come from broadly different childhood cultural experiences that give children discourse norms that seem inconsistent in certain settings with the dominant practices of formal schooling.

Some of the studies on key situations in the United States were reviewed in an earlier section. There are Australian and Canadian studies too suggesting that aboriginal students speak less often, speak more quietly, answer obliquely, and generally are on the receiving end of interactional inequality. In response, teachers are beginning to apply evidence of this kind by transforming classroom discourse to build in different interaction patterns and the values that go with them.[41]

Nevertheless these findings raise a further social justice issue about the research itself, very necessary though it is. Is there a risk of stereotyping aboriginal students according to the trends found in the norms of interaction for their group as a whole? Can researchers avoid creating stereotypes when they communicate their findings to teachers about discourse and other group norms? It does seem very important for teachers to know about research on discourse norms, but it is also important that they do not use that knowledge to stereotype their students. This raises two questions for me which are hard to answer conclusively:

- Is it better for teachers to note the differences found in research, but then try to treat children as if the differences did not exist?

● Is it better (or even possible) for teachers in culturally diverse classrooms to adjust their own interaction styles somewhat to suit what they know about norms of interaction for different groups of children?

The Kamehameha studies in Hawaii suggest the second approach, but there are many who urge dominant culture teachers to be very careful when they try to adopt the norms of cultures that are not their own. Again my preference is for more teachers from different cultural backgrounds to enter classrooms that try to cater for diversity, whether those teachers are qualified in the formal sense or not. Genuine fluency in a minority language, or real competence in the relevant culture, should count as much as a formal teaching qualification, at least until more aboriginal teachers have all three things in good numbers.

Every context and mix of students is a different one for dealing with all these difficult issues. However in general, the more knowledge teachers have about their students' likely norms of interaction and cultural values, the more likely they are to make the right choices in interacting with them from moment to moment. The most important thing that teachers can do in this regard is to think about their own discourse norms, and then ask themselves whether culturally different children are receiving an unintended message of domination, exclusion, or hostility from the way that they themselves interact with their students.

Conclusion

This chapter presents aboriginal education as the paradigm for reforming education for diversity. *This means that most of the material covered here is directly relevant to topics discussed in later chapters.* For example, the idea of 'voluntary and involuntary minorities' is a distinction that can be used to understand the situation of many students who come from backgrounds of diversity. Also, the history of treatment of aboriginal communities, right down to the present in many places, became part of a trend for the treatment of diversity generally in English-speaking countries. It set the low standard, and even now we are only beginning to leave that standard behind, as confirmed by the experiences of the five countries that were reviewed in this chapter.

Later sections of the chapter looked closely at the kinds of changes to classroom practices that teachers of aboriginal students are beginning to think about. Many of these things are also relevant to teachers of other diverse groups: changing teacher control and interaction styles; removing unfair assessment and evaluation practices; looking more critically at the approaches to literacy that schools use; making classrooms more compatible with the values and discourse norms of students; and doing away with stereotypes and other forms of bias against diverse populations that appear in the discourses of schooling.

The word 'control' figures strongly in this chapter. Indeed it provides a key motif for education for diversity of all kinds in places like Britain where diverse communities 'are increasingly voicing a desire to define their own problems and take their own initiatives' (Tomlinson 1984: 88). Moreover Britain has special problems that set it apart a little from all the other English-speaking countries. As the chief source country for English-speaking peoples, it is the oldest and the most affected by traditions and archaic structures that can too easily get in the way of reforms to education for diversity. Taken-for-granted ethnocentricity is more alive and well there than in most other places, and this means that the idea of culturally different groups in Britain beginning to control their own education is difficult for many people to accept. This is especially the case for people who believe that immigrant groups are really prepared to turn their backs on their own cultures, and want nothing more from their new country than to embrace its culture completely and finally. The truth of the matter is that the culturally different rarely want to be forced to choose between the culture of one world and the culture of another.

Above all, as in all forms of education for diversity, aboriginal students want the best of both worlds from their education. They want to see their own cultures celebrated and valued in schools, but they also want the other options that good forms of modern education can offer. This means that just replacing the aboriginal culture with the dominant culture is not good enough. Nor is it good enough simply to add the dominant culture to the students' culture. Instead, students need to start out with a strong sense that their own culture is valued in schools. Furthermore, getting the best of both worlds means students using their own culture as their vehicle for interacting with the majority culture. It means students using their own familiar discourses to make sense of the less familiar discourses of the dominant culture, and to integrate the best of both worlds, in their own way and to their own satisfaction.

Later chapters relate the same ideas raised in this chapter to the educational needs and interests of other diverse groups, both voluntary and involuntary. Chapter 4 looks at a range of diverse groups within immigrant communities who are often overlooked in policy discourse and in educational practice, partly because of their sex.

Discussion starters

1 What makes involuntary minorities different from voluntary minorities? Are there types of minorities that do not fit exactly into the distinction

between voluntary and involuntary minorities? Which minorities in your experience fit this distinction and which do not?

2 This chapter looked directly at aboriginal education in five countries where important changes have taken place. How could the Norwegian experience be used as a source of ideas for changing education for diversity in your country, or for changing education for diversity generally? Are there specific practices that you could borrow for use in your own teaching? What are these?

3 What ideas for changing education for diversity in your country, or for changing education for diversity generally, can be found in the New Zealand experience? Are there specific practices that you could borrow for use in your own teaching? What are these?

4 Does the Canadian experience offer any insights into ways of changing education for diversity in your country, or of changing education for diversity generally? What are those insights? Are there specific practices that you could borrow and use in your own teaching? What are these?

5 How does the Australian experience in changing aboriginal education differ from the Canadian? How does it differ from the American? Looking at each as a set of national policies, what might the three approaches have to learn from one another?

6 Do you agree that most of the work of reforming aboriginal education has to begin with school and system administrators themselves? What evidence or arguments can you provide to support your view? Specifically what can teachers do on their own to change whole schools and school systems?

7 What is a 'discourse norm'? What is an 'interaction style'? How can teachers in culturally diverse classrooms adjust their own interaction styles to suit what they know about norms of interaction for different groups of children? How far can they reasonably go? How far would you go?

8 Most aboriginal students will continue to receive their education in regular classrooms. If future classroom practices are going to accommodate aboriginal students more successfully, in what ways will the present practices that you are familiar with have to change?

four

CHANGING THE EDUCATION
OF GIRLS FROM IMMIGRANT
CULTURES

Perhaps the least visible groups in pluralist societies are girls who come from certain immigrant and refugee cultures. They are doubly marginalized: first as members of different cultures and then as females within those cultures. More than this, their invisibility in education is also increased by their marginal place in research and practice. This happens because the study and practice of multicultural education tends to treat members of any single culture as a homogeneous group, with little regard for sex. At the same time, early feminist theory and practices tended to minimize the cultural differences between women, because of the need to treat broad issues of gender discrimination that affect all women.

Although serious and multiple disadvantages do affect girls from immigrant cultures, this double effect receives only rare attention in the educational literature to date. This chapter collates the little that we know about this area at present. It opens with a survey of broad differences in school achievement between girls and boys, as revealed in recent research in English-speaking countries. It links this discussion with the different rewards or life chances that girls and boys tend to get from schools. These things again are linked to unequal discursive power arrangements in schools which affect immigrant girls unfairly. The chapter then collates some insights, from the research literature in several countries, into the special problems that first-generation immigrant girls can have. It argues from that evidence towards more worthwhile policies and fairer school practices.

Let me stress at the outset that individuals and groups of immigrant girls are very different from one another in their cultural values, their life histories, and their hopes about education. In assembling the initial evidence here, I am not making any claims that can be generalized to all immigrant girls, and especially not to all individuals within the groups described in the literature. Dealing with diversity means always treating every person with the expectation that he or she is uniquely different and lives a life independent of any stereotype.[1]

Fairness for girls and boys in the school context

Recent decades have seen many changes in educational policies and practices around gender issues. In some places, the historic injustices affecting the educational chances of girls have been softened somewhat, or even removed.[2] This trend exists in Australia, Britain and Canada (Ontario), but marked gender gaps in educational achievement still appear in the United States. In fact they may even be increasing there, especially in science achievement.[3] Research in Ontario gives some useful insight into the changing impact that gendered practices in education are having on educational success and failure.

Student achievement rates by sex have been studied in the very large Toronto Board of Education (Yau *et al.* 1993). Female students are now faring *better* than their male counterparts in secondary schools, regardless of programme level and regardless of race. Even in mathematics, which is often regarded as the weakest area of female performance, the improved pattern for girls still holds. Girls are also staying on in mathematics classes in numbers equal to boys. In spite of this, other studies suggest girls still have much lower confidence in their ability to learn mathematics, and they have higher levels of mathematics anxiety than boys. To remedy these matters, the researchers suggest that the evidence about girls' achievements should be circulated more widely among girls themselves. This could strengthen their self-perception of mathematics ability, and their self-esteem generally.[4]

Sex differences in favour of boys do emerge when the researchers look at science enrolment patterns. In chemistry, there is only a small discrepancy that favours boys' participation. At the same time, girls are much less likely to participate in physics at senior levels than boys (18 per cent of girls compared with 32 per cent of boys). On the other hand, at junior secondary level in the province of Ontario as a whole, female students performed much better than male students in reading and writing at ninth grade level (Ministry of Education and Training 1995) with *four times* as many boys as girls below the norm for their age level in reading.[5]

Immigrant girls

Some groups of girls are now more subject to risk of educational failure than others. In the United States, for example, research that looks at sex, race and ethnicity 'reveals critical vulnerabilities among various groups of girls'

(AAUW Report 1995: 34), yet little recent research has been done there link-ing sex, class, and culture with low achievement. Many groups of girls from low income but majority culture backgrounds are still in positions of unusual risk when compared with their male peers. They still hear narratives and stories, inside and outside schools, that close off whole avenues of life for them: avenues that include employment and lifestyle options which girls from more privileged backgrounds often take for granted these days. How-ever, the groups that seem most at risk again are girls from certain immigrant cultural backgrounds.

Schools often misperceive the preferences and abilities of immigrant girls because of stereotypes that circulate in societies and among teachers. No doubt some individual immigrant girls do hear life stories, in their own com-munities, about their future lives and opportunities that make them feel inferior to their male relatives. Although this is hardly the case for all girls from a given immigrant background, sometimes schools build on stereo-types of that kind. The false belief that immigrant girls are subjected to male power in every sphere of their home lives can create an image for these girls quite unlike the one that they experience outside school; it is also a very different image from the one that they would prefer for themselves.

In other words, while teachers may see many immigrant girls as passive victims of cultural forces, the reality of their cultural experiences may be life affirming. It may be positive in many ways, but unfortunately, as Tsolidis warns, 'rarely is the thought entertained that the source of ethnic minority girls' problems may be other than their cultures' (Tsolidis 1990: 58). These stereotypes, held by teachers and others about immigrant girls, can lead to a negative kind of differential treatment.

Differential treatment

There are two forms of differential treatment that education often practises. First, there is *negative* differential treatment, in which students are treated unfairly because of some policy or practice based on a prejudice or stereo-type about the students. Second, there is *positive* differential treatment, in which some students are seen as different in some educationally relevant way, and are treated differently from others out of respect for fairness.

The 'principle of equal treatment' in ethics is relevant here. According to this principle, people are obliged to treat everyone in life equally unless there is some relevant difference in the person or the setting that gives grounds for treating them differently. For example, specially improved arrangements for learning disabled children, and for those affected by other disabling con-ditions, are almost universally supported in educational systems. This is because an educationally relevant difference exists between these children and children in the mainstream. The question at issue is whether a child, or a group of children, are relevantly different in some way. If so, they are entitled to differential treatment.

As Chapter 1 argues, the acquired cultural, gender, and class interests of some groups of children do make them different in educationally relevant ways. Specifically, many girls from immigrant cultures can be different from other girls in relevant ways, especially in the school context. This means that they could be entitled to *positive* forms of differential treatment. To decide the forms that that treatment might or might not take, schools are beginning to look at culturally different students rather differently. They are getting new insights into students' home cultures. In particular, they are trying to understand the 'new culture' that forms as 'a product of the migration process and the power inequities integral to it' (Tsolidis 1990: 55). When children have these very different immigration experiences, their life chances can be affected. Discontinuities develop between the home and the school that can and do lead to educational failure.

Life chances: options and ligatures

Education usually gives people two types of life chances: additional 'options' in their lives, which give a greater range of choices in their future as a result of their education, and stronger 'ligatures', which are the bonds between individuals and groups that develop as a result of their experiences in education. Clearly there are gender and cultural differences in access to options and ligatures; these differences relate directly to gendered practices and norms that the institution of education helps to reproduce and reinforce.[6]

Western people, living among capitalist social relations, readily see the role that options have in offering increased life chances to those who have them. However many western people do have more difficulty seeing the place that ligatures have as life chances. This might be because the value of ligatures has become hidden for westerners in the rush to develop and extend capitalist economic options. So an example of the value that ligatures still carry in some cultures might help explain the point here.

In a newspaper article, Suzuki (1995) talks about the imposition of western-style capitalist options on Papua New Guinean communities. This twentieth century process has undermined the work of thousands of years building up ligatures which gave these people life chances beyond any possible quality of life that the options of global economics can now offer. Suzuki quotes a local social scientist, Faraclas:

> Imagine a society where there is no hunger, homelessness or unemployment, and where in times of need, individuals can rest assured that their community will make available to them every resource at its disposal. Imagine a society where the decision makers rule only when the need

arises, and then only by consultation, consensus and the consent of the community. Imagine a society where women have control over their means of production and reproduction, where housework is minimal and childcare is available 24 hours a day on demand.

Imagine a society where there is no or little crime and where community conflicts are settled by sophisticated resolution procedures based on compensation to aggrieved parties for damages, with no recourse to concepts of guilt or punishment. Imagine a society . . . in which the mere fact that a person exists is cause for celebration and a deep sense of responsibility to maintain and share that existence.

[Such a place is not fiction, says Faraclas:] When the first colonizers came to the island of New Guinea, they did not find one society that exactly fit the above description. Instead they found more than 1000 distinct language groups and many more distinct societies, the majority of which approximated closely to the above description, but each in its own way.

(Faraclas, quoted in Suzuki 1995: B8)

While these were hardly perfect societies, they did provide life chances that are important for the human condition. Yet, within 100 years of the introduction of western options, nearly all of the real gains in life chances are now badly eroded. The ligatures that bound these people to one another, and to their cultures, were traded for options that have destroyed those communal values built up over 40,000 years.

The Harvard Project on Human Potential also confirms a gendered dimension to the distribution of options and ligatures (R. Levine and White 1986). It offers the example of women in developing countries, who seem poor in options and richer in ligatures. But because ligatures provide some of the most important benefits in life, like support, structure, motivation, and a sense of respect and continuity, it is likely that women with few options in some developing country settings experience their lives as highly satisfying. Egbo (1997) reports that non-literate rural women in Nigeria are often very poor in options because of their lowly rated job and functional skills, while many are rich in ligatures because of their strong friendship and other support groups.[7] At the same time, western observers, weighing up the absence of options in the lives of these women, might think that their life chances as a whole were highly unattractive.

In some societies, and among some cultural groups, ligatures are positive ends in themselves, to be pursued as a goal in life. They are not just a means to other ends, like the ligatures that market economies value more highly. I am thinking of the aboriginal peoples discussed in Chapter 3 here. Even in the midst of the rich options that their countries extend to their citizens, it is often the ligatures that mean much more to these peoples, even when that valuing of ligatures leads to a reduction in options. Sometimes these ligatures that develop between ancestral people are so strong, as human interests, that they become almost physical needs, because their loss creates great levels of sadness, and even morbidity.

Most education systems in capitalist countries are good at providing students with options but very weak at providing them with ligatures. Nevertheless in English-speaking countries, in particular, many immigrants come from ethnic communities where ligatures are prized. For some, such as the millions of refugees from Indo-China, Africa, or the Balkans, ligatures of one kind or another may be all that remain to them. For others, like the ancestral peoples mentioned above, cultural interests support their ligatures, and often these interests are beyond the understanding of people from outside those cultures. Specifically, when these interests are those of women, they are often disguised by power relationships that make the interests of dominant males seem the universal norm.

Gender, discourse and power

Across societies, power is the variable that separates men and women. Female exclusion from public spheres of action also tends to exclude them from the creation of dominant ideologies and the sign systems used to express them. All of the many societies and cultures studied in Philips *et al.* (1987) have key public speaking roles and speech activities in which women participate rarely, or not at all. But in the same societies, men are not notably excluded from the key activities of women, and men are also able to define the activities that attract status.

As research into language and gender becomes more searching, the power of wider social structures is becoming a more important issue (Wodak 1997). It is clear that differences in interaction styles between women and men are affected by sociocultural practices and values well removed from language. Women and men usually belong to different subcultures that have different ways of empowering people. This is apparent in cultural groups where differences in male and female roles and activities are very ordered, as in some Islamic cultures, in Orthodox Jewry, or in fundamentalist Christian subcultures. The men and women learn different norms for interaction within and between the sexes. They then live out those norms and take them for granted. But there is more than subcultural differences at work here.

Powerful structures that reflect the outdated values of dominant male social groups, who lived generations ago, still affect the discourses of women and men in the 1990s. This happens even though people are far removed in time from those outdated values. Influenced by these things from the past, women, as a group, still get relatively few chances to reform practices that go much beyond surface forms of discourse. In other words, women have relatively little influence over the discourses that really control people's lives. History shows that control over discourse is the most important power to seize, if people want to escape the unwanted power of others (Foucault 1984). So all this carries a strong message for any group that wants to emancipate itself. To change imbalances in power, people have to control dominant discourses within the meaning systems that are relevant to the exercise of that power.[8]

At the same time, women usually have their own discourses that are not always defined in reference to dominant male norms or values. In societies with a high level of formal education, the high status models of language for women can come from educated women elites. Often female students from affluent backgrounds, in the Indian Sub-Continent or in East Asia for example, are better placed than other students to seize the rewards of English-speaking schools because of the cultural capital and the dispositions that they get from their upbringing. In contrast, other girls from the same regions often feel the effects not just of sex and culture, but also of class: this can affect their readiness to adopt the life chances that schools in their new country offer to them.

Another difficulty for immigrant girls is that the practices of schools in English-speaking countries, like everywhere in the world, tend to favour boys. Education rewards boys and girls in different ways for using their own gendered norms of interaction and behaviour. In fact, cooperative discursive practices, into which girls are socialized in their early lives, attract less and less value as children progress through schools.[9] Boys are favoured by schools that are still modelled on the competitive values of the dominant males who lived when modern schooling was introduced, more than a century ago.[10] These traditional schools are still very much the norm. As a result, during and after the middle childhood years, schools give more recognition to the competitive discursive practices that most boys learn to use early in their lives. As a consequence, girls from immigrant backgrounds, who are already affected by being culturally different, are doubly disadvantaged by the gendered practices that most senior schools still take for granted.

Girls from immigrant cultures

The following quote comes from an experienced secondary science teacher who talks about the many students in her London girls' school. She makes some generalizations that most teachers would agree with:

> Girls, particularly working class and immigrant girls, lack confidence in themselves and their abilities, especially in unfamiliar areas. Having spent a lot of time watching them, I have noticed that girls exert pressures on each other which reinforce this lack of confidence. There is

pressure not to brag, 'show yourself up' or make a fuss; otherwise you may be labelled 'big-headed'. Discretion and modesty are valued, while outspokenness and self-assertion are suspect, if not 'punished' by the group (unless they express anti-authoritarianism).

Imagine a girl attempting to formulate a question in a science lesson under such pressures. She is likely to expose her vulnerability in two ways. First, she risks the censure of the whole group. Second, she almost certainly risks being dismissed and thus unintentionally ridiculed by the teacher for failing to pose the question in a sufficiently abstract frame of reference to be recognized by that teacher. In such a context, girls may readily reject scientific knowledge wholesale as being at odds with their own experiences.

(Baran 1987: 91)

Structural arrangements in schools and classrooms can affect children from different cultural backgrounds very differently. Some girls and boys appear at home in the setting of the school. They are supported by the cultural interests and values that they share with teachers and classmates from similar backgrounds. These children are empowered in the setting of the school by the orientation to the world that they bring from the home. Accordingly they are ready to convert the already valuable and similar cultural capital acquired in the home, into the high status academic cultural capital that the school offers.

Other children are not empowered in this way, and their confidence in classrooms is affected. In particular, some studies of self-esteem are beginning to link wider social processes with the low self-esteem of many adolescent girls. These suggest that self-esteem 'is related to power and the ability to influence one's own destiny' (Tsolidis 1990: 63). I know that many immigrant students are acutely aware of their family's lack of power. They come from family circumstances where unemployment is common. Many others have parents who fill low status and intermittent jobs, often spent with others from similar immigrant backgrounds. Many have a family history set in a rural culture, which is the main life experience that the family draws upon.[11] Many have experienced war, or had first hand contact with violence before entering their new culture. Taken together, these experiences are filled with powerful symbols, and these become memories that can impact on immigrant children's perceptions of self. They are positioned in life by these sign systems, and the stories that they tell themselves about their place in the world tend to reflect all of this.

At the same time, these views of self and circumstance can be very different from the views that teachers believe immigrant girls hold about themselves. Teachers themselves in an Australian study believed that 'ethnic minority communities expected these girls to marry young and become young mothers, and this was the expectation they taught to'. But the teachers did not check with the girls to see if these views of theirs were misperceptions or not. So there is good reason to wonder 'how responsible are teachers for the creation of self-fulfilling prophecies?' (Tsolidis 1990: 65).

The evidence in the same study confirms that the immigrant girls were seeking greatly enhanced future prospects for themselves. In fact, these things were foremost in their minds. As important, their families also went well beyond simply agreeing with them on this. One girl's comment shows the *very high expectations* that immigrant families often have of education, and the pressure for success that it can place on their offspring:

> I honestly believe that my parents want to give me what they were deprived of when they were young. They often say that they wish that they were educated so they wouldn't be treated like 'dirt' by the boss. I can always see tears forming in their eyes when we discuss the matter. This makes me feel a bit depressed because you can see that being uneducated really has its hardships.
>
> (Tsolidis 1990: 64)

Students coming from backgrounds like this often want things from schools that teachers feel are inappropriate for them. Their family priorities and their own wishes may focus on a future quite unlike that forecast by their teachers. The teachers, working from good intentions but bad stereotypes, can become an obstacle to those hopes.[12]

Above all, immigrant girls want improvements in their quality of life. They want guaranteed access to the things that will give them good housing, health, and continuing education. At the same time, they want things from education that might not be readily available in the schools that they attend. Sometimes schools for immigrants are well below average in their quality, because of a poor location, or a cadre of stressed or burnt-out teachers, or a discriminatory tracking or streaming system.[13] For schools trying to make changes in what they offer, here are some items that are usually high on the list of things that older immigrant girls want from their school:[14]

- greater proficiency in English
- good academic standards in the school
- a concern for order and safety in the school environment
- a school guarantee of equitable and direct access to higher education
- planned and purposeful preparation for getting jobs.

A common theme in the literature, from the high immigration countries of North America and Australasia, is that immigrant families have very high aspirations for their offspring, much higher in fact than non-immigrants in the same income groups. Moreover for second and later generations, these aspirations translate into much higher success rates than non-immigrants achieve.[15] But first generation immigrant girls often bring cultural interests and norms of behaviour to schools that are inconsistent with what teachers ask from them. Clear and strong patterns of misunderstanding and mismatches in interaction between teachers and immigrant female students appear in Canadian, New Zealand and British research.

In Canada, Rezai-Rashti (1994; 1995) looks at immigrant female students in schools where racism and sexism are seen as 'systemic'. In other words, the discrimination in these schools was due not so much to the deliberately biased actions of people, as to biases in the structures of the schools themselves: in their rules, their taken-for-granted practices, their values. Here the relationships between the students and teachers are framed in what Rezai-Rashti calls 'colonial discourse', when the pressure to assimilate often leads the girls to reject their first language and culture. Instead they are urged to replace these things with the trappings of a capitalist consumer culture that the girls adopt only reluctantly, to fit in with dominant Canadian norms. However, the educators themselves miss the point of all this. Wrongly, teachers are 'likely to see students as rebelling against the perceived repressive culture of their communities. Seldom are students' problems seen within the context of the systemic racism present in the relationship between educators and students' (Rezai-Rashti 1995: 92). Furthermore, this readiness of the educators to find fault with the home cultures of the students allows them to overlook the sexism prevalent in their own English-speaking culture, while still blaming the sexism found in the immigrant cultures.

In a New Zealand girls' high school, working class girls from immigrant Pacific Island families receive only rare moments of teacher interaction, while middle class majority culture girls get most of the teachers' attention (Jones 1987). The immigrant girls explain their reluctance to engage in the verbal competition of class interactions as due to their fear of being singled out. They mention the cultural value of *ma* (modesty and shame) and their fear of being the centre of attention. In response the teachers react to this by being more sensitive to the discomfort that their questioning causes the immigrant girls. They reduce the public demands that they make on the girls, so giving them a negative form of differential treatment. Yet they do not substitute alternative pedagogies as a positive form of differential treatment. As a result, in a complex way, teachers reward European cultural norms and reproduce patterns in those students who have the disposition to receive them. At the same time, teachers discourage the cultural patterns of the Pacific Island girls while reproducing in the girls the same patterns that they discourage. Accordingly the immigrant girls do not get equal opportunities to learn, and they become more passive receivers of knowledge. In this way, they fit the image that their teachers create for them.

Some other evidence from New Zealand suggests that there is psychological reluctance and inability on the part of teachers to promote extended interactions with culturally different girls, even when they have much more extended interactions with other children (Cazden 1990). Elsewhere there are indications that it is the teachers' failure to create suitable conditions that cause these inequalities. A study of Panjabi new entrant children in Britain finds no differences in the patterns of interaction initiated by the children themselves with their teachers. However, there are significant differences in the patterns of interaction initiated by teachers (Biggs and Edwards 1991). The Panjabi children seek the teachers' advice and help, in much the same way as other children. In response, the teachers spend less time interacting with the children. In conclusion, because different amounts of time and different kinds of teacher interaction are associated with different groups of children, the reluctance seems to lie with the teachers.

These studies are interesting and important, but because some are impressionistic only, while others are small scale and rather limited in scope, they leave many questions unanswered about the wider lives of immigrant girls when compared with their lives in English-speaking schools. More thorough research is only just beginning to appear, especially research that looks at educational experiences unique to single cultural groups. This is why the study described in the next section seems so important to me. It provides a detailed and wide ethnographic investigation of immigrant girls from a single cultural group, attending the schools of one country.

An ethnography: Indo-Chinese immigrant girls in American schools

This ethnographic study looked at schools and girls in a medium sized mid-Western city in the United States (Goldstein 1988). It followed the education and integration of Hmong refugee girls from rural Indo-China. For the author of this study, understanding immigrant education means knowing about 'the interaction, conflict, negotiation, resistance and accommodation that occur among the different people who comprise a school's community context, internal culture and organisation' (Goldstein 1988: 1). She agrees that 'the educational practices and messages of school often conflict with those in the minority-culture home and community', but she warns that to understand all this, in respect to the education of immigrant girls in particular, 'it is essential to consider how gender mediates the point at which ethnic and dominant cultures intersect' (1988: 1–2). Goldstein's point here underlines the challenging task that teachers have when they try to make sense of the lives of the immigrant students who are in their charge. The conclusion seems clear to me: teachers need as much good information about their students and their wider lives as possible.

The Hmong culture places high value on formal education. As a result, male and female children are usually serious and committed students. The girls in this study said that they want two things from their education: integration into the dominant culture, and more expertise in that culture. However, these things are very different from the things they actually get from schools. In the American schools, they are almost exclusively socialized with other Hmong children. They take largely 'female courses' (home economics, health, typing, etc.) and they leave school before graduating. Goldstein explains this contradiction between the Hmong girls' stated goals and their real actions. As evidence she taps into the girls' own evolving construction of gender and personhood which was shaped by conflicts between their home and school experiences.

The Hmong culture is one where authority passes along the male line. Also its view of personhood is that the group is more important than the individual. Clearly in this respect, the culture is similar to the many aboriginal cultures discussed in Chapter 3. Moreover it is not unlike *the majority of the world's cultures*. But this emphasis on the group is very different from middle class North American cultural norms, and it affects individual behaviour differently too and in important ways. Hmong women also have a different relationship to their culture than men do, partly because in the rural Laotian setting, identity is inherited and affirmed through men.

Another key difference is that, unlike North Americans, the Hmong do not recognize adolescence as a special developmental period, which means that teenagers are considered adults. They have the same adult responsibilities as older people, but these responsibilities in turn are determined by their sex. Male adults are more involved in public roles, and females in private roles. In fact, in their home setting in Laos, females seldom leave their village neighbourhood.

Hmong parental expectations of their children's schools are also important for understanding their children's attitudes and actions. For Hmong parents, schools above all are settings where their children can interact with American people, culture, and institutions. As members of a preliterate culture in Laos, few of the Hmong adults had previous contact with formal education. When they could afford to send their children to Laotian schools, they sent the boys. This was consistent with the cultural norm in which males left the village environment while females stayed in the home. As a result, fewer Hmong women have had any education.

In the United States, the girls were encouraged to contribute to the Hmong community by reproducing it in its traditional forms. This meant maintaining the domestic sphere, and also getting married early in order to have children. But in sharp contrast to their parents' preferences, the girls wanted to integrate themselves into the American community. In this respect, they were also quite different from the Hmong boys, who dreamed of their future return to Laos, taking with them the technological skills needed to rebuild their country.[16]

The parents were also deeply distrustful of the 'loose morals' of American youth. They wanted the girls to keep close to their male relatives in schools, and insisted on them coming home immediately after classes. Eventually, once the needs of the family started to outweigh the need for education, the parents interrupted the education of the girls and finally withdrew them early from school. In fact, the ones who remained at school tended to be those coming from war scattered or split families who lacked the ligatures of their former home.

Nonetheless, the girls did have a real influence on their parents and families. They brought about gradual cultural changes in their home communities, especially changes in the traditional gendered expectations. In fact, Goldstein found this to be one of the chief aims and hopes of the girls. At the same time, their wish to be recognized as individuals in the dominant American culture was continually frustrated. This was largely because of the way they were treated in school.

At school, the teachers managed their classes in ways that blocked the integration of the Hmong girls, rather than encouraged it. In one high school, the Hmong girls were put in a bilingual programme that was specially targeted on the Hmong.[17] However, this created a major problem of negative differential treatment, because it isolated them from their American peers. It also labelled the girls as 'different' and 'inferior' to those from the dominant culture. In a second high school, the Hmong girls were placed in low level, transitional special education classes, where the academic content took second place to other disciplinary concerns. Again, because of the consistently good behaviour of the Hmong girls, they were separated once more from other students. In fact, the teachers encouraged the Hmong to work together, so that they could help each other and not trouble the teachers too much. In their turn, the teachers awarded passing grades for good behaviour, even when it came without academic success. Clearly their concerns for the Hmong children ended at the classroom door.

It seems, then, that in the one school there was negative differential treatment of the immigrant girls, but no positive differential treatment to compensate. In the other school, gender differences were not considered in the bilingual programme's organization of classroom interactions, or in the curriculum knowledge that was presented. At the same time, gender biases were clear in the teachers' presentations and in the selection of curriculum material. Although the Hmong girls had the usual problems of relating to the strange curriculum material, these problems were made worse because routine interactions with the American children, who might help them in their learning, were difficult. One Hmong student reported that she 'invariably ended up feeling like a child in their company' (Goldstein 1988: 17). Also, with few exceptions, the Hmong girls were socially excluded by the American students. This was made worse by the lack of knowledge that the

American students had about the Hmong and their practices. For the American students, the gendered separation of social activities by the Hmong was hard to accept, and this created further social distancing.

Although the experiences of these Hmong girls were unique to them as a group, there are many insights for changing the education of immigrant girls even in this one ethnography. Consequently, it would be valuable to have many more similar studies.

More finely tuned and focused studies are beginning to appear. Another ethnographic study from the United States looks at the lives of Cambodian women and girls in Philadelphia (Sylvester 1996). It discusses two different stereotypes of Cambodians in the United States that affect their lives as students in schools. First, there is the 'model minority' stereotype that people wrongly attach to all Asian immigrants (discussed earlier in this chapter). Second, there is the perception of Cambodian immigrants as poor, illiterate farmers who are unable to organize their lives for themselves in their new country or succeed easily in its schools. Sylvester finds that neither stereotype matches the reality of the students' lives, yet both affect the education that they receive. She also reports that schools treat the first language of these students as a problem to be removed, rather than as a resource to be built upon (see Chapter 6). At the same time, the students receive few opportunities to practise and learn the literacy skills needed to integrate into their new culture.

Summary

Although there are few studies that put sex and culture differences in schools together, the studies to date do more than hint at the special problems that first generation immigrant girls can have. In pulling all this together, I have done a lot of guesswork based only on this slight evidence. Therefore I should stress that *many groups of immigrant girls and many individuals within groups would not fit the summary below.* In fact, the summary is indented and bulleted to highlight how speculative and limited it all is. We can expect that future research will throw more light on the many different ways that education can affect girls from different cultures.

- In their upbringing in their own communities, some groups of immigrant girls seem to get fewer opportunities than other children to show communicative dominance or exercise their independence. At the same time, in schools, immigrant girls meet even worse imbalances in communication. Their teachers tend to leave them to their own devices, except when working with the whole class. In turn, the girls also find that the academic expectations that schools have for them are lower and they are affected by stereotypes. These paint immigrant girls, from some backgrounds, as passive, compliant, and lacking in ambition. In response to the stereotypes, their teachers tend to leave them alone. In fact, the teachers often feel sorry for the girls and prefer not to trouble them by insisting on the same high academic expectations that they have for others. Although the girls do less well in school than either they or their parents would like, they tend to accept this as their own fault.

- Treated in this way, immigrant girls can come to believe that school discourse in their new country moves along a single one-way channel. Knowledge passes only from the teacher to the students, with little return interaction. Although they see other children asserting their independence and interacting in lively ways, especially the boys, they see themselves mainly as spectators in all this.

- The immigrant girls also find that the special ligatures they share with other girls from similar backgrounds are missing from the public symbols and practices of schools. In their place, there are few opportunities to build close ties with non-immigrant girls and boys, who sometimes regard them as strange and even a little intimidating. Because there are few signs and symbols in schools that might open up alternative roles in life to them, they often accept roles for themselves that are more restrictive than they would like them to be. They come to accept that their place in life is very like the place decided for them in the stereotypes of dominant people in their community and in their school. The narratives and stories that they hear all their childhood lives give them few alternatives that they can easily identify with.

Changing the education of immigrant girls

Textbooks and reading materials

Although I could find no research specifically linking textbook bias with immigrant girls, many studies do examine cultural and racist portrayals and many authors argue that bias continues in textbooks.[18] Others list strategies to eliminate cultural and racial stereotypes from textbooks and reading materials.[19] Taken together with the mass of evidence about gender bias in textbooks,[20] it is clear that in this area girls from immigrant backgrounds are being doubly disadvantaged by their sex and by their culture.

Children have wide and early encounters with bias in the textbooks used in schools, and these books are often reread by generations of students. The representations of gender and race in beginning reader texts, and in graded reading schemes, help create models for later language use and for students' perceptions about how the world is. Early reading texts are the first contact with books that many children get, and they are presented in an institution that carries official authority. It is true, historically, that textbooks have always excluded certain groups of children. Yet as the authoritative texts of the school, school books are always critical agents of socialization in every country.

There is good evidence that non-sexist and non-racist children's books can have a positive influence on achievement, and also reduce harmful stereotypes (Stones 1983). Frankly this is the easiest area of reform for schools to deal with, because it is the most tangible, and schools are now giving careful attention to how they go about selecting reading texts for the very young. They try to choose textbooks that are more inclusive in theme and character: books that have children and adults from diverse backgrounds as central actors; and books whose themes represent the cultural interests of diverse communities.[21] Schools are also choosing books for older children more carefully, by looking for books that avoid painting a falsely rosy picture of conditions in society. Some recommend selecting books that provide a non-sexist and non-racist context, even if that context contains language which in the interests of social realism is not gender or race neutral. But others suggest choosing books for older students that highlight social injustices and fairer practices, and then ask readers to reflect on the book itself as an example of the point that it makes.

Immigrant girls need to see people like themselves as characters in textbooks and curriculum materials, doing community activities that might suggest alternative roles in life to them, and also give them status among their classmates. If these can also be high quality bilingual books, which can be lent to children by the school for use in their homes, then many good things can result:[22]

- immigrant children get a clearer vision of their ethnicity
- the books help establish a sense of security for children in their own background
- their sense of empowerment in the setting of the school increases
- the books become a bridge between the parent and the school
- they motivate parents to learn to read in the new language
- teachers themselves become more committed to multicultural literacy
- positive intercultural moments centred on the books occur in classrooms and schools
- the books help prepare all students for life in a multicultural community.

Unfortunately few of the books presently used in schools are likely to be multilingual. For the rest, and for younger children in particular, here is a list of questions that teachers can ask about the representation of gender and race in the language of children's books:[23]

- Does the book use 'man' or 'men' to mean 'people' or does it use 'men and women' instead (e.g. the inclusion of Boadicea and Joan of Arc in a book titled *Fighting Men*)?
- Does the book caricature the members of racial or ethnic groups by giving them unfairly stereotyped roles, attributes, or personalities?
- Is the book imbalanced in giving heroic and other leading roles to actors from elite backgrounds while putting ordinary people in the background?
- Does the book use sexist or racist terminology?
- Does the book use the pronoun 'he' to refer to males or females?
- Does the book use a two-value system in the language it applies to female and male characters (e.g. girls 'giggling' while boys 'laugh')?
- Does the book use a two-value system in the way it characterizes people from different cultures (e.g. 'brave colonists' struggling against 'blood-thirsty savages'; 'hard-praying ancestors' versus 'troublesome renegades')?
- Are females and the culturally different described in demeaning terms (e.g. 'the women and children'; or 'a hen party'; or 'jabbering away in their language')?
- Are females described as male appendages rather than as people in their own right (e.g. 'the clever wife' or 'the wise daughter')?
- Is the female member of a partnership presented as unequal (e.g. 'the farmer' and 'the farmer's wife')?
- Does the resolution of the story depend on whether a character is 'pretty', 'ugly', 'strong', 'handsome', 'rich', 'titled'?
- Are the characters' problems set against a real background of social inequality and social problems?

As a stimulus to wider changes, it is important that professional users of books communicate their needs and their views to publishing houses. In some places, teachers and schools make a point of communicating with publishers and their agents about any strong satisfaction or dissatisfaction felt for particular books. Informed criticism of this kind is a powerful force in the literary marketplace that can have a real impact on change.

Teacher interaction styles

An earlier section described studies of mismatches in teacher interactions with immigrant girls. When this evidence is coupled with the huge amount of evidence on gender bias more generally in teacher interaction styles, the difficult situation for immigrant girls becomes clear. In all countries studied, female and male teachers tend to pay less attention to girls than to boys at all ages, in various socio-economic and ethnic groupings, and in all subjects. Girls also get less criticism for their behaviour, fewer instructional contacts, fewer high level questions and academic criticism, and slightly less praise than boys. Male teachers give more attention to boys than to girls. But while girls volunteer to answer questions as often as boys do, they are less likely to initiate the contact. Boys initiate more contact with teachers in classroom talk itself, while girls tend to contact the teacher outside this context. Teachers also read and respond to the behaviour of boys and girls quite differently. Although they tend to respond to the form of girls' contributions, they respond to the content of boys' contributions. Slow achieving boys get more behavioural criticism, but high achieving boys get 'the best of everything'. In contrast, low achieving girls get the least teacher attention of all in classroom talk, although some studies have also found that high achieving girls get the least.[24]

Many suggestions in Chapter 3 about teacher interaction styles with culturally different children also apply here. As mentioned, female discursive norms are often different from male norms. Females tend to place high value on strengthening affiliative links between people, rather than competing with them. Boys do the same of course, but their greater tendency to compete in discourse makes this behaviour seem the typical male response. Nevertheless, it would seem that dominant male norms of competitive interaction are really the more unusual variety, in spite of their dominance. In other words, they are a norm which most people, including most boys, would not prefer if they were allowed the choice. As a result, perhaps the real interests of boys too would be served by changing classroom norms. For example, schools could reduce or cut entirely the following authoritarian teacher–pupil interaction practices. These things do create imbalances in power that give status to competitive norms, while disadvantaging girls in general:

- the unrestrained use of the imperative (by the teacher)
- the use of the (absolute) right to speak last
- the use of the (absolute) right to contradict
- the use of the (absolute) right to define the world for others
- the use of the (absolute) right to interrupt or to censure
- the use of the (absolute) right to praise or blame in public.

These negative things are deeply ingrained habits that many teachers think are part of the very stuff of teaching. I believe this teacher ideology would not withstand critical inspection and challenge. It is an area for change.

More comprehensive changes are also happening in North American schools. These are aimed at improving the performance of immigrant girls in mathematics and science, and the planned intervention programmes list their changes under five headings:[25]

- group instructional approaches
- tutoring

- test preparation and study skills
- teacher training
- parental participation.

First, in changing group instructional approaches, the programmes are finding that problem focused and activity based learning helps to promote learning among immigrant girls if it follows these strategies:

- if it adopts practices that are consistent with recent evidence about students' developmental needs
- if it links achievement with motivation in direct ways
- if it gives more attention to problem solving than to product or outcome.

Second, in changing peer tutoring or teacher tutoring for remediation or enrichment work, the programme aims to give mastery over previously presented material. Specifically, it uses interactive exchanges with a significant other who scaffolds the task in his or her own discourse.

Third, in complementing tutoring, the programme highlights activities that teach students strategic knowledge about test preparation and study skills. This means helping them get inside the peculiar culture of schools, where American forms of evaluation and assessment often present a way of life that seems strange to culturally different students.[26]

Fourth, the programme stresses the training and renewal of teachers themselves. As the evidence shows, too often teachers' interaction styles give girls biased messages about their place in the academic programme. This is especially the case with mathematics and science where a range of research studies confirms that better opportunities go to boys than to girls. Also cultural bias in the treatment of culturally different students, in science classes in particular, promotes a self-fulfilling prophecy of student success and failure.[27] Some teachers see culturally different female students as much less able than majority culture males in these areas, and they deliberately or unintentionally create barriers for students because of these stereotypes. The programme uses intervention activities like workshops and seminars to give teachers ideas for improving the performance of immigrant girls in these areas.

Fifth, it is known that parental participation in the management of schools gives parents a sense of their own efficacy in relation to the school and its environment. This translates into higher achievement by children coming from the same cultural background. It is especially important for parents, who may feel alienated from the school and its middle class culture, if they see other culturally different parents involved in this way and if they become involved themselves.

Also relevant here are the many suggestions made in Chapter 5 about the fairer treatment of children from inner urban, low income backgrounds, and in Chapter 6 about the fairer treatment of children from second language minorities. Also the issue of fairer assessment is an important area of reform. Perhaps most important of all, for changing education for diversity, is the reform of early childhood education. Chapter 6 discusses this.

Whole school planning

If these many recommendations are going to work in a coherent way, they need to be inserted into some sort of corporate plan at school level. The critical policy making approach in Chapters 1 and 2 has this sort of planning in mind. However, for school plans to have much chance of changing things, they need to be thoroughly negotiated with relevant people. A high level of agreement among participants allows the plan to become an action statement, whereby the plan (or policy) lays out precisely how a school is going to do what it hopes to do, which in this case is to reform the education of girls from immigrant cultures. Certainly girls from immigrant cultures are a worthwhile focus for school planning in culturally different communities.[28]

Planning by asking the girls

This kind of planning aims to bring the sociocultural background, the skills, knowledge, and gendered interests of immigrant girls directly into the school and to place more value on those things. It tries to increase the girls' pride in who they are and where they come from. Planning could begin by consulting the interests of the girls themselves and their parents. For example, from a survey of opinion the school might discover that immigrant girls want priority given to learning English well, instead of training in self-assertiveness or self-esteem. Not speaking English can be limiting in a range of ways that undermine self-esteem. Also, integration into the mainstream is an overriding concern for most children, while a weak command of English stands in the way of integration.

Unexpected insights into the interests of immigrant girls could also come to light if schools consulted the students directly. Adolescent girls often point to the absence of safe places in the school's programme for exploring sexuality (Fine 1988). In particular, they might confirm that the standard sex education classes available to them give too much attention to the sexual needs and interests of heterosexual boys; while more serious matters like conception, contraception, abortion, teen marriage, and motherhood are overlooked. Also sex education programmes often bypass difficult issues to do with consensual sexuality, discursive resistance, and imbalances in power. Grappling with these issues depends on open dialogue and critique, which means that successful courses are usually interactive, not didactic. School-based health clinics also have an important role in complementing the work of sex-education courses. In fact, only positive things come from these clinics.[29]

Planning for education and work

Staff in secondary schools in English-speaking countries often have problems deciding on strategies to use for advising children about their futures (Rudduck 1994). In contrast, in Japan, an entire department in secondary and vocational schools is set aside for smoothing this process of school-to-work transition and ensuring that all students are placed in jobs (Okano 1992). Perhaps as a result of this, Japan is a society where youth unemployment is consistently close to zero. Elsewhere, though, in the more openly multi-ethnic societies that English-speaking countries have become,[30] there are complex issues of fairness involved when schools provide professional advice and direction to students. Moreover young women often get less than fair treatment in this area (Griffin 1987). Therefore dealing with these complexities when planning means asking some serious questions about gender, race, and culture:

- What sort of printed material on careers will give just the right message to every group of students?
- How can the interests and preferences of parents be balanced with those of students?
- What should be done about jobs in areas of the workforce that remain persistently male or female?
- Should immigrant female students be encouraged to enter occupations that do not offer the same standards of fair treatment to girls that schools themselves try to provide?

'Education for work' is a dynamic and growing area of school practice, although its theoretical base has a long history.[31] Again, a key issue for immigrant girls is how to improve their participation and performance in mathematics and science so that a different range of job prospects from the traditional range opens up for them (Branson 1991). The programme already described above, in the United States, targets four areas for changing attitudes and expanding immigrant girls' knowledge:[32]

- role models and mentors
- career awareness activities
- exposure to extracurricular science and mathematics activities
- providing a supportive environment.

First, one practice that proves effective is helping girls make regular contact with role models and mentors who have had favourable experiences in mathematics and science. Two points emerge from the research: exposing students to women scientists influences female students' attitudes positively towards scientists in general and towards female scientists in particular; and reading and discussion units that look at famous culturally different, female mathematicians or scientists give girls a way of identifying with the early life experiences of these famous people which lifts their own horizons.

Second, career awareness activities at middle school level are fostering vocational maturity and career competence. Here schools are contesting the powerful stereotype that it is unfeminine to study mathematics or science. In exploring this area researchers in the United States keep their interests focused on the individual student in a single context. But wider discourses of social control also need to be challenged by the school, if immigrant girls are going to resist becoming part of the stories that they hear told to them on every side. Counselling strategies are useful, especially when focus groups look at the experiences of older students who have had some success.

Third, extracurricular activities make use of industry tours, cooperative work placements, and vocational planning. These are more valuable if they are done in the company of people who really know about the effects of negative discourses, and who have managed to challenge those discourses themselves. In other extracurricular activities, students are mixing recreational with problem solving activities. They visit exhibits at museums and galleries, make trips, do special projects, and join after-school science clubs.

Fourth, a broadly supportive school environment helps students cope with many sources of intimidation. A strong climate of individual and group efficacy develops when teachers use feedback that is constructively positive, but academically challenging. Also contacts with significant others, who reflect a sense of self-worth, are important for all children, but especially for immigrant girls who may be unsure of their place and reception in a school.

Planning change for classrooms

The micro-context of classrooms is where the obvious changes appear. In England, for example, adolescent girls engaged in craft, design and technology courses have more contacts with their teachers than boys, and they are also longer contacts. The girls interrupt more, and they make more unsuccessful attempts to initiate contact. In general, in this setting, they are more competitive in their interactions. Also in these practical sessions there is a change in the usual ratio of teacher-to-pupil contacts found in formal classes, where teachers usually control interaction (Randall 1987). However, in the same school setting, wider structural changes also help explain these differences: The teacher, the head teacher, and the local authority were all strongly committed to equal opportunities for girls. As a result, projects of equal interest to the sexes were available, and there was minimal gender stereotyping in the way lessons were handled. In this positive context of female empowerment, where teachers valued the interests of girls and boys equally, the girls received a fairer distribution of interactive opportunities, and more control over the discourse.[33]

Planning that involves parents: countering the effect of the marketplace
Studies in the United States often report that immigrant girls receive relatively little encouragement from their mothers, get little motivation for doing science and mathematics from their female teachers, and are given negative differential treatment by their male teachers and counsellors. Also community members and classmates seem to reinforce these negative attitudes.[34] Although this evidence from the United States seems to conflict with the anecdotal evidence from Australia, where people urge students to 'dare to be different',[35] it is likely that immigrant girls are affected by these negative things more in the United States, where the highly conservative culture of the marketplace creates powerful discourses of conformity within which people have to live their lives.

At the same time, immigrant girls in the United States are known to pursue science-related careers after getting encouragement from significant others. Clearly schools need to take a real interest in the wider contexts of an immigrant girl's life. They need to combat the negative messages students receive from a marketplace biased towards maintaining its own status quo. A starting point is in educating parents, by sending them strong messages that their daughters do not have to conform to marketplace expectations about their roles or their actions.

Another step in working with parents is to involve them actively in the girls' mathematics and science education. This can happen if teachers find a place for them in homework activities, perhaps by asking them to play with apparatus and to speculate about solutions to problems. Parents need to have high expectations for their daughters, but not expectations that burden the girls unrealistically. For example, Asian immigrants sometimes believe that everyone is equal in ability, and that hard work is all that is needed to succeed in almost anything. This could be a factor in the success rates of Asian immigrant students in English-speaking countries, which has become a stereotype with its own negative effects.[36] Taking this view too far can be harmful, as reports of the pressure-cooker school experience in Japan and its links with teenage suicide suggest. Again parents can help by exposing children to good role models, who offer optimistic and emancipatory life stories that immigrant girls can picture themselves inside.

Planning through professional development
The key to effective implementation always lies in professional development work. In fact, a whole school plan will have professional development work

as a key subheading. To meet the needs of immigrant girls, some areas of professional development work stand out. It is clear that different students receive very different messages and discursive treatment from their teachers. So matters of anti-racism and anti-sexism deserve special attention, because outside agencies tend to be lukewarm in their support in these areas. A study of 37 school boards, covering most of Ontario, confirms that many boards have no policies for dealing with non-sexist education, and many of those that do limit their policies to employment equity for professional staff rather than worrying about their students (A. Gilbert 1990). Very few school boards have evaluated their programmes and materials for sexist content. Furthermore there is limited support for teaching staff in this area, and few efforts to educate students about sexist and racist stereotypes.

Teachers claim that they treat students all the same, yet teachers expect different things from students depending on their sex and culture, and few teachers make any effort to assess their own teaching styles in these areas. Because teachers in general are very resistant to the evidence of discrimination in this area, a process of information sharing followed by professional development activities is one way to go. As a starting point, there is a place for collaborative action research projects, conducted by willing teachers with one another, and then shared more widely. These use observation studies or audiovisual media to examine whole class practices.[37]

When grappling with these issues, teachers are embarking on a school research task that could provide a target for a whole year of professional development work, and its effects could be lasting ones. Action research activities in anti-racist and anti-sexist education provide an essential knowledge base for planning change.[38] A whole school plan can set out the kind of research that is needed, and the responsibilities and professional development activities that come from it.[39] Guskey (1986) offers three goals for the in-service training of teachers:

- changes in teachers' behaviour
- enhancement of student learning
- changes in teachers' attitudes and beliefs.

Although these three goals may seem out of order, changing teachers' behaviour has priority, because this impacts on student success which in turn changes teachers' beliefs about their own behaviour. Teachers are often unconvinced by research evidence showing that their practices are unfair to immigrant female students. But if the same teachers are encouraged by a school-wide plan of professional development to try some new techniques, the second and third goals shown above can be reached more easily: student achievement goes up and then teacher attitudes often change.

Specifically the topics of classroom interaction, raised throughout this chapter, are areas that schools are concentrating on in professional development work. Some activities look for key situations where immigrant girls get negative differential treatment.[40] In response, they ask teachers to change their own behaviour. Other activities look for key situations where immigrant girls need positive differential treatment, which involves teachers finding out more about the girls' family and cultural backgrounds, and blending that information with the knowledge obtained from the girls themselves.[41]

Conclusion

What I am suggesting are changes to whole school structures. In their range and scope, these could even approach many of the changes discussed in Chapter 2, at Richmond Road. Indeed, for reform to occur, these things do have to begin with schools themselves, because, in general, wider school systems are rather uninformed about the realities of the cultural diversity that they contain. At the same time, these wider systems create the framework of policies that schools and teachers have to operate within. Therefore teachers and administrators, in individual schools, may need to press for system wide research that can provide a useful knowledge base for all schools to draw on. This sort of research ranks among the priorities of system wide school reform.

Schools themselves in high immigrant areas are beginning to find out much more about their local communities, but because they have worked for many years with the children of a community, teachers often assume that they are experts on the local context. However, the reality can be rather different. Teachers themselves can be highly biased in their views about their school's social context. This can happen if they are not members of the local social and cultural networks; or if they travel into the community each day and base their views on the filtered impressions that they get from the descriptions that often circulate in the staffrooms of schools. Sometimes teachers are so affected by their own lack of success with children from certain backgrounds that they see those backgrounds in a prejudiced way. Replacing these stereotypes with information closer to reality, means studying the context in great depth and then taking action. There are a range of ways to do this,[42] although here I concentrate on only the most relevant and useful.

Those who have used ethnography to study children in natural contexts[43] say that teachers can understand student learning much better in schools if they know more about children's daily lives in their own community settings. A few schools in some parts of the world have made radical changes to their pedagogy, assessment, and curriculum procedures after doing ethnographic research in their local communities. Good ethnography of schooling has the following criteria:[44]

- it involves prolonged and repetitive observation within the actual context
- it disturbs the process of interaction as little as possible
- its instruments are developed in the field
- questions emerge as the study proceeds
- its major task is to understand the sociocultural knowledge participants bring to the context and generate within it.

Ethnography comes in several guises. These include classroom ethnography (Watson-Gegeo 1997), ethnography of communication (Farah 1997), micro-ethnography (Garcez 1997), and critical ethnography (May 1997a).

This chapter has already shown the value and point of ethnography. Goldstein's searching study of Hmong girls in American schools was very relevant to the theme of this chapter. Nevertheless other ethnographic studies could go further, by setting the life experiences and norms of behaviour of female immigrants alongside the unfamiliar economic and sociocultural pressures that their new countries bring. These different things often make it difficult for immigrants to understand the working of the new culture. As Bottomley says about immigrant women in Australia, they often develop 'their definitions of reality and of themselves within rural societies where the family, as a unit of production, was sustained within concentric spheres of activity'. In contrast, in postmodern Australian cities 'these activities are dispersed and perhaps contradictory' while the social and economic conditions of urban centres 'create centrifugal forces that fragment the family' (Bottomley 1977: 309). Chapter 5 looks more closely at the fragmented education offered in these urban centres.

Immigrant girls are among the most vulnerable human beings: they are exploited, ignored, and denigrated in many social settings. The school should not be one of those settings; changing the discourses of schooling in ways that give immigrant girls a sense of their own empowerment is important. In doing this the example set by professional staff, especially male teachers and administrators, is vital: 'men teachers have a particular responsibility and opportunity here, because what they say and do influences what kind of masculinity is hegemonic in the school' (Kessler *et al.* 1985: 47). At the same time, to begin the process of changing this still taken-for-granted educational patriarchy, the following suggestions for teachers and administrators could make schools and classrooms fairer places for everyone: for boys and girls, and for men and women. They do seem important courtesies for schools to extend to everyone, as part of their classroom and administrative discourses:[45]

- reducing the use of impersonal or bureaucratic language in official and informal communication
- softening formal messages with more humour, less pomposity, less condescension, and a use of vivid metaphors linked to the real world of the school

- sending messages to students that personalize the recipient
- using the first person as subject, and only the occasional passive verb in oral and written communication with students and staff
- introducing a language of school and classroom symbols that expresses collaboration rather than competition, cooperation for shared rewards rather than winning for personal glory
- taking positive policy action to end the denigration of girls by boys in the school and the classroom
- speaking openly about issues of race and discrimination[46]
- taking positive policy action to challenge the pervasiveness of verbal sexual abuse
- fostering a classroom environment where laughter is common, where frequent greetings are given using people's names, where real achievements are recognized through public expressions of congratulation
- creating a classroom environment filled with displays of students' work and where people are relaxed about giving and taking criticism without fear or offence
- giving higher priority to reshaping the sexual distribution of interaction in classrooms
- singling immigrant girls out for more recognition, and remembering their names and using them
- creating a comfortable and non-threatening environment for interaction[47]
- withdrawing from a centre-stage pedagogical role more often as a deliberate pedagogy, and rearranging the structures of classroom interaction in ways that favour the language rights of girls
- giving more attention to the purposeful and regular use of oral language by students, as a key pedagogy in all areas of learning across the curriculum.

Discussion starters

1 What is the difference between positive and negative differential treatment? How can schools justify providing one, but not the other? What common classroom practices illustrate these two forms of treatment?

2 Do you find the distinction between 'options' and 'ligatures' a helpful way of looking at the life chances that people get from their education? Why or why not? Are there important ligatures, as well as just options, that conventional schools pass on to their students? What are those ligatures? How could classrooms be rearranged to build ligatures?

3 What are the options and ligatures of the teaching profession? How do these interact or conflict with the work that teachers do with culturally different children?

4 Review the studies that confirm that boys and men tend to be more competitive in their interactions, while girls and women tend to be more cooperative. Does this match your own experience in mixed sex interactions? Can you give examples of experiences that illustrate your points? Are there exceptions to this in education? Where do they occur?

5 Consider the schools that the Hmong girls attended in the United States. What changes could have been made to the policies and practices of these schools to give the immigrant girls consistently fairer treatment? Would the changes be fairer for all immigrant girls, or not?

6 Based on the evidence provided in this chapter, how true a picture of the situation for immigrant girls is the summary on pp. 96–7? Explain your response and be as critical as you like.

7 This chapter suggests that immigrant girls are doubly disadvantaged because of mismatches in their interactions with teachers in class? On the basis of your own experiences, do you agree or disagree with this statement? Why? Can you give examples from your own experience?

8 Mathematics and science are areas that seem to need special attention when considering the needs of immigrant girls. Are there other areas of the curriculum or other levels of schooling where immigrant girls need special help? How could the changes in practices for mathematics and science mentioned in this chapter be reapplied in other areas?

9 In this chapter I have suggested that dealing with cultural and gendered differences is a complex and difficult matter, but that the starting point for teachers is to be as knowledgeable as possible about their students and their wider lives. Is this true? If it is not true, how else might teachers address these matters?

five

CHANGING THE EDUCATION OF THE URBAN POOR

Urban education is a well established area of inquiry in Europe, Australasia, and North America. Its focus is on schools in inner-city areas, especially in places sometimes described as 'ghetto' sites. Policy and practice in this area usually addresses the needs of urban schools using an economic deficit or compensatory approach: urban schools are seen as lacking the resources needed to bring them up to the same standard in opportunity and outcome as schools provided elsewhere for the more affluent and privileged.

This chapter looks at the issue from another perspective. While it recognizes the pressing need for increased funding for inner-city schools, it also presents the urban poor as groups who have their own distinct values, norms, and cultural practices.[1] In fact, all these things mean much more to them than just cultures of poverty that need to be escaped. These urban neighbourhood cultures can be just as systematic and regular in their practices as any culture, and they deserve the respect that any culture should receive. I agree that there is much to do in tackling the glaring structural inequities that affect the lives of the inner-city poor.[2] But for these reform efforts to work, they also need to respond at every point to the expressed wishes of local people themselves, telling of the things that oppress them and the things that they value. Indeed, the neighbourhood cultures that often exist in the vicinity of a single large school can include many things that are highly valued, highly distinctive, and also highly relevant to the real work of the school.

My point is that good urban schools, wherever they are found, are as organic to the local neighbourhood cultures as they can be. This means that the schools, in their formal curriculum and in their informal message systems, recognize and respect any important aspects of the neighbourhood cultures that seem educationally relevant. Although every school should guarantee a level of quality in its educational provisions that is close to that of other schools in the system, a school that is not organic in this way is probably not providing that quality of provision in any case. This is because it represents, in the eyes of its students, an island of cultural isolation removed from many of their pressing interests and values. Accordingly, borrowing ideas from Chapter 3, the opening questions for this chapter are these:

- How can inner-city schools become more organic to their neighbourhood cultural communities?
- How can they do this while also offering high quality education to all their students?

This chapter argues for a *very different* accommodation to the needs of inner-city students. It begins with the important equity factors that affect different community groups, especially in societies where ideas like a level playing field and no special interest groups are part of the rhetoric that sustains inequalities. The chapter's four major sections then follow. The first two sections raise many of the issues that are central for teachers in urban schools. The last two sections suggest reforms to policy and practice that integrate equity with high quality education.

Equity matters

Formal education is mainly concerned with students' ability to put meanings together in thought, to communicate them in words, and to learn from the discourses around them. But many other factors have a role in educational success. Matters of race, culture, gender, region of living, and social class often affect educational progress. Even wide participation in a literate culture is not enough to guarantee educational success. On its own, participation in a literate culture does not provide all the cultural capital that schools base their criteria of success upon.

Often, as Chapter 4 shows, several sociocultural factors combine to affect children's educational success and failure. A study in a cosmopolitan Australian city looked at immigrant children (Italian, Spanish, Portuguese and Macedonian) from low income backgrounds who had learned their English in school only as a second language. Yet these same ESL students outperformed their Anglo-Australian classmates from equally low income backgrounds on language tests and also in school achievement examinations.[3] In Canada, groups of Canadian-born children from immigrant language backgrounds (Italian, Chinese, Ukrainian and German) outperformed groups of working class children whose mother tongue was English (Cummins

1984a). Clearly class, culture and language interact here in complex ways. And this complexity grows when gender or race are added. In the present-day world, the effects of race are best seen in American education.

School achievement in the south-west and west of the United States is stratified by race, with African Americans as a group at the bottom, Hispanics in the middle, and Anglo-Americans at the top. Although the African Americans speak English as their first language, it is Hispanics who achieve better as a group than African Americans in schools.[4] Clearly, there are other influential factors at work beyond race: bilingual Hispanic children have experiences in two languages, a contact that monolingual African American children do not have. This might give real advantages to the Hispanics. But there is another factor at work here suggested in the account of a twentieth-century social historian.

During the 1970s and 1980s, 'Black immigrants into the USA from the Caribbean and Hispanic America behaved, essentially, like other immigrant communities'; they were not 'extruded from the labour market to anything like the same extent' as the ghetto society of many native-born Black people in the United States. In contrast, the latter became 'the textbook example' of 'an increasingly separate and segregated "underclass" whose problems were de facto regarded as insoluble, but secondary, since they formed only a permanent minority' (Hobsbawm 1994: 415). How can we account for the difference between these two groups of people, both from the African diaspora?

Some of the reasons can be found again in the differences between voluntary and involuntary minorities. Applying this distinction of Ogbu's,[5] the voluntary Caribbean immigrants usually knew what they had to do to succeed in their new country: they had to adopt the new culture and fit into it as much as necessary. But African Americans are already part of the culture of America; in important ways, linked closely with racism, that culture does not serve them well. Yet they cannot easily change their own culture and obtain educational success without changing the rest of the culture of America itself, along with themselves. So this creates a dilemma that holds back the complete emancipation of African Americans. Underpinning this dilemma is the fact that powerful discourses of racism, dating from a much earlier time, perpetuate themselves even in the culture of present-day America. In doing so, they affect almost every aspect of African American lives. Taken together, these things highlight the desperate need for anti-racist and anti-bias education in American schools, so that African American young people can better become the agents of their own emancipation.

The role of discourse, including the many different sign systems that people encounter in their lives, are the all important factors here. But language on its own, as the chief public discourse, is not the cause of educational inequity. Language has little power when it is separated from powerful institutions and people. The power of language comes from what it is used to do: the discursive practices in which it is sited. Labov (1987) is categorical in claiming that the primary cause of educational failure for children of diversity is not simply language difference, but institutional racism. The evidence suggests that the unjust use of power in maintaining stereotypes and class distance is the chief factor in educational failure, not language. But even these things operate through the wider discourses that surround us all; because of these discursive patterns that circulate in societies and limit people's actions, even literacy itself can seem a vain achievement to those approaching it from a poverty background. Bourdieu observes that individuals from some backgrounds find that achieving 'success' in schools involves a rejection of their social origins, so different are the cultural practices of schools.

Indeed North American studies reveal the pressures on students to choose between rejecting their identities in order to succeed, or giving up on school success in order to retain a sense of who they are.[6] D. Smith (1986) echoes this view, listing the social factors that often hold children from marginalized backgrounds at a distance from literacy:

- they quickly come to believe that there is little truth in the claim that school success for them will lead to a better life
- they recognize that there is a ceiling on their achievements held there by aspects of cultural capital that have little to do with being able to read and write
- they often conclude that to learn to read and write is to subordinate themselves to a game whose rules are set by a culture that they themselves are forever excluded from.

Problems and issues 1: bias in urban schooling

Following on directly from the discussion of equity matters, this section looks at four key areas of bias for children from low income backgrounds in urban schools: racism and its associated biases; treatment of non-standard language varieties; labelling and stereotyping children; and the treatment of different discourse norms. These four areas overlap to form a syndrome of factors that make many schools very unattractive places for the children of the poor.

Racism and its associated biases

'Prejudice against the other' is one way that racism is defined.[7] A definition that is also a partial explanation would link racism with the role that discourse plays in shaping the human mind, and positioning people in certain social locations. A key term here is 'stereotypes' and I discuss stereotypes of various kinds and the way they work in a later section. The mind of a person who holds a racist view is shaped by a great many past situations and discourses in which stereotype-reinforcing properties appeared that were connected to the stereotyped racial group, seen as individuals or collectively. As a result, any sign system linked to members of that race (such as their bodily appearance, dress, public bearing, or language) then becomes overlaid with meanings that cannot be separated in that person's mind from the stereotypical and racist view.[8]

I think it is clear from this expanded definition that once individuals and groups hold racist views, it becomes very difficult for them to change those views. This means that racist views tend to persist even when there is overwhelming evidence that they are wrong. In addition, people often use racist views to rationalize actions that are basically irrational. Clearly too these views can easily be circulated among the members of closely knit groups, especially if the formal structures of prominent organizations and social systems allow the views to circulate freely. In fact, the most notorious example of twentieth-century racism illustrates the point well.

A study of the discourses of National Socialism that were developed in the 1920s and 1930s in Germany shows how effective these 'stories' were when circulated within their limited and highly structured space.[9] Any power in the battle of discourse that took place, lay with the discourses of German ultranationalism, racism, and militarism. This is because any contrary discourses at the time were increasingly forbidden a public airing, while the fascist discourses, notably here the discourses of racism targeting various groups, were officially encouraged and rigorously promoted. Indeed German schools themselves were especially important in doing this evil work, just as the discourses of schools in today's world are important for good or ill. Schools everywhere can play a positive role in encouraging and promoting anti-racist discourses.

Understanding racist practices, like understanding any system of oppression, begins with the reasons and accounts of those who are affected by them. To get some insight into the views of students themselves who are affected by racism in school, I looked closely at a study whose focus was on the impact that racism had on the readiness of students to pull out of school: to dropout.[10] Here a team of researchers talked to many Black Canadian students about any racist aspects of the schooling that they experienced. Below is a summary of some of the practices that they and others identify as contributing to a racist school environment:

- teachers with low expectations of certain groups of children as students
- teachers ranked in the school hierarchy on the basis of the social status or abilities of their students[11]

- open teacher disrespect, especially using racially offensive remarks
- a sense of being overly visible or targeted for misconduct by school personnel
- careless labelling and categorization of students by race
- deliberate teacher inaccessibility and lack of encouragement to the poor or the racially different
- a depersonalized school environment[12]
- alienating curricular content, with no representation of Black identity
- a sense of invisibility, that no one cares if certain students go or stay
- inappropriate disciplinary methods, like suspension from class for skipping classes
- teachers who avoid or ignore discussions of race and discrimination[13]
- school and classroom organizational styles that promote individual competition rather than peer support groups.[14]

A later section presents a list of *positive* practices that try to balance this list. It describes ways in which real schools are reforming their own practices, partly in response to the kind of evidence offered by students themselves.

Some people affected by racism can change their appearances, blend into the background, and so reduce acts of racism against them.[15] Usually even this is impossible. Few societies have been as stratified by race as the former South Africa under apartheid, where appearance provided no escape for those who were on the more powerless side of the colour bar. In fact, most people who are subject to racism cannot change their appearance any more than they can change the language variety that they were raised with. Second only to a person's appearance, it is the public use of language that impacts most heavily on teacher assessments of student potential.

Treatment of non-standard language varieties

In many settings, the non-standard language of marginalized people is used as a guide to their potential for achievement and to their worth as human beings. This occurs in any stratified society where many variations in vocabulary, syntax, accent, and discourse style are socially marked, so that even a basic conversation between individuals can suggest their place in the social structure. For example, to people from Philadelphia a change in one aspect of a single vowel in an utterance can be enough to make a White speaker sound Black, and a Black speaker sound White (Fasold 1990).

In any language community, closely knit social or ethnic groups use a range of language varieties.[16] These varieties come into the work of the school in one way or another. Children coming from these backgrounds can have two or more varieties which they use in their everyday language, perhaps one variety used in the home, another in the peer group, and a third in the school. Largely as a result of the school's influence, this last variety may come to be very close to the standard variety.[17] At the same time, many children arrive in schools with little or no contact with the standard variety used as the language of formal education. Often these children are penalized for having a language variety that is different from the variety that has high status in the school. Indeed this discrimination is so severe in some places that Dannequin (1987) describes very young students who are non-standard speakers of French as 'gagged children' in their own classrooms.[18] Elsewhere this kind of discrimination has even led to legal sanctions being applied to schools.[19]

The state itself helps maintain an ideology of 'correctness' in language. Governments legitimize a particular form of language by making that variety obligatory on official occasions and in official settings, like schools, public administration, and political institutions. This prestigious form of language then becomes the standard variety against which all other linguistic practices are measured, including especially the practices sanctioned in schools. In the wider societies of the English-speaking world, except in England itself, this ideology of correctness has been declining in recent decades (Herriman and Burnaby 1996), especially where non-standard varieties have never been stigmatized or socially marked to the degree that they are in Britain. However in the United States, the debate over the use of 'ebonics' in the mid-1990s suggests that bias there is still rampant (Baugh 1997).[20] Furthermore discrimination against a range of non-standard varieties is easily disguised in other countries too, even in one like Canada that prides itself on its reputation for linguistic tolerance (Corson and Lemay 1996).[21]

In his early work, Labov (1966) found that the non-standard language varieties used by diverse peoples varied systematically and regularly. In other words, the varieties were entirely regular codes of the language, and they are in no sense inferior to the standard variety in matters of syntax, accent and pronunciation. Labov's studies made people aware of the need to give fairer treatment to non-standard varieties in education. This is best shown in the Bullock Report (Department of Education and Science 1975) in Britain which recommended that schools begin to value whatever language variety children bring with them to school, while adding to it those other forms, functions, styles, and registers that are necessary acquisitions for educated people to make. As a result, a search began for ways to make teachers in English-speaking countries more aware of their own prejudices about non-standard varieties, and of the range of varieties that do coexist in monolingual societies. More recently it also led to the idea that students and teachers should become much more critically aware of language varieties and their role in activating stereotypes.

Labelling and stereotyping children

The evidence of language is central in confirming stereotypes and activating prejudices. Negative teacher attitudes towards the speech of culturally and socially different children affect teacher expectations, which affect pupil performance (J. Edwards 1989). A long-standing finding of research is that teachers' perceptions of children's non-standard speech leads to negative expectations about the children's personalities, social backgrounds, and academic abilities (Giles *et al.* 1987). Although teacher awareness of this key injustice stretches back over a generation, in practice this has not lessened the injustice very much. In Britain in the 1990s, there are doubts about teachers' ability to be objective when formally assessing oral language ability at senior school level. Findings reveal that the standard variety is rated much more favourably than non-standard varieties,[22] thus routinely discriminating against non-standard speakers. Moreover it seems that teachers bring these stereotypes with them into the profession. V. Edwards (1986) reports student-teacher evaluations of anonymous children's speech where both the academic and the interest level of speakers of non-standard varieties was viewed less favourably.

Like anyone else, teachers are prone to the influence of these and other stereotypes, but because of the kind of work that teachers do with children, they are in a unique position to put their stereotypes to work, sometimes with harmful effect. Hewstone and Giles (1986) offer four descriptive statements about stereotypes:

- stereotyping stems from illusory correlations between people's group membership and their psychological attributes and traits
- stereotypes influence the way information is processed about the members of groups (i.e. more favourable information is remembered about ingroups and more unfavourable information is remembered about outgroups)
- stereotypes create expectancies about other people and the holders of stereotypes often search for information and behaviours in others that will confirm those expectancies
- stereotypes constrain their holders' patterns of communication and promote communication which confirms the stereotypes held (i.e. they create self-fulfilling prophecies).

Remarkably, there is now evidence that teacher attitudes to children's non-standard language use are more critical in judging the quality of language use than the children's language itself. There is even evidence to suggest that the stereotypes that beginning teachers from the majority culture hold about children from poor and culturally different backgrounds cause them to 'hear' those children as non-standard in their language, regardless of how standard their speech actually is (Fasold 1984). These stereotypes endure because of simple ignorance among teachers about the range of varieties that coexist in a single linguistic space. I return to this and the other issues raised here later in the chapter.

Stereotypes, though, are more than just an outlet for prejudices *about* language. They are intricately caught up in language and in other forms of discourse. In other words, discourse is the substance in which stereotypes survive and are transmitted. As Ryan (1998) notes, every social group has a vocabulary of images that they use to designate the externalized 'other'. These webs of signs mark out large or small differences between people, and they reflect the contexts that give rise to them. For example, one way in which some people respond to perceived or real threats from others in their environment is to search for differences in appearance and make much more of these than the differences usually warrant. These exaggerations are shared with others from the same ingroup. In this way, everyday talk and other sign systems transform personal prejudices into the views of an entire group. In their turn, opinions based on stereotypes and put into words permeate, define, and redefine social situations. They create structures of systematic discrimination.

Even 'positive' stereotypes have negative effects on people. For example, students from some Asian backgrounds find it difficult to live up to the 'myth of the model minority' that circulates in English-speaking countries. Because of the academic success that some Asian students achieve in difficult areas like mathematics, music, and technology, others from similar backgrounds meet unreasonable expectations about themselves. Maclear (1994) describes the problems that journalists and editorial writers create for Asian children by overemphasizing academic success stories. These stories overlook the fact that children of Asian backgrounds are no different in their natural talents and skills from any other group of children, and success in education comes no more easily to most of them than it does to any others. Clearly stereotypes of any kind are best avoided. Their effects can never be controlled or even predicted.

Another problem of bias against inner-city children is in the labelling that educational professionals often engage in, which is really a form of well intended stereotyping. This happens with labels like 'dropout' where the school's failure to provide for a student is reconstrued as the student's own failure in the school. It also happens with labels like 'mentally retarded' where inappropriate assessments lead to placements that convenience the school, while often dismaying parents and disabling children.[23] Elsewhere I discuss work by Edelman (1984) and Fairclough (1985) on the labelling of disadvantaged and other students.[24]

Treatment of different discourse norms

Many educational difficulties for culturally different children are due to sociolinguistic interference. Yet teachers are often unaware of the impact on school learning of subtle differences in the language norms that minority children bring to school. Teachers sometimes see culturally different children as unresponsive, as disruptive, or as slow learners. They tend to overlook the fact that members of a different culture bring an understanding of their culture's own participant norms for interaction that may be very different from the dominant pattern. These norms are expressions of the culture's values. They provide informal rules which govern speaking, listening, and turn-taking behaviours.

Many studies now confirm the prevalence of inappropriate classroom and school contexts of interaction for culturally different children.[25] Information about these subtle differences in children's language norms appears only rarely in the professional training of teachers and it often falls outside the taken-for-granted reality of professional policy and practice in education. As a result, this is a prime area for unintended bias in the everyday practices of teachers working with socioculturally different children.[26] As an example, ethnographic studies confirm that there is no single way to tell stories, even in one culture. Children begin with the rules for storytelling that their unique socialization has given them. When called upon to use that skill in key situations in classrooms,[27] young children can adopt a very different set of norms from what the teacher expects.

One key situation that has received lots of attention is 'sharing time'. African American children sometimes manifest quite different discourse norms in this activity, and elsewhere too in school and community (Michaels 1981).[28] Some children use a 'topic associating' or episodic style, in which a string of personal anecdotes makes up the discourse. The theme of these strings is not made clear to the listener and its relevance to the teacher's understanding of the topic often seems obscure, because there is no end, no middle, or any clear beginning. Majority culture teachers are sometimes much more successful working with children who use a topic-centred style. When working with the African American children, teachers can have trouble seeing the point and predicting the speaker's direction. While African American professionals can be more helpful in rounding out and organizing the topic-associating children's accounts, even excellent teachers have difficulties with this approach to storytelling. Therefore the problems are not due to teacher incompetence. Instead the students seem to be negatively affected by their distance from the school's accepted norm.

This and other research on key situations suggests that inner-city children can meet a very structured form of discontinuity between the practices widely used in their own communities and those demanded by the school.

Nevertheless, these things are still not well understood by teachers, even by those who have spent long careers working with children in inner-city schools.

Problems and issues 2: entering academic meaning systems

Success in education is highly dependent on people's ability to 'display' knowledge, usually through the spoken or written use of words. Young children's display of the signs of a language is often the first contact teachers have with them. In later stages of education, verbal contact through formal or informal assessments is the main link between students and the assessors who decide their educational fate. In fact, formal education is largely a process of teaching the rules for using words, and the other signs used in academic meaning systems, and then judging how well those rules have been learned.

Clearly 'language' touches every aspect of education, and it could be no other way, because language is the medium of instruction in schools, it is the content of instruction, and it provides the pedagogical means by which that instruction is realized. In fact, every outcome that schools try to achieve depends on the language ability of students: students need high level skills in apprehending and using language; they also need to acquire the concepts at the heart of the curriculum that are expressed almost exclusively in language; and they need to make sense of the complex uses of language that teachers and texts employ in the process of passing on that curriculum knowledge.

More than all this, though, beyond school, the life chances of students are determined by their ability to interact with the discourses around them. The language all around children teaches them who they are, what their place is in the world, and what they need to do to become autonomous and valuable citizens. If they are unable to interact with those discourses with critical insight, they will be less autonomous and so they will become a burden to others. Language development is empowering for people, because the brain does not create language: language creates the brain.

Many other factors do affect educational success. Race, culture, gender, region of living, and class often affect people's educational progress. But if these could be taken out of the equation, one thing would stand out as the most important factor in educational success or failure: the more diverse the meanings that people communicate, and the more appropriate those meanings are to the academic meaning systems given high status in education, the more rewarding the institution of education will be. So does educational success depend largely on students having the words, wanting to use them, and being able to use them?

Words: the taken-for-granted markers of educational potential

It is the content of language, the use and the diversity of vocabulary in particular, that teachers look for when their students are communicating meaning.[29] They do this believing that the skilful use of those signs against a background of publicly meaningful rules is the most important evidence available about the quality of student thought. Yet they do this while knowing that the special vocabulary that they target is very culturally bound and very unevenly distributed among the population. In particular, many children from poorer working class backgrounds seem to be unmotivated in using the formal vocabularies of education in the context of schools themselves.[30]

While many teachers are aware of this problem, others take academic vocabulary more for granted in this way. In fact, there is much evidence that vocabulary diversity is the most consistent marker of proficiency used routinely throughout education. In written work, what teachers currently see as 'good' narrative writing is closely linked to vocabulary diversity (Grobe 1981). In reading, it is content knowledge, especially knowledge of word meanings and the rules for their use, that is the key to mastering texts and gaining entry to the culture of literacy (Chall 1987).

Similarly, studies of academic success in a second language confirm that in learning another language, vocabulary knowledge is 'the most important aspect of oral proficiency for academic achievement' (Saville-Troike 1984: 216), while lack of adequate English vocabulary severely affects ESL students' reading comprehension and their academic progress (Garcia 1991). The reading performances of Latino students in the United States, for example, differs mainly in vocabulary range when compared with non-ESL students; these differences begin to grow rapidly at around 10 years of age (Applebee *et al.* 1987).

Sometimes alarms are raised about the overemphasis on vocabulary skills in education. There are reasons to target the verbal sections of the *Scholastic Aptitude Tests* (SAT) that are used in the United States as gatekeeping measures for entrance to universities and colleges. Daniels (1983) describes these verbal tests as little more than a measure of 'lexical formality'. Maylath (1994) adds that the SAT is mainly a test of fluency in the Graeco-Latin vocabulary of English. Yet, in the United States, this vocabulary has almost second language status for many people, so remote is it from their everyday language practices. Maylath also observes that high school marks, based largely on tests of the Graeco-Latin vocabulary, 'combined with college entrance exams, like the SAT, do much to cull out those students who have avoided the Graeco-Latin vocabulary, usually well before they might step into a college or university classroom' (Maylath 1994: 198).

The academic culture itself of senior schools, in English-speaking countries,[31] is marked out by specialist vocabularies and other signs. Gaining access to that culture means learning the rules of use for the words used within it. While many children bring many of these rules of use to school with them, many others rely on the school itself to give them these rules of use. So what factors affect access to these rules of use that are so important for school success?

Sociocultural factors

Culture and class together create the conditions of upbringing and the alternative forms of linguistic capital that formal education often discounts. Class systems, based on occupation and income, exist in all modern societies. In relation to language, Labov's point is a good generalization to make about the relationship between language and sociocultural background: people who are sociologically similar are linguistically similar. Furthermore the academic culture of schooling is much more linguistically similar to the dominant groups in society than it is to others. So what makes the discursive practices of some groups of people so different as to keep them away from academic meaning systems?

The effect of social stratification upon the dispositions, experiences, and activities of certain social groups is central. It is true that the history of social class relations and their impact on the vocabularies of the poor varies across and within countries. Many commentators describe the unique link between 'the making of the English working class' in England, and the differences in cultural meaning systems between the social classes there.[32] Indeed the 'division of labour' in society is the key factor in all this in every country (Durkheim 1964[1893]). This produces social class divisions and great differences in wealth and lifestyle. In doing so, it creates and sharpens differences in sociocultural meaning systems.

Common influences on the language experience and vocabularies of adults in low income, inner-city families are listed here; these things, of course, tend to impact directly on the vocabularies of young members of those families:[33]

- monotonous and enervating nature of physical labour
- effects of small incomes on life experiences
- relative absence of outside language contacts
- relatively low levels of parental education and access to continuing education
- relative absence of outside influences on routine and habit
- social class-based housing common in English-speaking societies
- frequent and lengthy periods of unemployment.

When the lifestyles of broad sections of an adult population direct their experiences, activities, and language contacts in certain ways, rather than in others, and when this reoccurs from generation to generation, then sharp differences in cultural meaning systems are likely to arise between groups. Moreover if people's lives are unaffected by outside influences, these differences are passed on across the generations in people's discursive practices. They become markers of group values and vital aspects of group solidarity and identity.

Other life experiences also go with these differences in sociocultural positioning. There are differences in access to reading materials, especially books and periodicals that introduce the basics of academic vocabulary; and there are different everyday contacts with the kind of discourse that uses a wide vocabulary drawn from the school's culture of literacy. As a result, many children develop vocabularies very different from the vocabularies given high status in the school. In fact, there is much evidence to show that differences in children's vocabularies do correlate with their parents' levels of education and with levels of quality of life generally.[34] Research also confirms that early differences in achievement increase with age;[35] there is evidence that schools still do little to narrow these differences. In other words, children from affluent families get the early advantages in learning academic vocabulary, and they keep on getting them. So what can teachers in inner-city schools do about this?

Along with Gramsci, I believe that the best way for people to emancipate themselves is for them to have access to the most powerful and useful meaning systems available. In most of the English-speaking world, these are the meaning systems of education. The urban poor need access to those meaning systems, but it has to be an access that complements not replaces their own meaning systems. In other words, the task of schools is to integrate that academic culture of literacy into the cultures that the culturally different already value, not substitute one for the other, or merely add one on top of the other. If schools do want to bring everyone inside the academic culture of literacy, teachers have to find new ways of presenting that culture of literacy to all students, so that it meshes with their own lives and integrates with their own cultural meaning systems. As later discussion shows, in some settings schools are doing this by offering students a positive kind of differential treatment.[36]

The academic culture of literacy

Like any set of meaning systems, academic systems are open to change, challenge, renewal, reform, or decay. But moving freely within those meaning systems is much easier for those students reared within and around the institutional forces and experiences that produced them. For these students, the academic meaning systems are already an important part of their acquired cultural capital.

Meanings are marked by arbitrary symbols. The words of a language are the symbols most often used in shared meaning systems. Accordingly thinkers in any culture are competent managers of systems of signs, and our most efficient signs are the words of a language.[37] At the same time, meaning systems go well beyond the sum of the meanings of all the words that they contain, because they penetrate life forms, material conditions, and human relations.[38]

The special culture of literacy that is given high status in schools, is made up of many meaning systems that are well removed from the cultural capital valued by many people. Compared with the culture of poorer working class people, the dominant group's cultural capital in a society is usually an 'academic' one:

> Those whose 'culture' . . . is academic culture conveyed by the school have a system of categories of perception, language, thought and appreciation that sets them apart from those whose only training has been through their work and their social contacts with people of their own kind.
>
> (Bourdieu 1971: 200)

This causes problems for people crossing over from one side of the academic divide to the other (including teachers working with many students from low income backgrounds). Discussing the French working class, for example, Bourdieu notes that when intellectuals put themselves in the place of workers without having the world-view and dispositions of workers, they see 'the working-class condition through schemes of perception and appreciation which are not those that the members of the working class themselves use to apprehend it' (Bourdieu 1984: 372–3). Again, within single societies, the key to this process of stratification is the division of labour. This is what separates people into various class categories: those who create the routines, those who supervise the routines, and those who carry them out.

Coincidences of social, educational, and linguistic history have created a situation in English that is unique among languages: most of the specialist and high status vocabulary of English is Graeco-Latin in origin,[39] and most of its more everyday vocabulary is Anglo-Saxon in origin. Relative to other languages, English has a fairly clear boundary drawn between its everyday and its high status vocabularies. Relevant to education itself, children from certain sociocultural groups, in their final years of schooling, have unequal active access to the words that have high status as cultural capital in the 'field' of education. At the same time, teachers assess their students' grasp of the culture through their public use of this vocabulary, on the grounds that its use displays entry to academic meaning systems. As a consequence, it seems that high status word usage stands as one key mediating factor between sociocultural background and educational success or failure. So what can be done?

Instead of changing children from diverse backgrounds in some way, to suit the school, I prefer to think more about changing the forms of education that undervalue the things that many children bring to school with them. Just making slight changes in educational contexts can affect sociocultural groups differently. Therefore educators really need to know how different children's entry into academic meaning systems is affected by changing the context of schooling in some way. Using this knowledge, teachers can then change the contexts that they create and promote greater levels of success among the culturally different. Specifically this applies to the acquisition of literacy itself.

Literacy and the academic meaning systems

The problems of those trying to master literacy are only superficially matters of linguistic behaviour. In becoming literate, people pass through a sequence of cognitive, linguistic, and social adjustments rather like those that occur in communicating across cultural boundaries. As a result, children progress unequally towards academic literacy and towards success in the special literate culture that the school tries to create.[40] Literacy is learned in specific settings and the purposes, effects, and types of literacy for any single group can be very different from those established and recognized in schools. Thus children's potential for achieving academic literacy and quick success in the literate culture of the school will vary, as sociocultural factors interact with cognitive factors in complex ways.

Heath (1983) looks at the ways of 'taking' from printed material that young children learn from their home settings. Often these ways of taking are inconsistent with the patterns of literate culture expected in schools. These patterns established in the home leave many children unconnected with the usual rewards that come from school literacy: things like job preparation, social mobility, intellectual creativity, and information access. As a result, the motivation for reading and writing for many children is different, and many children are little motivated by the apparent academic usefulness of literacy. Outside schools, they often develop other culturally relevant skills, including access to other meaning systems, that are not required of them until later stages of schooling, if at all. However, by the time these skills are needed, many children have missed the basic literacy needed to present their special insights in school-acceptable ways.

At the same time, different children acquire a system of signs that is very different from those favoured by the special literate culture of the school. Although we know little about the concrete effects of literacy on the lives of individuals (Kaestle 1991), it is likely that the acquisition of literacy in schools does little to change the active vocabularies of children who are at a distance from the kinds of cultural capital given high status in the school.

The importance of this point, for urban schooling, is that displaying access to academic meaning systems depends largely on having access to the signs used to represent those systems. Access to those signs is unevenly distributed among groups of people according to their sociocultural backgrounds. How can schools do something about this?

Oral participation in an English-speaking culture of literacy may rank more highly than literacy as a factor in English vocabulary growth (Olson 1997). Even without acquiring literacy, oral participation in a culture of literacy seems at least as important for vocabulary acquisition as some of the work that schools concentrate on, in the formal teaching of reading or in direct vocabulary instruction. Indeed, a rather worrying finding, from a study of children's out-of-school experiences, suggests that *just participating in the discursive practices of a literate culture* is more important for academic vocabulary growth than most school related things.

Looking at thousands of students in New York, Hayes and Grether (1983) compared all the students' vocabulary development during the vacation period with their vocabulary development during the school term. Remarkably the vocabulary gap between high achieving and low achieving students increases more during the holiday period. Most of the difference in word knowledge performance comes from events outside school, not from school itself. This raises the question, can schools ever make up for the effects of society in this area? For me, the first task of schools is to integrate an academic culture of literacy into the various cultures that students bring with them to schools. Although some already bring key aspects of this academic culture with them to school, most inner-city students do not. I believe that most, if not all, inner-city families rely on schools to provide their children with this academic culture of literacy. But many schools do not do this because they do not know how to bring the very different cultures together in educationally valuable ways.

So what can schools serving the urban poor do about this? The two answers to this question offered below try to complement one another. They anticipate the fuller discussion of ways of doing these things that follows in the next two sections and in the Conclusion to this chapter:

- The first is for teachers to value the home and community cultures that children bring with them to school. This includes initiating them into anti-bias ideas and practices, so that they can recognize and respond prudently to racism and all the other forms of bias that they will likely encounter in their lives; and so that they can begin to feel that their own sociocultural background is valued and valuable. Critical language awareness activities are one part of this.
- The second is for schools to integrate the academic culture of literacy, and all its key meaning systems, into their students' life experiences and

discourses (i.e. their own cultures) so that they can draw on that academic culture whenever necessary to improve their life chances and their lives as autonomous citizens.

Changing policies and practices 1: valuing sociocultural differences

Teachers and school administrators meet children who are vulnerable in many different ways, especially in schools that serve the urban poor. Urban students from low income communities often come from a background that is very different from the dominant culture. Usually their parents' occupations or unemployment place them among the poorer working classes in society. Sometimes they have a religious background that is different from the mainstream. Sometimes the life histories that they have experienced are very different from the lives of other children and from those of their teachers in particular.

Dealing with bias: the need for anti-bias policies and practices

To cope with this range of relevant differences, schools in some places are developing more general and wideranging anti-bias policies and practices. These policies go beyond those covered by 'positive discrimination' or by 'affirmative action'. As valuable as those social practices may have been, their effects in removing social injustice have been patchy, to say the least. Often they have given equitable treatment to a few people, while many others remained discriminated against, or became new victims of discrimination. In contrast, anti-bias policies confront racist, sexist, and all other forms of discrimination. For me, there are several reasons why broadly based anti-bias policies are more likely to 'work' than single dimensional policies:

- because anti-bias policies extend to all the different groups of people who meet bias in school systems, many more people can be convinced of their relevance
- children who are targets of bias can more readily see how forms of discrimination operate against other groups, as well as against their own[41]
- more people will appreciate the need to reduce bias of all kinds in society, not just the kinds of bias that affect them
- when one group of people are the victims of several kinds of bias at once, the real injustices for them tend to multiply, yet they are sometimes seen as discriminated against on only one dimension.[42]

These points seem persuasive on their own, but another important point is that anti-bias policies and practices all depend on a single ethical principle that has great generalizability: the 'principle of equal treatment' maintains that we should treat everyone equally unless there are relevant reasons for treating them unequally. If children learned to respect and apply this principle prudently in their lives, then many of the biases that affect the human condition might begin to lose their effect. Here are some practices that teachers working in schools for the urban poor are already adopting.

Cultural bias: valuing home cultures

While many teachers are not members of the dominant culture, few can avoid bringing an ethnocentric perspective to their work because the things that each person values are usually the residue of knowledge, beliefs, and experiences received from a single culture. A few students in inner-city schools have teachers from their own culture and the numbers are growing gradually. But most enter classrooms where their home cultural values contrast markedly with those of their teachers. In addition, sometimes their teachers are unaware that this is the case; they miss the point that in their work giving students knowledge of the academic culture of literacy, they are also giving prestige to aspects of the dominant middle class culture which is similar to school culture in many respects. How to teach the academic culture, without devaluing the children's own cultures, is no simple task.

The best place to start, whatever the age group, is with educational experiences related directly to the children's own cultures: cultures that have their roots locally, or cultures rooted in some other country. In a school organic to its community, these community cultures are at the centre of the school's world, not at its fringes. For example, if students are African Americans who come to the school from a local African American community that identifies strongly with its African heritage, then that heritage is respected and widely recognized in the school's curriculum, pedagogies, and modes of assessment (Boykin 1994). Children are constantly reminded, in the discourses of the school, of that respect and recognition so that they are confident about who they are and what place they have in the world. In these and other respects, today's education is beginning to learn from the tragic episodes of culture-stripping that aboriginal people experienced in almost every setting.[43]

This valuing process asks teachers to open up and explore the discourse around non-dominant definitions and categories. If the students come from distant cultures, it involves looking at non-western definitions and categories. If the students come from neighbourhood working class cultures, it means allowing those cultures and their meaning systems to enter the school in formal and informal ways. In both cases, it means drawing on indigenous or neighbourhood knowledge systems wherever possible.

Nevertheless this is no easy pedagogical formula. There are dangers in the power relationships that cross-cultural teaching of this kind creates. Only teachers in real contexts of their own can detect and minimize these dangers. Not least is the problem of creating a sensitive context where 'voices' can be raised. Painful memories of abuse, racism, or danger can plague the lives of inner-city students and even make them ambivalent about valuing their own cultural background. Fortunately there is now a body of work that points in positive directions.[44]

Valuing children's culture, in engaged ways and in sensitive settings, enhances the educational opportunities of inner-city children. Moreover there is growing evidence for both sides of this 'valuation' equation. Nieto (1995) mentions a study of Cambodian refugee children in the United States whose culture was not valued in the school and whose emotional adjustment worsened the more successful they were at modelling their behaviour on other American children (National Coalition of Advocates for Students 1988). Another study looked at other Indo-Chinese students whose levels of school success matched the extent their culture was valued in the education process (Rumbaut and Ima 1987). Nieto also mentions a programme for Latino youth in a large urban US high school, where the students' cultural values were the basis for everyday classroom interactions. These values linked into the Hispanic concept of *familia*, and students from this school had a very low dropout rate compared with Latinos in other school systems. More than 60 per cent went on to higher education (Abi-Nader 1993).

Cultural bias: building on youth cultures
Inner-city schools often serve communities that have their own distinct youth cultures. These are brought into the school in influential ways. Walker (1988) argues that youth cultures in the secondary school setting provide a basis on which to build aspects of the curriculum. In particular, adolescent problems relating to work and the world of work can be better understood by teachers who are familiar with the various youth cultures in schools. To understand youth cultures, it is important to address both the perceived and the real problems of students by consulting the students themselves.

As examples of youth cultures at the borders between school and work, Walker draws on two ethnographic studies conducted in inner-city Sydney: one looked at boys in a youth culture styled 'the footballers' and the other looked at girls in a youth culture styled 'the troublemakers'. Members of these youth cultures had a wealth of knowledge and experience of real work situations, commonsense knowledge that contrasted markedly with the more obscure knowledge of work found in teacher cultures. To tap into this everyday knowledge in educationally valuable ways, Walker recommends the creation of curriculum 'touchstones' between teachers and pupils, and between pupils and work. These are points where different cultural bodies of knowledge come together; they provide avenues of communication across pupil and teacher cultures based on the sharing of problems, interests, experiences and standards of behaviour.

The central method Walker recommends is negotiation: making deals with students about solving mutual problems and acting upon them. He offers steps towards curriculum development of this kind (Walker 1991) which suggest a process rather like the critical policy making that I introduced in Chapter 2. The views of those with interests at stake, especially the children themselves, need to be consulted and taken into account at every stage. How could these ideas be generalized to urban schooling in other places?

Elsewhere teachers link these ideas with what the teachers know (or can find out) about local gang cultures whose activities often reach into schools.[45] Gangs, and other loosely organized youth groups, are easily identified in most secondary schools. They find their identity in ethnic street gangs in New York, in rival football code supporters in Sydney, in rival football clubs in Britain, or in quite formal organizations of some kind outside the school. Sometimes these in-school groups imitate outside groups. In New Zealand, Polynesian young people in schools often form groups that imitate the behaviour of the highly organized motor cycle gangs that are widely dispersed about the country.

A valuable piece of work for North American schools is Vigil's study (1994) on gangs. He uses long term ethnographic studies of Mexican American, African American, and Vietnamese American gangs to describe the ethnic gangs that operate in many urban communities. For him, solutions to youth problems depend on recognizing that gangs fill real socialization voids for young people. They offer attachments, commitments, involvements, and beliefs to their members that are missing elsewhere in their lives. If schools exclude gang cultures from the culture of the school, then they risk excluding many of the important things that have meaning in the lives of inner-city youth. It follows that integrating academic meaning systems into the lives of many young people means integrating those systems into neighbourhood cultures that can seem very distant from the things that traditional schools value.

One approach in doing this is for staff to redefine the group's attributes, so that what were once seen as undesirable traits are given recognition closer to the status that the group itself places on those traits.[46] A burden that many African American students face in school is the constant devaluation of their cultural styles by teachers who link those styles stereotypically with poor academic performance: 'The student who identifies with "hip-hop" culture may be regarded as dangerous and/or a gang member for whom academic success is not expected' (Ladson-Billings 1995: 485). In fact, this is one of the classic ways that stereotypes do their work. In this case, the stereotypes overlay the perceptions that teachers have of those students and link the students unwillingly with negative meanings that directly shape their identities in the world of the school.

Going beyond just 'rewording' the traits of youth cultures, schools in some places are meeting the challenge of different youth cultures by seeking out rituals and activities performed by the groups that can be given a place in school life. The more secure and positive that members of a group feel about their identity, the more accepting they are likely to be of members of other groups (Gudykunst and Schmidt 1987). Some groups of African American children in New York, of Jamaican children in London, of Chicano children in Los Angeles, of Caribbean children in Toronto, of Aboriginal children in Sydney, and of socially marginalized children everywhere resist the work of schools much less if their youth cultures are more publicly valued in this way. The removal of unwanted controls in other areas of school management is also part of the package.

Studies in Canada and New Zealand (Kehoe and Echols 1984) looked at schools that had the lowest levels of truancy, vandalism, and anti-social behaviour, and which also had the potential for higher levels of achievement. These schools were those with a clearly drawn and widely known philosophy for cultural relations in the school. Teachers in these schools

- modified their textbooks
- changed their teaching styles
- expected good results from their pupils
- avoided giving offence to their students on cultural matters
- changed their programmes in the face of pupil failure
- favoured praise and reward for good behaviour, instead of punishment for bad.

In contrast, schools which practised assimilation of youth cultures had higher levels of truancy, vandalism, and anti-social behaviour. They also had problems from ethnic gangs, from teams selected on the basis of race, and from widespread negative stereotyping.

Other relevant changes in teacher behaviour are mentioned elsewhere in this book.[47] For the school as a whole, the most important change is to make the curriculum more relevant to the future lives of the students, by integrating it into the many things that their students look forward to or worry about. In secondary schools, this means two things above all: linking school more with the world of work; and making students confident that they can succeed in the culture of that world.

Cultural bias: studies in work across the curriculum
The idea of 'studies in work across the curriculum' suits the interests of inner-city secondary school students. They are often anxious about future work opportunities for themselves, and they can be motivated in the school

setting by almost anything related to the world of work. At the same time, in their senior years students need to be confident that their own culture, race, gender, or class background does not disqualify them from successful entry to the world of work. A school policy for 'studies in work across the curriculum' could extend into a number of areas:[48]

- the way that work is practised in the local community and the kinds of work available affects the kind of curriculum strategies that are most suitable
- the kinds of 'youth cultures' found in the school are major considerations for planning
- any resources for vocational guidance and careers counselling need to be integrated into a policy to ensure that the particular needs of individuals are not overlooked[49]
- the nature and scope of transition-to-work programmes operating locally influence school policy decisions and there are often opportunities to relate these more closely to the school's formal programme.

The development of a school policy in this key area depends on a number of factors. All of these are well within the school's control:

- the commitment of the teaching staff to the needs of 'education for work'
- a willingness to undertake some research into 'education for work' possibilities in the local community
- the openness to consult with parents and the wider society in deciding possibilities
- leadership of administrators and the enthusiasm of the whole school community in making the policy work.

Again critical policy making seems to suit this kind of policy development. Indeed the creation of a whole school plan for studies in work across the curriculum could provide on-the-job professional development for the whole staff of a secondary school.

Cultural bias: school size and lack of community
Cultural bias thrives in settings where power is dispersed and fractured. But power is not only negative: it has a positive and a negative moment. By building internal structures more suited to diversity, the power exercised in a school begins to have an emancipatory effect that can even help compensate for oppressive influences outside the school. These new structures become key bearers of the academic culture of a school. Things work even better when a school's values and its structures are already influenced by some sort of positive moral direction external to it. So by putting these internal and external structures together, some 'cultures of schooling' are

much better than others at compensating for oppression outside the school.

Catholic schools in the United States and elsewhere seem very successful in certain areas. They retain students that public schools tend to give up on, and they provide a better education for children from dysfunctional family backgrounds. In fact, the evidence for all this is substantial.[50] That evidence suggests that something important happens in Catholic schools that other schools are not always providing. So why should children from poorer working class and other marginalized backgrounds do so much better in Catholic schools?

Without fine-tuned ethnographic research, it is not easy to identify the precise features of Catholic schools that set them apart from many public schools. Therefore by listing some basic features, I am not suggesting that these are present in all Catholic schools, or missing from non-Catholic schools, or that they are important, in any cause and effect way, for rescuing the children of the poor from educational failure. At the same time, they are suggestive of things that other schools and school systems could probably give more attention to.

- Catholic schools tend to be smaller
- they tend to be less bureaucratic
- principals and staff often have a free hand within the broad constraints of parochial rules
- the schools tend to have formal and regular links with parents and community
- they give deliberate attention to creating an environment of care and responsibility
- they insist that students see themselves as sharing responsibility for that environment
- the staff and students meet for regular school functions in a culturally supportive way
- even non-religious teachers see their work more often as a vocation, rather than just as a job
- teachers tend to pay special attention to the 'at risk' students: they act as 'mentors'
- there is a strong tendency towards value consistency among parents
- this value consistency creates shared parental expectations about educational outcomes.

These features also appear in other alternative forms of schooling.[51] Many were built into the reforms at Richmond Road, and also in other schools that strive to be more organic to their cultural communities. The problem of school size seems very important.

The very size of inner-city schools often stands in the way of constructive policies and practices. One attempt to offset the impersonality and size of large schools is the 'charter' movement that has been developing in Philadelphia (Fine 1994).[52] In this approach, charters are 'schools within a school', not unlike the 'houses' that operate in some New York City high schools, but rather more functional than the 'houses' in British and Australasian schools. In Philadelphia, each charter has between 200 and 400 students, working with 10 to 12 core teachers throughout most of their secondary education. Teachers have a common preparation period daily; they share responsibility for a cohort of students; and they collaborate in planning and teaching towards a common goal. With the students, they make up an autonomous body that includes counsellors and parents drawn from all the communities represented in the larger school.

In this approach to charters, teachers concentrate on discipline based work and on building interdisciplinary links. They are involved with administrators and parents in school based policy making and in continuous seminars of in-service training. The effects have been impressive: these charters 'enhance teachers' professional development, parents' level of involvement, and students' academic and social outcomes' while the 'teachers' sense of themselves as intellectuals, as professionals, and as relational [professionals] has been enhanced' (Fine 1994: 6, 10). Many teachers report being 'reinvigorated' by the challenges of making these work, and the charters themselves struggle to become learning communities that model the following desirable qualities for school reform more generally:

- democratic governance
- school based and ongoing professional development
- student centred teaching
- authentic assessment
- deep parental involvement
- long term relations between teachers and students.

In fact, steady improvements in student achievement confirm the value of these charters. They get better attendance rates, better results in core subjects, and very dramatic increases in attempted entries to higher education. Girls seem to do slightly better than boys, and African American and Latino students do slightly better than majority culture students. However, there are many factors at work here apart from the structural. The stress on giving all students broadly based access to academic meaning systems seems a major factor in their success. Another is the change in teacher behaviour that these smaller organizations promote. The teachers become much more relational and empathetic. Problems of cultural and racial bias fall away, as the educational challenges that confront all students begin to take centre stage, and of course, the neighbourhood cultural discourses of the students integrate more naturally with the academic discourses of the school.

Racial bias

Cultural bias is directed against people displaying the values and the practices of another culture, but racial bias is most often directed against people
who have a different skin colour. Earlier I offered a definition of racism
which also has explanatory power in the school setting (see p. 114–16).
Teachers themselves can begin to deal with racial bias by constantly reflecting on their own teaching practices and changing things that might alienate
students and lower their self-esteem. Above all, anti-racist teachers are critically aware of their own discourse practices, which means more than just the
way that they use natural language itself.

Any of the sign systems that students take meanings from can suggest
racial bias: gestures, looks, silences, bodily movements, and actions of all
kinds. The good model that teachers offer, in their own discursive practices,
is the starting point for helping children handle racial bias and develop their
own 'critical language awareness'. Young perpetrators of racial bias and also
those on the receiving end are highly influenced by the model of a respected
teacher, and this influence can work for good or ill. Racially different
students themselves suggest a range of positive school conditions, based on
their own school experiences.[53] Furthermore the conditions below work
against both racial and cultural bias. I have added some other points to this
list which tries to balance the list of *negative* practices given previously:

School organization and climate
- a climate of belonging, community, mutual respect, and appreciation
- the presence of racial and cultural diversity in the school
- administrators who speak openly about issues of race and discrimination[54]
- forms of organization that involve children in peer support groups[55]
- cultural role models offered by guests who are honoured in the school.

Curriculum
- a curriculum enabling children to affirm their group identification with
  people of similar descent[56]
- a curriculum containing fully integrated minority culture history and
  studies
- a curriculum enabling children to maintain the world-view and values of
  their group heritage[57]
- literature and curriculum aids representative of diverse cultural values and
  interests
- narrative materials and styles like those used in the local community (i.e.
  proverbs, maxims, etc.)
- a sense of achievement (in mastering the formal curriculum) that is communicated to all students

• extracurricular activities celebrating self-worth and group accomplishments.

Teachers

• teachers with high expectations of them as students
• teachers familiar with the neighbourhood community and comfortable in it
• the presence of teachers from students' own racial backgrounds as mentors and role models
• teachers who speak openly about issues of race and discrimination[58]
• culturally similar teachers working in mainstream classrooms who are able to use non-standard language forms in relaxed and non-mocking ways.[59]

Bias against non-standard varieties of language[60]

This is a special form of bias in low income urban areas, and elsewhere too where different varieties of a language are used. I deal with the matter at length here and also say more about it under 'critical language awareness'. Like other discontinuities between communities and schools, this one arises because schools place high status on an academic culture of literacy, *including all its associated signs*. This culture excludes many of the signs used in non-standard varieties. The non-standard issue is an important one, partly because language differences are tied to cultural and identity differences, and partly because human language is the thing that most constrains and emancipates human action.

Many inner-city children who do not use the standard version of the language enter schools where a standard variety is considered 'correct'. Some children start out in schools with more of the standard variety than others, and they are rewarded for its possession. Often standard English is used uncritically as the model of excellence against which other varieties are measured, and non-standard users come to see their own varieties as things of lesser worth. So it is important to value the language variety that children bring from their home community into schools. It is also important to do this in ways that enhance the critical awareness that all children have about the social and historical events that create language varieties. What are schools doing about the difficult issue of valuing non-standard varieties?

Valuing non-standard varieties is not an easy thing for many people to do, especially if they are only vaguely aware that non-standard varieties exist. For experienced teachers, it may be contrary to a professional lifetime of quiet prejudice.[61] However critical language awareness (CLA) asks teachers to go even further than this.[62] CLA asks teachers to value the varieties that children bring to school, but for that 'valuing' of varieties to really count, it needs to be carried out in a genuinely *critical* context. In other words, children need to become aware of the social, political, and historical factors that combine to make one variety of the language seem more 'appropriate' in contexts of power and prestige like the school, while allotting non-standard varieties appropriateness only along the margins of prestigious usage. Clearly there are two issues here.

First, students need to be aware that their use of less prestigious forms and expressions will be judged unfavourably in many social contexts, so that their use can cause them to be disadvantaged as individuals in those contexts. Second, in the interests of their own critical language awareness, children need to know that a non-standard variety used regularly and systematically by people for their own purposes is not incorrect (or necessarily inappropriate). Even adults find it hard to understand this point, because everyone seems biased to a certain extent on this issue by the language varieties that they have acquired. Perhaps students can be helped to grasp this difficult social paradox by giving them some examples of language forms that are widely judged to be 'incorrect', but whose use is more frequent among language users even than the so-called correct versions.

For example, 'I done it' is usually seen as a mistaken form of 'I did it'. This happens in spite of the fact that 'I did it' is normally used by no more than 30 per cent of native speakers of English.[63] The much more common form 'I done it' is seen as mistaken, usually because of the social background of those who tend to use it. Its users are rarely those with wealth, status, power, prestige, and education. In addition, their lowly regarded linguistic capital is stigmatized by those who have the high status capital, which includes the power to say whose language is right (or appropriate), and whose is wrong.[64] Accordingly there is a valuable instructional principle in all this:

> *While discrimination may result in many contexts from a use of forms like 'I done it', which is reason enough to urge students to be aware of the stigma that may attach to them, students also need to be aware that by avoiding their use they are doing so for social reasons, and not for reasons of linguistic correctness.*
>
> (Based on Anderson and Trudgill 1990)[65]

A good place to begin reform is teacher education itself, which means that the circle turns back fully to the selection of those responsible for orienting teachers in their professional practice. For change to occur, it is certain that a more explicit and thorough discussion of questions of power and social justice needs to enter the curriculum of teacher education.[66] Blair (1986) offers some teacher education guidelines for valuing varietal differences. He says teachers need to:

- learn to appreciate non-standard varieties as assets rather than hindrances in the acquisition of the standard [variety]
- extend the range of children's skills by showing them that in certain situations it is appropriate to use certain forms of language, while others suit other contexts
- teach the features of the standard [variety] that do not exist in the children's variety, looking at genuine communication needs rather than teaching isolated features artificially
- pay attention to differences in the rules of interaction between the children's community environment and in the more formal environments where the standard [variety] is used
- learn as much as possible about the children's cultural and linguistic traditions
- avoid testing procedures that favour the standard [variety] since these may not reveal genuine ability, only knowledge of the standard [variety].

There is much to agree with in these suggestions. However, critical language awareness would want to take teachers-in-training even beyond this point. For beginning teachers to become critically aware of non-standard and standard issues, they need to study the critical practices of critical practitioners themselves: they need to work with other teachers who have put themselves inside these issues and changed their practices. It is difficult to see widespread change happening quickly, because most schools see their role as passing on the cultural heritage, including some standard variety of the culture's language. However, inner-city schools that serve poorer working class groups can hardly afford to wait. By postponing change they are gradually but surely alienating people who rightly place value on their own language varieties.

Giving every student critical language awareness (CLA)
This curriculum reform increases students' awareness of the real-world features of language and its place in people's lives, so that this awareness can help them organize and take control of their own lives. Beginning in England, CLA now affects curriculum planning in Britain, the United States, Australia and South Africa.[67] The main ideas that CLA tries to get across to students are as follows:

- people have the power to shape the conventions that underlie discourse, just as much as any other social practices
- although we tend to accept the way language is, and the way discourses operate, they are changing all the time
- forms of discourse receive their value according to the positions of their users in systems of power relations

- struggles over the control of discourse are the main ways in which power is obtained and exercised in modern societies.

To provide some direction for a curriculum, CLA uses three activity themes.[68]

Promoting social awareness of discourse

The aim here is to encourage students to approach meanings more critically, rather than take them for granted. Students examine why access to certain types of discourse is restricted, and how imbalances in access affect individuals and groups. For example, students might examine the routine imbalances in communication that occur between teacher and student, doctor and patient, or judge and witness. If handled skilfully, students can come to see how power that derives from justified authority, from knowledge, or from expertise, often results in an unequal distribution of access to discourse. At the same time, students become more alert to those occasions when an unequal use of discourse in special contexts is used unjustly.

Promoting critical awareness of language variety

Working within this theme, students can examine a number of issues that are very central to the concerns of people living in inner-city settings:

- why some language varieties are different in status from others
- why some language varieties are valued differently in different settings
- what historical events have produced different valuations of language varieties
- what are the effects that devaluing a language variety has upon its users.

There are many possibilities for pursuing this theme, because every community contains examples of language variety. Varieties may be the relatively subtle markers of status that distinguish groups in monolingual societies.[69] Or they may be significant boundaries that make cultural and subcultural groups distinct from one another, even while sharing the same social space.[70]

Promoting practice for change

CLA also encourages students to help improve wider practices and to use their own discourse responsibly. Working within this theme, students can examine a range of complex issues that they can easily relate to their own lives:

- how social struggles and changes in power relations can change language
- what potential for language change exists in contemporary societies

- what constraints on change exist in contemporary societies
- how improvements can be brought about.

The best examples of CLA in use with secondary students are found in South Africa, a country where two dominant colonial languages vie with one another, and in doing so keep other new and ancestral languages in subordinate positions. Two sets of CLA materials have been published in South Africa by international publishing houses.

The series *Level Best: An English Course for Secondary Schools* provides a graded set of texts for English that integrates CLA ideas into an attractive format for adolescents.[71] The first of these texts, for the beginning secondary grade, has units of work on things like 'getting to know each other', 'all our languages', 'winners and losers', 'living in families', 'talking not fighting', and 'bodytalk'. This last unit, for example, asks students to

- think about how they feel about their bodies
- look at images of young people in advertisements
- discuss what affects body images
- learn how to cope with difficult words.

The *Critical Language Awareness Series* has five booklets of classroom materials, entitled Languages in South Africa, Language, Identity and Power, Language and the News, Language, Advertising and Power, and Words and Pictures.[72] In her Foreword, the author describes the series as follows:

> What the series hopes to do is to teach students how to become critical readers. Critical readers resist the power of print and do not believe everything they read. They start from a position of strategic doubt and weigh texts against their own ideas and values as well as those of others.
>
> (Janks 1993: 1)

Changing policies and practices 2: entering academic meaning systems

This second overview of changes offers alternatives to 'compensatory education' as ways of reforming the education of the urban poor. The section concentrates on ways to give students motivated access to the high status academic meaning systems that are so often closed off to inner city students. It begins with 'critical literacy', which seems the key goal of any form of education, especially of education at more senior levels.

Critical literacy

Planned attention to reading and writing may be even more necessary in the secondary curriculum than in the elementary curriculum where a concern for literacy development infuses everything in any case. Very often reading and writing development gets a lower priority with older children. There is usually no single staff member responsible for literacy development in a secondary school, and few of the 'at risk' children get planned attention. They tend to fall through the cracks, especially where policies of streaming or tracking are in place, so I discuss these policies later in this section.

Because of this common management gap that exists across the curriculum of secondary schools, children leaving earlier grades with poorly developed literacy skills will likely continue at functionally inadequate levels of literacy development throughout their secondary education. Some even lose much of their reading and writing proficiency during adolescence.

As young adults, students overlooked in this way make up the majority of candidates for adult literacy education, even in highly affluent countries (Corson 1978). In particular, the effects of poverty and low income background are very important here: literacy itself can seem a vain achievement to those approaching it from certain class or cultural backgrounds. To acquire academic literacy often involves a rejection of their social origins. So this large group of students needs to find something else in their literacy education, if it is to be motivating and relevant to their lives and interests. If literacy's only purpose is to entice students into an academic culture that they do not want, then they may spend their school careers resisting literacy:

> Looking at [literacy] as a means of transmitting our culture to our children, we give it priority in education, but recognizing the threat of its backfiring we make it so tiresome and personally unrewarding that youngsters won't want to do it on their own . . . The net effect of this ambivalence is to give literacy with one hand and take it back with the other, in keeping with our contradictory wish for youngsters to learn to think but only about what we already have in mind for them.
>
> (Moffett 1989: 85)

Instead of this, the literacy that schools offer needs to be 'critical' so that it becomes a tool for young people to use when exploring their own real-world situation and for taking control of their lives. There is much to say on this topic,[73] but let me summarize what this literacy curriculum would look like for me.[74] It would be

- *grounded in the lives of students*: using and creating texts to probe the way their lives connect to the broader society and also are limited by that society
- *critical*: asking who makes decisions? who benefits? who suffers? what alternatives are possible? how can change occur?

- *multicultural, non-racist, non-sexist*: a social justice literacy curriculum addressing the lives and experiences of every social group
- *participatory and experience-based*: focused on creating and using texts that invite questions, collaborative problem solving, challenges, and decision making
- *hopeful, joyful, kind, visionary*: developed within a curriculum that presents learning experiences in ways that make children feel significant and cared about
- *activist*: using texts that reflect the diversity of people who have helped to improve the human condition, from all of the community's cultures and from all its social strata
- *academically rigorous*: inspiring levels of academic performance in students far higher than those motivated or measured by grades or test scores
- *culturally sensitive and inclusive*: using and creating texts that give insights into cultural circumstances beyond the experience of most teachers themselves.

Accelerated schools

Many students in inner-city areas are so far behind their classmates when they arrive in high school that critical literacy is difficult for them to achieve. This happens because their previous education or a history of interrupted schooling has left them with underdeveloped levels of functional literacy and poor academic general knowledge. To counter this, impressive reforms are taking place in elementary or primary education that target students from poverty backgrounds who may not otherwise catch up without some sort of intervention. However, this educational intervention, before high school, is no more than transitional: it is 'designed to close the achievement gap so that students can benefit from regular instruction after some period of intervention' (Levin 1990: 9). In summary, this 'new approach' has these features:

- high expectations of students
- deadlines by which they will be performing at grade level
- stimulating and challenging instruction
- careful planning by teachers
- the use of every resource available, including parents.

This Accelerated Schools programme in California uses transitional schools to bring students up to grade level by the end of their elementary education. Its aim is that graduates from these schools are prepared by the programme to take full advantage of regular secondary schooling. Moreover after closing the achievement gap, it aims to lower the dropout rate at high school level. How is the programme succeeding in doing this?

The whole organization of the accelerated school focuses on this one aim: bringing all children up to the achievement norms for their age group. Because there are no withdrawal or remedial classes, there is none of the stigma that sometimes attaches to those kinds of provision elsewhere. Instead, students are assessed on entry to the school; a personal programme, based on their forecast development, is drawn up for each one. By using periodic evaluations, including standardized tests, carried out on a range of competencies, the school tracks every student's progress through each strand of the curriculum. The programme has these other features:

- a heavily language-based approach across the curriculum, even in subjects like mathematics
- peer tutoring arrangements
- a heavy use of group work and other oral activities
- early introduction of reading and writing with a focus on reading for meaning
- a stress on the usefulness of what is being taught and learned
- a devolved professional model of school governance that is attractive to teachers
- an agreement signed by parents setting out the obligations of parents, staff and students
- training given to parents to help them provide active support for their children
- an extended day programme with extracurricular activities and homework time
- college students and senior citizens working as volunteers alongside individual students.

For Levin 'these broad features of the accelerated school are designed to make it a total institution for the disadvantaged, rather than just grafting on compensatory or remedial classes to elementary schools with a conventional agenda' (1990: 10). Specifically this approach tries to avoid the compensatory model of educational change that has been common for younger children who are at risk of failure, and which has also been the main strategy used in the high schools of English-speaking countries.

Failure of compensatory education at secondary level

Compensatory education locates the causes of failure in underachieving children themselves, rather than in the way traditional schools are arranged. After many years of use in inner-city schools, its results have not been impressive. In fact, instead of lifting the performances of underachieving high school children, it often reinforces their underachievement by using remedial programmes with a curriculum that is reduced in scope, and which is delivered more simply and at a slower pace. Clearly this does little or nothing to help underachievers actually catch up.

Compensatory programmes thrive because they fit into the policies of tracking or streaming that are widely used in the high schools of English-speaking countries, but their effects on low stream or low tracked students have always been severe. These students rarely catch up to other students from affluent backgrounds. Instead they often receive a cheap and watered down curriculum, delivered by unmotivated teachers, and in the eyes of other students they are stigmatized by their participation in low track courses.

The alternative is to give all high school students widespread entry to academic meaning systems without discriminating between students. To me this seems the only fair course for schools to follow, because it is clear that policies of streaming and tracking tend to discriminate between students largely on their social class and cultural backgrounds, rather than on their long term academic potential. I grant that it is true that the introduction of comprehensive schooling, with its patchy history in England and Wales, Canada, Australia, New Zealand, and the United States, went part of the way towards reversing these policies. Yet the problem remains with us, because of the widespread belief that large sections of the children of the poor, and of other marginal groups, will routinely drop out or fail in the literate culture of schools. In fact, this is quietly accepted almost everywhere as an educational given.

Britain, for example, enjoyed egalitarian trends in its postwar education. Mixed ability grouping of children for the early years of secondary education became quite common, and more general forms of comprehensive education became available. But these reforms came to an abrupt end when elitist educational policies were reintroduced in the 1980s and 1990s. These policies returned many schools to their former role. They became centres of sociocultural positioning and stratification that shaped children's access to academic meaning systems to match people's prejudiced expectations about their futures.

Modifying school 'ways of talking' and 'tracking'

As a widespread practice, North American schools track or stream children for most of their secondary education. The students go into basic, or vocational, general, and advanced tracks. This practice herds the children of the poor into the less demanding basic and general tracks in hugely unequal numbers. In effect, it excludes many children from the high status meaning systems, that are the chief output of schooling, at the very time they are almost ready to enter them.

Tracking is a deeply ingrained structure in North American schools that seems almost part of the continent's educational world-view. Many of the 'charters' established in Philadelphia to give greater equality of outcome ended up looking more like tracks than charters: 'Beliefs in tracking, in the need for homogeneity, and in categorical groupings are more deeply embedded in schools than we anticipated' (Fine 1994: 18). Nevertheless evidence is growing that there are ways out of tracking and streaming; one approach in the United States is called 'untracking'.

'Untracking is the process of assisting a small number of students to move from general and vocational tracks to the college preparatory track' (Mehan *et al.* 1994: 2). This reform contrasts with 'detracking' which is a more holistic process of dismantling the tracking system in one go (Oakes *et al.* 1993). So perhaps untracking could be the first step towards a policy of complete detracking. Based on extensive case studies in the San Diego school system, *untracking* can be successful with underachieving students from different linguistic and ethnic groups, and low income students generally. It motivates and prepares them to perform well in secondary education and to seek higher education.[75] How does it work?

Students meet every day in one regular class period over three years and receive a distinctive approach to curriculum and teaching. This focuses on three things:

- In *writing*, students learn a special form of notetaking in which they jot down detailed notes from their academic classes in one column of a notebook. As homework, they develop questions based on these notes in a second column. Students also note their thoughts and reactions to their classes and their studies
- In *inquiry*, tutors, who are students recruited from local higher education institutions, lead study groups in each subject. The group activity is based on the notes and questions that the programme's students keep, although the tutors do not give answers. They lead inquiry, help clarify thinking, and aim to develop independent thinkers
- In *collaboration*, groups or study teams of students work together to achieve curriculum goals under the guidance of their teacher in the programme. They act as sources of information and feedback for each other, interacting in purposeful ways with each other and with the teacher.

The programme includes development activities for the professionals involved. It uses workshops at system-level for principals, counsellors, coordinators, and instructional leaders. Furthermore the programme's results seem to justify the investment of effort. In summary, students who participated in this trial reform are enrolling in higher education in numbers well above American national and local averages. So what factors help promote this result?

Most credit goes to the 'explicit socialization into implicit academic culture' that the programme provides. In other words it provides access to academic cultural capital and the dispositions needed to make use of it.[76]

Certain ways of talking, thinking, and acting are demanded in the conventions of secondary schooling. These are connected to things like the following:

- a fixed body of knowledge that has to be mastered within its own meaning systems
- factually correct information
- styles of question and response based on 'known information'
- talking about text (see pp. 148–52)
- high value placed on activities of labelling and categorizing, away from any real-world context.

Other studies confirm that activities like these are used more in some subjects than in others. Certain 'ways of talking', for example, are seen as unsuitable for 'proper' participation in some subject areas. For instance, in the high school science classroom, students and teachers usually avoid the following discourse forms:[77]

- colloquial language
- figurative language
- emotional, colourful or value-laden words
- hyperboles and exaggerations
- stories
- humour
- references to individual human beings and their actions.

Instead, students and teachers in science and other formal academic subjects aim for a more impersonal and expository style of talk, even though this tends to exclude many students from participation, especially students whose life experiences of talk have been very different.

This discussion suggests that secondary schools could give more attention to introducing students to school 'ways of talking'. Another good approach tries to change some of the talk conventions of the school to suit the students, rather than always expecting the students to change in order to suit the school. Two North American researchers find that by relaxing the demand for formal language use in science classrooms, students can be brought more easily into academic meaning systems.[78] Their studies are based on records of immigrant students doing science activities while working in their own first languages.

In both studies, the students managed to stay 'on task' in their academic topics. However, they did this while talking in the same way as they would at home, or in the playground. This prompted the teacher in one study to allow more of this informal type of talk into his classroom, because it seemed a good way to get the students to participate. The same students usually said very little, but under their teacher's more relaxed classroom approach, their own private discourses began to make contact with the discourses of science. These different ways of talking that represent different values and different approaches to knowledge began to bump up against one another. As a result, the classroom talk became much more authentic for the students, as multiple perspectives from the teacher and the students came into contact, and the academic culture melded with the students' own culture.

As Bakhtin (1981[1975]) says, the process of individuals making a new discourse their own really involves populating it with their own intentions and purposes. Therefore it should not be surprising that many students never get inside the academic discourses of schooling. Indeed this seems a special problem for classrooms in English-speaking countries, where the pressure to use a formal style of language is often more traditional than necessary. It is also interesting that in drawing their conclusions, both North American studies had to look at ESL students who were not using English, but instead were working in their own first languages.[79] Perhaps schools in English-speaking countries do need to compromise much more in their classroom discourse styles and change their practices in this way: they could bring benefits to all students.

The untracking approach does suggest one way out of the tracking or streaming dilemma, at least for those who are able to experience it. In particular, this successful untracking programme seems to be suppressing the widely acknowledged effects of social class on student academic achievement. Its results suggest that schools can make a difference, that students are not necessarily trapped by their social class backgrounds, and that what schools do can be rearranged to give greater educational opportunities to those who underachieve in traditional education. In the rest of this section, I suggest other changes in 'ways of talking' that clearly give students easier entry to academic meaning systems.

Talking about text: extending classroom 'conversations'

Earlier in this chapter, I mentioned Olson's point that oral participation in an English-speaking culture of literacy, and its mediated benefits, probably ranks much more highly than literacy itself as a factor in English vocabulary growth.[80] Certainly the role of print exposure is still very important, because reading experience does a great deal to build knowledge bases within meaning systems.[81] But in the main, children acquire the academic vocabulary range necessary for school success, by taking part orally in the discourses of a literate culture. This gives them regular contact with the rules of use for words and other signs. These rules of use become part of the individual's cultural capital, and the display of this linguistic capital then distinguishes those who have taken wide part in the practices of a literate culture from those who have not. In fact, assessing this very thing is what schools do when they evaluate students' performance.[82]

As their central goal, schools need to provide this participation, especially where the lives of students outside school cut them off from wide participation in the practices of the academic culture of literacy. Once the other matters discussed earlier in this chapter are addressed, then 'talking about text' becomes the secondary school's curriculum foundation, just as it is the foundation of education for younger children.

This idea that student dialogue is at the heart of education is still making its way forward rather slowly in educational practice. But it is not a new idea. In *The Concept of Education* (1967), Peters recommended a wider use of the *ad hominem* method used by Socrates. Peters advised that the classical way of ensuring an integrated outlook is not through explicit learning situations, not through courses, but through conversation. In *The Relevance of Education* (1972), Bruner argued that the crucial way in which a culture aids intellectual growth is by internalizing dialogue in thought; this led him to conclude that the courtesy of conversation may be the major ingredient in the courtesy of teaching.[83]

The use of oral discourse in classrooms is perhaps the most dynamic and thriving area for research and practice in education at present. This seems true for first language education, for ESL programmes, and for other second language contexts.[84] This research points to the danger of excessive teacher control of talk in classrooms. In question-and-answer whole class sessions, speakers' rights are distributed so unequally that students have few opportunities for any sustained interaction that might allow them to put new concepts to use, or even learn their uses.[85] The one-sided claims that teachers make, and which students must accept uncritically when drawn into these interrogation sessions, often mean that the classroom is little more than a site of intellectual indoctrination.[86] Recognizing this, many students are turned off academic work and remain hostile to it for all of their lives. Specifically for secondary school students, several conclusions follow from the research on classroom talk:[87]

- normal high school classroom interactions are removed in style and meaning from interactions in the everyday world
- to master the unusual patterns involved, students need wide opportunities to engage in the kind of talk that uses the patterns
- the formality, strangeness, and abstractness of academic words contribute a great deal to the 'other-worldliness' of classroom language
- over-formal uses of discourse in academic subjects discourages students from bringing their own meanings and theories, expressed in their own informal language, to the curriculum.

What does all this mean for the role of the teacher? Does increased oral language use by students make teachers less necessary? The difference between what students can do on their own in using language, and what they can do with the help of an older or more experienced language user, working closely with them, is still very important. It makes the teacher indispensable in formal education. In fact, the informal 'scaffolding' that the teacher's dialogue provides is the most basic kind of assistance that academic learning can get. Talk and display by a teacher, working with a class or large group, is necessary for giving initial access to academic meanings. But for most students, it gives little more than this.

The later use of dialogue gives the necessary elaboration. This talk can be with classmates, or even with friends or family outside the class. It provides the much more important series of reconceptualizations needed to master rules of use across different contexts, and across the many subtle changes in sense that words and other signs have when they appear in different texts. Therefore group work, or some other dialogue activity, needs to follow the initial conceptualization to add the more important benefits that come when quality language input is followed by quality output. These conclusions are also supported by research on second language learning and use.[88]

Another matter is deciding what 'texts' secondary students need to talk about. Outside the English curriculum itself, every subject's special textual material needs to be talked about in this way, if students are going to master its concepts. Inside the English curriculum, literary texts provide the traditional subject matter for talk, but media texts provide the essential subject matter for operating in the contemporary world. I look at literary texts here, and at media literacy in Chapter 6.

Talking about text: the study of literature

There is little consensus in deciding the place and the type of literary texts that all secondary students need to talk and write about. There are teachers who defend the canon of English literature as the only valid vehicle for civilized education. Similarly most parents want their children exposed to good books, but are unsure what those books should be. Part of the difficulty is captured in Mark Twain's definition of a 'classic': 'It's a book that everyone praises, but which no one has read'.

Professors in universities seem to have the strongest views of all, and some of them have had a powerful impact on secondary school curricula. Hirsch's *Cultural Literacy: What Every American Needs to Know* (1987) seemed to set the scene, in North America at least. He listed 5000 traditional and classical texts that he saw as essential foundations for understanding an American culture that has its roots in European civilization. These have become the basis for secondary curricula, in places like Florida. At the same time, opponents of this cultural literacy approach describe it as 'intellectualizing xenophobia':

In our view, this notion of *cultural literacy* constitutes *cultural illiteracy* in a profound sense. It takes no account of the fact that cross-national and cross-cultural cooperation is crucial for economic, scientific, and environmental progress and for ending ethnically based conflicts around the globe. Cultural literacy in Hirsch's sense is vacuous unless it becomes part of a broader intercultural literacy. This is true as much for white middle-class children as for any other ethnic or racial group.

(Cummins and Sayers 1995: 10)

Most teachers working with secondary school students feel that a small number of university bound students of English and the humanities need a rich immersion in the traditional and classical canon of literature. But the great majority of graduating high school students, including the inner city poor, do not need the canon and probably would no longer tolerate it in any case. Those days seem long gone. As a result, what might a literary curriculum provide?

The trend seems to be away from choosing the literature of high culture and more towards choosing the literature of the popular culture that is closer to the students' lives. Teachers are selecting from a much wider range of materials, better reflecting the cultural diversity of where they live, and more contemporary in style and theme. Here is a possible range of coverage:

- fiction drawn from the English literature of the British Commonwealth and the United States
- quality fiction in translation, representing the cultural diversity of the school's context itself, especially more recently published works
- works written by groups of authors who are underrepresented in the canon
- non-fiction materials, including travel, adventure, historical, and biographical themes
- high journalism, especially lucid interpretations of world events and issues
- contemporary drama and poetry
- a sample of pre-twentieth-century materials, including exposure to Shakespeare.

Whatever texts they choose, teachers are now doing much more with students than asking them to read texts and write essays about them. There has been a dynamic change in literary studies in recent decades. It ties directly into the talking about text theme:

Modern approaches to reading now mean that oral discourse in literary contexts includes not only talk *about* texts but also talk *within* them, whether through imaginative responses to character and conflict or . . . through critical awareness of the intrinsically dialogic nature of literary language.

(McGonigal 1997: 249)

The trend is already seen in the use of a response-oriented curriculum which stresses critical and informed analysis of personal responses and the responses of others. It uses groupwork in the cooperative classroom to clarify the roles of participants and mixes groups according to task, and it follows a more dialogic exploration of literary texts using the views and interests of the real audience at hand.[89] However, problems of student evaluation are important here too.

A major reform of the Scottish high school examination system in the 1980s looked at the assessment of oral approaches to literature. The changes included the following features:[90]

- literary texts as the unifying focus for the secondary English curriculum
- broad grade-related performance criteria which are shared with learners
- assessment of group or individual talk activities centred on texts
- teacher development supported by exemplary videos of methods in action
- attention to accent, dialect, and the standard variety, using Scots literary texts.

In England and Wales, adolescent students in oral English examinations show their proficiency by using collaborative discussion. Attainment targets at various levels use talk activities based on literary texts: it seems that oral language assessment policies have become an essential part of the secondary curriculum throughout Britain.[91] Teachers are using self and peer assessment more with students, which for inner-city schools seems consistent with the aim of producing autonomous citizens, rather than just scholars.

Linking both spoken and written approaches to literary studies, the Teaching and Learning of Argument Project in England and Wales sees the teacher as 'discourse leader' who models different ways for students to present their viewpoints on texts. Here *rhetoric* is revived as a unifying force for literary discourse, so that children learn to speak and write persuasively themselves about the content and style of the text they are reading (Costello and Mitchell 1995). The aim here again is to turn out young graduates who are empowered as citizens by their secondary education. In contrast, earlier approaches to literary writing classes often left students with an acute sense of their own inadequacy.

Conclusion: participation in making it work

In conclusion I discuss the importance of participation by parents and the wider community in putting this chapter's ideas to work, especially again through critical policy making. Communicating with a school's community and promoting a strong sense of local autonomy are central to making a school organic to its community and for getting the community to support the school, and to work in its interests. In fact, the evidence is beginning to mount that 'participation' in policy change that brings only the teachers and administrators into the dialogues of reform tends to reinforce unhelpful discourses and even maintain practices that need urgent changes (Lipman 1997).

We know already, from British research comparing different kinds of schools for students from diverse backgrounds, that the organizational quality of the comprehensive school itself can make a real difference for children from different backgrounds, including those students that schools sometimes abandon as almost hopeless (J. Smith and Tomlinson 1989). Changing arrangements and redesigning structures in schools can help improve the educational prospects of students from every background, not least those who come from marginal backgrounds. To do this, certain additional things need doing.

The ideas presented in this chapter would not be easy to implement in a single school unless they were put to work as part of a negotiated and corporate school plan.[92] A plan of this kind is thoroughly negotiated with stakeholders. Its success depends on finding out about the needs and wishes of the local community, and that community also takes part in its implementation.[93] This planning also pays careful attention to the strengths and weaknesses of teachers. It covers programmes of professional development to address weaknesses and to capitalize on any strengths.[94] It critically weighs the requirements of external agencies that oversee the work of the school. It also gives people in the school special roles and responsibilities to see that it all works.[95] Above all, it allows the school, if necessary, to become really 'different' and organic to its local community.[96]

Modern schools everywhere are trying to reduce the social distance between themselves and the communities from which their students are drawn.[97] They are trying to extend participation in policy making to parents and others. But even affluent people can be reluctant to take much part in school governance, and in advanced industrial societies parents too willingly concede authority to professionals. It also takes persistence on the school's part to overcome this reluctance to participate. Moreover it takes strength of purpose not to cater simply to the needs and interests of the politically active in preference to the apathetic, of the rich in preference to the poor, or of the culturally similar in preference to the culturally different.[98]

Implementing a whole school plan needs careful communication to those critics of a school who demand product rather than process from its curriculum. At the same time, when 'educators define their roles in terms of collaboration with culturally diverse parents and communities, they are challenging the all-too-prevalent coercive discourse that attributes students' academic difficulties to apathetic and uninvolved parents' (Cummins 1996: 152). In fact, culturally different and working class parents, in my experience, are pleased to take part in school affairs, if only schools will give the lead and tell the community about what they do and why they do it.

In every urban school community, there are social groups who bring their own ways of knowing the world to schools. Instead they find that the school demands something different from those ways of knowing, something which they do not have, and which the school does not even identify explicitly. Accordingly school-based studies of local attitudes and knowledge about education can uncover wide variations in children's cultural backgrounds. Often parents hold misinformed views about education, based on their own unhappy experiences of it, and these views can have a harmful impact on their own children.[99] So a key task for inner-city schools is to 'educate parents about education'. Community education, as well as the community-based education described in Chapter 2, is part of urban school reform.

Some neighbourhoods present special problems in involving the community in dynamic educational change. Devolving decision making down to the local school and its community can produce action at a greater pace than many communities can possibly absorb. The sudden devolutionary reforms in New Zealand in 1989 faced this problem in many places.[100] Clearly, careful community education needed to come before these reforms. Local people often need training to manage new responsibilities, and no two communities are the same in their need for expertise and leadership.

New forms of communication are also needed: leaflets, newsletters, and questionnaires written in local minority languages. But even this communication itself can be handled by influential people from the local community, who are esteemed in its cultural circles, and knowledgeable about its practices and customs. Where all this works, the goals and reality of the school are communicated to the community over a long period, as at Richmond Road, as an integral part of the change process. This begins in small ways, but grows until regular two-way communication becomes the natural thing, making the school more and more organic to its cultural community.

By involving its community, the school begins to do more than manage a dominant curriculum using the standard organizational and teaching styles that so easily disadvantage children from backgrounds of diversity. In this process, the real power of outside agencies over the school is also affected. There is always pressure on schools to submit to system wide coordination and uniformity, and often attempts by the wider system to make schools less uniform serve only the system's 'interest group politics, balancing off segments of the community against each other to create a tenuous semblance of harmony' (Lipman 1997: 32). This challenging act of bringing the community into a school as partners means taking a stand on school autonomy, which may decrease the pervasive tension that exists between external agencies and the individual school that many see as 'a critical problem of practice in urban education' (Tallerico 1993: 212). In contrast, a vigorous assertion of local autonomy over all the things that are best decided and managed at school level, gives a school legitimacy in the eyes of its community. The approach used at Richmond Road, for example, is a model of resistance to unwanted external pressures.[101]

Elsewhere other policies are used to lessen this tension between schools and school systems. In the United States teacher contracts have been renegotiated in some places to allow schools greater freedom of movement in staff hirings.[102] In New Zealand, in the Australian States of New South Wales and Victoria, in Chicago, and in the Canadian provinces of New Brunswick and Ontario, specific legislation now gives schools much more autonomy. In these and other places, especially in England and Wales, the 'autonomy' has been more apparent than real, proving that tensions with external agencies are not removed by one legislative or industrial action.[103]

Safeguards to guarantee equity across the whole system are essential in any devolution attempt. Inequities can easily develop in single schools if guidelines on matters like a non-racist or non-sexist curriculum are not handed down from the centre. Clearly deciding what levels of administration should decide these things depends on where those powers are best exercised. Some things do need system wide policies if key rights and interests are to be guaranteed. This includes guarantees about the equity issues that opened this chapter, and about other educational standards. Many other matters, however, are better dealt with in local policies that take local needs and interests into account.

The communities around inner-city schools have neighbourhood cultures of great resilience and sophistication, and these cultures are usually valued by the local people themselves. Although they are much more than 'cultures of poverty', it is common for social planners and others to describe them in that sort of way. But in the people's minds, it takes only a few improvements to the local area to make those cultures much more worth living. It is easy to guess what those improvements would be:

- emancipation from the threat of crime, drugs and violence
- emancipation from hate filled bias and discrimination
- emancipation from poor treatment by service providers
- emancipation from the threat of unemployment or from its reality.

Nevertheless when asked to name it, adult members of inner-city cultures always rate *quality education* very highly, because they see education as a way of winning these other forms of emancipation, not for themselves, but for their children. This is no surprise, because the poor are acutely aware of the value of good education. More than this, many are prepared to help make schools work for their communities, if the schools would only show the leadership necessary. In summary, schools that do manage to involve parents and communities in shared decision making tend to have the following characteristics:[104]

- strong support for shared decision making across the staff
- collaboration among all the leadership team in the school
- a staff that is confident about their own educational effectiveness
- willingness among teachers to go beyond the classroom and address school wide issues
- strong collegial relationships among the school staff
- a shared sense of purpose or vision among the school and its community.

Discussion starters

1 On pp. 115–16 there is a list of racist practices that students say they experience in their schooling. How close is this list to your own experience of schools and classrooms? What other practices could be added to the list? Which of these are deliberately racist practices and which are more systemic?

2 Consider the four descriptive statements about stereotypes on pp. 118. What other things in children's behaviour or appearance create stereotypes that disadvantage them educationally? Which of these apply in inner-city schools in particular? How can teachers guard against these stereotypes in their work?

3 In your own experience, are there other examples of schools placing value on the youth or community cultures of students in ways that improved the students' chances of success? Draw up a list. Can these be used in other school settings as well?

4 Placing value on a youth culture seems educationally valuable, but as a practice it has pros and cons attached to it. What are those pros and cons? How could a school overcome some of the negative effects of this practice?

5 Critical language awareness makes sense to many people. Yet most people continue to accept language as a given: as something that they are born into, and which exists in nearly final form before they exist. What problems does this raise for introducing CLA to the staff of a school, and also to its parents and other community members? How could teachers overcome these problems?

6 D. Levine and Lezotte (1990) review the impact of programmes that try to give children from low income backgrounds more access to higher education. They list the following key elements as necessary for success: early intervention; sustained involvement by a mentor; and financial assistance. How highly do you rate these factors? Why? Are there other factors that you see as important or more important?

7 What are the organizational problems in using oral language more widely in schools? What are the attitudinal problems? How could teachers overcome these problems? Are any of the problems insurmountable?

8 What would a critical literacy curriculum look like in practice?

six

CHANGING THE EDUCATION OF MINORITY LANGUAGE GROUPS

This chapter looks at the education of communities whose first or preferred language is a language other than English. These groups fall into four categories:

- immigrant students receiving bilingual education
- immigrant students learning English as a second language
- linguistic minorities who are not recent immigrants[1]
- signing Deaf students.

Longstanding bilingual programmes exist in the old multilingual democracies in Europe and elsewhere. More recently other educational systems in Britain, North America, and Australasia have begun to look at providing bilingual education for students who might benefit from it. Although in most places English as a second language (ESL) education is still the standard provision for immigrants,[2] major changes are under way, especially for younger children.

The first section below looks at the education of immigrant children up to middle childhood. It concentrates on bilingual education, because most forms of bilingual education are aimed at younger children. The second section concentrates on ESL education, because this is the more common provision for immigrant children at secondary or high school levels, and also looks at some wider areas in the language curriculum, like media education and language awareness that are relevant to all students. The third section looks at the education of linguistic minorities who live permanently inside the borders of several English-speaking countries but have cultures and languages that are different from the majority of the population. It will be clear to readers that these first three sections again stress the point that 'talking about text' is the key practical activity of schooling. The final section looks at the special educational needs of another language minority, Deaf signing students, who talk about text in another way.

Bilingual education of immigrant children up to middle childhood

Curriculum theorists of the mid-1960s put together ideas that still shape the curriculum in every English-speaking country. Moffett's *Teaching the Universe of Discourse* (1968) set the scene with the key idea that our ability to think depends on the many previous dialogues that we have taken part in. Research in a range of disciplines now confirms the accuracy of that key idea. It puts language and discourse at the very heart of education.

The same ideas drew people's attention to the fact that schools make too little use of students' own language, especially their informal and expressive talk and writing, as a learning resource in the classroom. These ideas are just as applicable to the education of second language learners of English as they are to students of English as a first language. Specifically, the following four points have been supported widely in studies of the observed behaviours of students and teachers:[3]

- language develops mainly through its purposeful use
- learning usually involves talking, writing, shaping, and moving
- learning usually occurs through talking, writing, shaping, and moving
- the use of discourse is basic to intellectual development.

Here and throughout this book 'discourse' refers to the full range of meaning filled events and sign systems that we encounter in life: the words of a language are the most common systems of signs that people meet. Although many systems of signs, inside and outside education, have shared meanings, words provide most of the important symbols for forming and refining thought.

Up to middle childhood, English-speaking students are rather similar in the words that they need and which they choose to learn. Later, however, things become different. After 12 years, children begin to acquire the shared meanings of tens of thousands of new words and the other signs that they need to succeed at higher levels of formal education.[4] Many students do not acquire enough of those shared meanings to succeed in senior education. This has little to do with innate ability or the present efforts of schools themselves. It happens because an adequate foundation for that academic learning is not laid in many children's early life experiences.

Language development and early childhood education

It is no surprise, then, that *early* language development is the secret to intellectual growth, including later language development and educational success itself. The most important foundation for any system of education is a strong and universally available system of early childhood education, beginning at around 3 years of age. Yet for all their wealth and educational commitment, many English-speaking constituencies still lack this provision, and their educational outcomes are inevitably lower than they could be.

We know that later attainment leaps when children have pre-school education: the huge benefits for later education of early childhood education are among the most widely attested findings in educational research. In answer to the question 'does early childhood education do any good?' a broad range of longitudinal studies in Europe and the United States followed children's careers throughout their schooling.[5] They found these lasting beneficial effects for school leavers who have had early childhood education at 3 and 4 years:

- improved cognitive performance and achievement throughout education
- greater aspirations for education, motivation, and school commitment
- decreased delinquency, crime, and lower arrest rates
- decreased incidence of teenage pregnancy
- increased high school graduation rates[6]
- higher enrolments in post-secondary education
- lower rates of unemployment.

The main factor is the opportunity that quality early childhood settings offer *for using discourse*. In fact, we can tell what schools need to be doing at every level by looking at what good early childhood education offers: *the widest possible exposure to experience based language use.*[7] Through their interactions with classmates and teachers, young children are introduced to new meanings, and they get constant opportunities to use talk in making those meanings their own. Moreover this is as true for children using a first or a second language. For young immigrant children, it is much better educationally to be engaged in discourse that uses their first language than to be sitting in silence listening to others use a language which is not yet their own.

The first languages of immigrant children

Clearly, discourse plays the central role in learning. No matter what the subject area, students make new concepts their own largely through the use of language; when they listen and talk, read and write about what they are learning, and relate this to what they already know, they are learning. Like early childhood settings, junior and primary schools that provide bilingual education to immigrant students need an environment that encourages students to use language to explore concepts, solve problems, organize information, share discoveries, formulate hypotheses, and explain personal ideas. Students need frequent opportunities to interact in small group discussions that focus on exploring new concepts. They need regular opportunities to work together around shared media, to shape new media creations, and to interpret the creations of others.

All these things happen easily if young children are surrounded by others who speak their own language. But for most of the history of schools in English-speaking countries, immigrant children have not had this valuable start to their education. Almost everywhere in the English-speaking world, the standard practice after enrolling immigrant and refugee students is to ignore their minority languages and give them as much English as a second language as possible. Often teachers and administrators go beyond ignoring the minority language. Sometimes they forbid its use in the school environment, arguing that to allow its use in any way would interfere with the learning of English and prevent students from becoming fully involved in the majority culture.

Recently much more thought has been given to the fairness and the educational effectiveness of this policy. People are more aware of what happens when schools do not build on children's first languages in the early to middle school years. They realize how important the signs and symbols that children experience in learning their first language are for brain development. These signs, especially words and other expressions, shape the early brain development of the young. Although this is not a shaping in any final sense, it is wrong to think that the different encounters with cultural signs that immigrant children have had, are irrelevant to their learning in the new setting. Acting on this false belief is likely to disadvantage children intellectually. It also stops them from making use of the best vehicle available to them for engaging with their new culture: their first language.

There are intellectual and cultural benefits in maintaining young children's first languages.[8] By giving immigrant students carefully designed bilingual education, schools give them benefits that go well beyond those offered by ESL education.

The advantages of being bilingual

A helpful definition of bilingual education contrasts it with second language learning: 'Bilingual education is distinguished from foreign or second language education, including the study of community languages, in that bilingual education is the use of a non-dominant language as the medium of instruction during some part of the school day'.[9]

Until the 1950s, most research on bilingualism saw it as a rather unhelpful human possession, useful mainly for professional interpreters. Bilingualism was seen as a problem for education to remove, mainly through intensive teaching in the majority language and by bringing students quickly into the majority culture.[10] Highly successful programmes in the 1960s, especially those provided for anglophones in French immersion programmes in Montreal, helped to bring about change. New theories developed that took account of sociocultural factors in the development of bilingualism. They also looked at other things like motivation, language mastery, the status of languages, and matters of demography (Hamers and Blanc 1983). This work added weight to the growing body of evidence suggesting that there are real intellectual and sociocultural advantages in having a bilingual education.

The aims of schooling in respect to bilingualism fall into two categories, introduced into the bilingualism debate by Lambert in 1975. The first is 'additive bilingualism', when a second language is acquired with the expectation that the mother tongue will continue to be used widely; the second is 'subtractive bilingualism', when a new language is learned with the expectation that it will replace the mother tongue (the minority language).[11] Additive bilingualism is a 'maintenance' form of bilingual schooling, which sets out to use both languages as media of instruction for a reasonable amount of the children's school career; it aims to preserve and extend proficiency in the minority language. Subtractive bilingualism is a 'transitional' form of bilingual schooling which usually lasts for only part of the early years of schooling, and then the majority tongue takes over as the means of instruction; it gradually replaces the minority language as the children's preferred language.

The bilingual education issue is complicated by sharp differences in the value placed on minority languages in schools in different places. Even the early bilingual research studies, from 1910 to 1960, were affected by bias and distortion. Widespread racism in the early twentieth century helped make minority languages unpopular, and the users of these languages often became ashamed of them. So in some countries, whole generations of people refused to use their minority languages in public. Minority languages were also thought to pose a threat to social cohesion and national solidarity. As a result, in formal education, efforts were made almost everywhere to replace minority languages with the dominant language. To fit these established patterns of preference, policy makers selectively preferred research evidence showing the negative effects of bilingualism, while other positive research was ignored.[12] Although recent research confirms the great benefits of bilingual education, the effects of the earlier distortions continue in some places.

Since Peal and Lambert's study in 1962, evidence has been growing to confirm a point that may seem obvious with the benefit of hindsight: bilingual children have much more exposure to using language, which should translate into improved performances in most of the areas of activity where language and thought converge. Research in the physical sciences has long supported this claim: bilinguals are said to mature earlier than monolinguals, both in the development of cerebral lateralization for language use and in acquiring skills for linguistic abstraction (Albert and Obler 1979). But there are other advantages too. Maintaining the minority language is said by many to develop a desirable form of cultural diversity in societies; it promotes ethnic identity; it leads to social adaptability; it adds to the psychological security of the child; and it develops linguistic awareness (Crystal 1987).

Bilingual research also shows that becoming bilingual has cognitive advantages for the learner. While Baker (1988) warns against overestimating these advantages, especially in relation to everyday mental functioning, there is good evidence for the following:

- bilinguals are superior to monolinguals on divergent thinking tests
- bilinguals have some advantage in their analytical orientation to language
- bilinguals also show some increased social sensitivity in situations requiring verbal communication
- bilinguals have some advantages in thinking clearly and in analytical functioning.

These advantages of bilingualism prompted further questions about the value of offering bilingual education more widely. The main question to address is whether schools for language minorities are better at what they do if they offer bilingual programmes. The evidence suggests that they can be.

The advantages of bilingual education for young immigrant children

Quality bilingual education is a recent development which even now is in its early stages of evolution. But these programmes are developing rapidly in some places to serve very different national needs: as a step in moving towards recognizing a single or several national languages; as a way of making national contact with a world language; as a way of putting to use the multilingual resources that immigrants bring to a country; and as a way of extending language rights and social justice to linguistic minorities. Chapter 2's discussion of Richmond Road shows a school using bilingual education as a way of extending language rights, cultural identity, and social justice to immigrant and indigenous communities. This kind of bilingual education is still not widely available in English-speaking countries for reasons that are partly historical and partly ideological.

Cummins and Swain (1986) provide a guide to the research in bilingual education itself. Their review overturns some earlier views about bilingualism and education:

- they offer strong evidence that quality bilingual programmes have been influential in developing language skills and building academic achievement generally

- they show the common view to be mistaken that immersion programmes are effective only with the very young
- they suggest that in some respects older learners have advantages over younger ones
- they report evidence that lower ability children also benefit from immersion programmes
- they conclude that a quality bilingual programme will support and aid development in the first language.

Cummins' two hypotheses
Two theories developed by Cummins provide a backdrop to recent research. In 1976, he published his 'threshold hypothesis', which has become influential in explaining differences in the achievement of students in second language programmes, and its conclusion is widely supported by research studies in many places, notably in Australia, Italy and India (Cummins 1996). According to this theory, there may be minimum or threshold levels of competence that bilingual children must attain in their first languages to avoid cognitive disadvantages and to allow the potentially beneficial aspects of becoming bilingual to influence cognitive functioning. This hypothesis helps explain many different things about the educational success and failure of minority language groups. As a basis for educational policy, it suggests that minority language maintenance should be available to all minority children until the years of middle childhood, if their academic achievement is not to suffer.

Cummins' 'interdependence hypothesis' is also relevant here; it looks at the relationship between the learner's first and second languages. There are aspects of language proficiency that are common to both first and second languages: aspects that are interdependent. As a result, less instruction in the second language often results in higher second language proficiency scores for students who are young users of a minority language. But more instruction in their second language results in higher second language proficiency scores for majority language students.

Three key points about minority bilingual education follow from these two theories:

- a high level of proficiency in both languages is likely to be an intellectual advantage to children in all subjects, when compared with their monolingual classmates
- in social situations where there is likely to be serious erosion of the first (minority) language, then that language needs maintaining if academic performance is not to suffer
- high level second language proficiency depends on well developed first language proficiency.[13]

Arguing from these three points, Cummins and Swain conclude that young children from immigrant minority groups profit from bilingual programmes if their first language plays the major role, because this lays a language foundation that cannot otherwise be guaranteed. This contrasts with the findings for children from majority language backgrounds, who benefit from bilingual programmes in which the second language is used more frequently; a firm foundation in the majority first language develops quite naturally, because it is the language of wider communication in the society. Similarly, older immigrant students, whose first languages are already well developed, get the most benefits from English-only programmes where their first language is not supported.

Maintenance bilingual programmes at work

Increasingly maintenance bilingual education programmes are living up to the research on bilingualism itself. Bilingual programmes for minority language children are the subject of extensive study and development in many places (Cummins and Corson 1997). In the Netherlands a bilingual maintenance approach to the education of minority children is favoured because it proves as effective in promoting majority language learning as other approaches, and even requires less time to be devoted to the teaching and learning of Dutch (Vallen and Stijnen 1987). Other Dutch programmes for the young children of Turkish and Moroccan immigrant workers suggest that minority language teaching for children from these backgrounds has no negative educational or social effects (Appel 1988). Also in the Netherlands, Verhoeven (1994) finds strong support for Cummins' interdependence hypothesis in two programmes where Turkish background children improved their first and their second language literacy, following a heavy stress on instruction in Turkish.

An overview of developments deals with programmes over twenty years in Mexico, the USA, Sweden, and Canada. In each of these, children began school speaking a minority language and that language was used as the main or only medium of instruction. Later there was a gradual transition to instruction in both the minority and the majority language. Academic progress achieved in each case was much better than in programmes where minority language children were taught entirely in the majority language. Student self-esteem, pride in their cultural background, and group solidarity also increased in each case (Moorfield 1987). In other settings too, where bilingualism and biliteracy are important social advantages, initial and advanced literacy in two languages becomes possible and full bilingualism becomes a natural acquisition for all children (Garcia and Otheguy 1987).

A long term comparison study in the United States examined three approaches to bilingual schooling for Hispanic children (Chamot 1988):

- immersion strategy, in which content subjects are taught through simplified English
- early exit or short term transitional bilingual programmes of two to three years
- late exit or long term transitional bilingual programmes of five to six years.

Researchers report that long term bilingual programmes are most effective in promoting progress in both Spanish and English, and that immersion programmes lead to a greater use of English by students in school itself.[14] Elsewhere in the United States, Spanish dominant children benefit academically and in their English language acquisition when their mother tongue is used as the language of instruction in the early school years.[15] A synthesis of research, covering all of the United States, finds that bilingual education is much more effective than monolingual approaches. It promotes long term academic gains, and it also leads to improvements that grow in consistent ways (Collier 1992).

In Sweden, a policy of 'active bilingualism' has been the goal for immigrant pupils' language learning since 1975, and it has been a legal right since 1977. Every immigrant child, from any minority group large enough, must have the opportunity to attend a mother tongue medium class. Classes for the large Finnish minority in suburban Stockholm are among the longest established. These are segregated into classes using Finnish as the medium of instruction, with Swedish taught as a second language (Hagman and Lahdenperä 1988). After nine years of operation, researchers base their conclusions on comparisons with other Finnish children and with other immigrant groups who have not had this history of instruction in their mother tongues. By the end of compulsory schooling, the segregated Finnish maintenance children still managed to integrate themselves into their Swedish comprehensive school, while building up their academic self-confidence, identity, and their proficiency in Swedish too. The students from the Finnish maintenance classes show much higher figures for entry into further education.

In Britain, the MOTET project in Bradford (Fitzpatrick 1987) reports the effects of bilingual education in a one-year experimental programme with infant children whose home language was Panjabi. The class programme aimed to preserve a 'parity of esteem' between English and Panjabi by giving equal time and space to each language. The study concluded that there were no negative effects from bilingual education. Instead, there were the positive effects of mother tongue maintenance, as well as a level of progress in English equivalent to a matched control group who had not had a bilingual programme.

In anglophone Canada, the more longstanding attention given to the needs of francophone minorities also led to research and changes in policy and practice for immigrant children. Clearly, subtractive bilingual education is unsuitable for francophone Canadians who live in anglophone areas.[16] They certainly need English to live in that environment, but the evidence confirms that strong French-maintenance approaches are the best way to ensure that they get this. Francophone minority children in Ontario schools, who get most of their education in French as the medium of instruction, tend to achieve much better in education and succeed better in the world of work than those submerged in English or in only nominally bilingual schools (Churchill *et al.* 1986). Although this finding is relevant not only to Canadian-born linguistic minority children, but also to immigrant Canadian children, maintenance forms of bilingual education for immigrant Canadians are still rare, as they are too for immigrants in Australia, Britain, New Zealand, South Africa, and the United States.

Providing bilingual education

Where programmes are available, different responses are made to maintaining and developing immigrant children's first languages. In general, they are of two types: first, 'bilingual immersion education' which aims to maintain children's mother tongue and culture as far as possible; and second, add-on 'heritage language programmes', which try to maintain the minority language to some extent, while still allowing quick transition to the dominant language if necessary through ESL classes. In later subsections, I look at each of these approaches.

Bilingual education: supporting first languages in school and classroom

Schools and teachers are addressing many basic questions when they plan bilingual education. The planning involved is complex because it asks teachers to support students' first languages while giving them English at the same time. Here are some of the questions that have to be considered.

What needs to be done to staff the first language maintenance and development programme?

- Staff–pupil ratios to provide teaching in both languages?
- Community involvement to support minority language use in the school?
- Itinerant specialists proficient in both languages?
- For how much time and when will minority languages be used in school and class?
- What materials and resources can be used to present the minority first language?
- Is there technical written material in the minority language?

- Is there an available literature in the minority language?
- Should literacy in the minority language be a priority, or just spoken competence?
- Can a working group prepare written materials for literacy development in the minority language?

What in-service provisions are being made to develop staff proficiency in language maintenance

- for helping transitional students?
- for learning about differences in methods for majority and minority language learning?
- for pupils who are linguistic minorities or dialect speakers in their own homelands?
- How can each minority language be used to build relations between the school and its community?

What procedures can be introduced

- for community consultation?
- for recruiting bilingual teacher appointees?
- for providing aids and resources?
- for attracting adequate funding?
- What can the school do to encourage minority parents to maintain and use their languages?

Sometimes schools are frustrated in their efforts because minority families are reluctant to use their language outside the home. Often this happens because they feel ashamed of their first language, following several generations of minority language intolerance in English-speaking countries. Children can easily lose their motivation when they see that their first language has no place of prestige in the wider community. Clearly the school itself has an important role to play here. Fishman (1980) suggests 'reward systems' to stimulate the use of the minority language. Where bilingualism is supported officially in a country, the school system, government, the law, libraries and other instrumentalities all show by their actions and policies that minority and majority languages have equal status. Inside schools, similar approaches are possible on a smaller scale, even in non-bilingual countries:[17]

- using the language resources of the community in the school's official programme of events
- treating adult speakers of the minority language with respect in the school's curriculum
- deploying signs, written in all the languages of the school
- having older bilingual children work with younger ones in vertically grouped classes

- asking children to compile the emigration patterns of each others' families
- developing narrative stories of family histories.

The help of minority parents themselves is central to all this. Consequently, teachers in bilingual schools are often interested in finding answers to the following questions:

- What sort of role can parents have in the school to supplement what teachers can offer?
- Would parents value an introduction to the bilingual approaches used, or even training themselves?
- How can parents mix regularly with students in lesson time?
- How far can the school extend into the home in language matters?

This last question is more important for some children than it is for others. If the minority language is not maintained outside the school to a high level of fluency, then the school needs to make special arrangements.[18]

The costs of providing bilingual education can also be a concern. In dealing with this, partial immersion programmes, like those used in the prairie provinces of Canada, are less expensive and they seem more effective than heritage language programmes (Gillett 1987). For this reason, Gillett suggests that an expansion of bilingual immersion education should be the next step in the development of immigrant language education in Canada. Similarly the Richmond Road type provisions in New Zealand were not expensive to introduce. Although they were demanding of the time of the professionals involved, those provisions also managed to extend well beyond language and teach about cultural differences as well. A problem apparent in many bilingual education programmes is that the minority languages are treated in isolation from the context and culture of students themselves. This treatment of language in isolation from its context was also a characteristic of the early bilingual research.

Cultural factors

In most of the early studies on bilingualism, cultural factors other than the minority language itself were discounted. Other aspects of cultural capital that minority children bring to school got little attention. Yet these were often the very things that caused the discontinuities and inequalities in school performance that were measured but never explained by researchers. Even in more recent studies of bilingual classrooms in the United States, instruction in the minority language for some of the time is the only accommodation that seems to be made by teachers to the cultural differences of the children (Iglesias 1985). Few of the recommendations, from sociolinguists for example, about matching participation styles with appropriate cultural styles, are actually put into practice.[19]

A key point that comes from research on this matter is that the pedagogical styles and organizational arrangements adopted in schools need to be matched, as closely as possible, with children's home cultural values, especially in classes for the very young. To do this, and so reverse the educational failure rates of some language minorities, could involve major policy changes, similar in kind to reforms in schools serving aboriginal students that were described in Chapter 3. Again the Richmond Road example in Chapter 2 suggests the degree of change that may be needed in pedagogy, in school organization, and in serious professional engagement with minority cultural knowledge.

Assessing bilingual students

These cultural differences become influential when bilingual children are receiving assessments. Often culturally different children come to school knowing very different kinds of things from other children. When they meet the assessment methods that teachers use, they are sometimes asked to display knowledge about 'x,y' when what they really know about is 'y,z'. Often in regular schools, they are never asked to display their knowledge about 'y,z'. Furthermore they are usually asked to display their knowledge in unfamiliar ways. For example, many children from Polynesian cultures seem more 'oral and aural' in their interactions with the world, because these senses are highlighted in their cultural practices. But the formal schooling they usually get is mainly 'visual', with a heavy stress on literacy and few opportunities for group work.

At Richmond Road, this different cultural orientation was taken into account in the school's planning. Dance, drama, groupwork and music were central to the programme, because teachers could see how central they were to the cultures, and to the children's real interests. They also became more central in the school's assessment system and in its professional development programme where teachers themselves began to engage with the children's cultures. All this suggests that being able to see the world from the different culture's point of view is an ability that teachers need to strive for. In other words, as far as possible the culture of the child needs to be in the mind of the teacher.

Cummins' work provides a key reference for the assessment of bilingual children.[20] He draws attention to the overrepresentation of minority language children in classes for the 'learning disabled'. Other North American writers also confirm that this is a serious issue which especially affects African Americans and Latino-Americans (Artiles and Trent 1994).[21] Cummins attributes this overrepresentation to routine mistakes using psychological tests with linguistic minority children.[22] In particular, he warns against tests that measure only things that count as 'intelligent' within the dominant group, while excluding any culturally specific ways that minority children have learned as 'intelligent'.[23] He suggests that intelligence tests tell us little about previous learning, because the previous learning experiences of culturally different children are not fully sampled. At the same time, he warns against testing children in their first language, if it has not been recently used or if it is affected by heavy and recent exposure to the dominant language.

Cummins (1989) also discusses bias-free language testing. For fairer assessment, one of the trained people testing minority children's language should be a fluent user of the children's mother tongue. Assessments made in the second language need to be used with care and never as the sole basis for placing the children in special education classes, even for long term residents of the country. He warns that teachers can be overoptimistic about minority children's language ability. Often the students understand undemanding English in relaxed conversations, but their ability to use English in the classroom might not meet the demands of academic proficiency.

Assessing and teaching exceptional minority language students

For assessing exceptional minority language pupils, Cummins (1984b) offers the following main points:

- For children already diagnosed with language disorders, assessment and instruction should mainly concentrate on helping them to interact either with others or with a written text, rather than on the production of language forms. The task is for teachers to separate the effects of the children's language barrier from the effects of their language disorders, and this can come only from attending to their practical competence in both the first and second languages.
- For children already diagnosed as hearing impaired, descriptive assessment in both languages (including perhaps a sign language) is of more value than assessment that compares them with others or with norms. The focus is on what children can do rather than on what they lack.
- For candidates for gifted and talented programmes, teacher observation is central. One piece of evidence may be the child's rapid progress in learning the majority tongue (assuming that five to seven years is the average time needed to catch up in their language use for academic work). A major motivating factor is curricular and extracurricular activities that encourage that display; gifted and talented children will be no less represented among the language minority children than among the majority.

Students with few literacy skills in their first language also fall under the 'exceptional' category. Similar teaching approaches seem to suit students who arrive in a programme with insufficient literacy in their first language, and also students who have a learning disability of some kind. Hamayan (1997) summarizes some of the better approaches that do not involve watering down the curriculum. These make use of the following strategies:

- meaning-based instruction
- instruction in the student's stronger language (i.e. usually first language maintenance)
- literacy instruction that allows literacy to emerge holistically and developmentally
- a curriculum connected to the students' homes and personal experiences
- lessons structured to focus on tasks
- lessons structured to cluster new concepts together
- lessons structured to allow students to learn collaboratively
- lessons structured to allow students to use technology
- lessons structured to allow students to learn by doing.

Heritage language programmes

Heritage programmes can operate as an appendix to the regular school timetable, or they can be integrated into the school day. Established programmes operate in parts of Australia, Canada, and Britain. They are taught by fluent speakers of the immigrant language who are sometimes trained teachers, but often not. The heritage language programme in Ontario has been a source of controversy since its introduction.[24] The uncertain goals of the programme contributes to the controversy, fed especially by the mistaken view that the programme creates cultural divisiveness. Joshee and Bullard (1992) claim that a large majority of immigrant community members in Ontario support heritage language maintenance through the school, but the majority culture population opposes this.

These programmes can be unsettling for other reasons too. R. Young (1987) observes that heritage language programmes represent significant changes to the structure of schooling. This is because they stress community languages and redefine what counts as legitimate school knowledge and practice. ESL programmes are seen more positively by people, because they link immigrant students into the traditional curriculum. In contrast, heritage programmes value the linguistic capital of minority groups. These programmes also redefine the qualities that teachers need to have (Cummins 1985) which leads to some opposition among regular teachers. Teachers are sometimes frustrated by the complications involved in putting the programmes into the school timetable, but there are wider factors to do with racism and cultural privilege that also affect the success of these programmes.

The power of the dominant cultural group decides the language of school classrooms. It is difficult to break this power (Mallea 1989), especially where economic control is involved, so most heritage language programmes are offered outside normal school time, often at weekends and outside the school itself. But this only increases their distinctness and makes people see them as an educational frill, designed to appease the interests of sectional groups; and the opposition grows if minority language communities themselves are lukewarm about wanting the programmes (J. Edwards 1993). As a result, all these things contribute to the problems that heritage language programmes meet. At the core is the question of making the programmes more meaningful and this already exercises the minds of teachers themselves. Feuerverger (1997) interviewed a wide range of heritage language teachers in Toronto and she highlights the marginal professional existence of these teachers. Based on the views of her respondents, her suggestions underline the urgent need for changes in policy and practice:

• professional development to give teachers a sense of their professional identity and importance
• the forming of partnerships between heritage language teachers and regular teachers
• regular teachers who themselves place value on the heritage languages
• credit status within the school's programme for heritage language courses
• more integration of the programmes into the regular school day
• more attention to the heritage cultures, as well as to the languages
• supportive administrators who express that support to the students and other teachers.

Others who have studied current heritage language programmes are not very enthusiastic about them. Richards (1991) wonders if the programmes actually support a more assimilationist model of education, rather than an integrating one. Cummins and Danesi (1990) cite visiting experts to Canada who warn that heritage language programmes could encourage regular teachers to ignore matters of linguistic and cultural diversity during ordinary class time. The solution to several of these problems is to integrate the programmes into the regular school day and into its timetable. But even where this happens, in one large Toronto Board, the courses are usually aimed only at the languages of established groups, and not at the languages of recent arrivals who may need urgent language maintenance. So while these programmes do serve a purpose, it may not be the purpose that their supporters expect. Also it is far from certain that they are the best way for changing the education of immigrant language minorities.

The ESL education of older immigrant children

By the time children reach middle childhood, their first languages are usually well enough maintained to support the learning of a second language without first language support. As a result, secondary and high schools meet most of the needs of adolescent students by giving them the widest possible academic and informal exposure to English, taught as a second language.

Students needing ESL support range from those with little or no knowledge of English, who have just arrived in the country, to those who are fluent in social communication in English but have difficulty with their academic communication. Students placed between these two points differ in more than just their experience of English.

There is as wide a spread of academic potential among ESL children as among other groups of children. For example, immigrant children with specific learning problems get encouraging results learning English if they are given the same special conditions that they would receive in first language education. These children with exceptional needs learn English as a second language with no hindrance to their first language or to their general development (Bruck 1984). Accordingly there is no need to exempt students with disabilities from second language study, as is often done, for example, in the United States (Hamayan 1997).

There are many other ESL priorities that schools try to balance. The list below is a summary of responses from principals and ESL specialists in Australian schools who were asked to rank the different groups of immigrant students seeking help in English (Commonwealth Schools Commission 1984). The students most in need come first:

- recent arrivals with hardly any English skills
- students unable to participate in mainstream classes, due to lack of English language proficiency
- students whose parents speak no English
- students unable to participate in mainstream classes due to lack of subject content knowledge or skills
- students in transition from junior to secondary school and from lower to upper secondary school
- socially isolated students
- students in the early years of primary and secondary school
- gifted and talented ESL students.

Nevertheless, even getting to the point where this sort of ranking is possible means completing certain tasks of identification, placement, and assessment by dealing with questions like the following:

How are ESL students to be identified?

- Consultation between administrators, ESL teachers, and class teachers?
- Interviews with parents and students?
- Diagnostic tests for determining ESL proficiency?
- Liaison with intensive language centres outside the school?

- Liaison with feeder schools?
- A combination of methods?

How are their needs to be assessed and how will progress be evaluated:[25]

- What ESL learning needs do the children have?
- What functions of language need most attention?
- What language modes are priority areas (speaking, reading, writing, comprehension)?
- Are their numbers sufficient to set up groups at different stages of ESL development?
- What linguistic distance is there between the children's first language and English?
- Are students literate in their first language?
- How much education have they had in their home country?
- Are they speakers of a non-standard variety of their first language?
- Have they studied English as a foreign language?
- How long need a programme continue before proficiency is likely?

After doing these preliminary things, schools begin to plan the teaching approaches they will use. This leads to questions like the following:

- What ESL support outside the classroom will provide adequately for students?
- How can their first languages be used in learning the second?
- What non-threatening environment can be provided for language learning?
- What type of motivation to learn English suits the students?
- What ESL teaching styles suit the students?[26]
- How will ESL learning be linked with the wider reward systems in the school?
- What provisions for using language for listening, speaking, reading and writing would give a balanced approach to learning?
- How many ESL hours per week is a fair allocation of time at the various levels and phases?
- How will students get feedback on their performance in English?

Certain arrangements outside the classroom are also necessary. To support, monitor, and evaluate the ESL programme, school administrators address questions like these:

- How can the school display a positive attitude towards the students' first languages and towards users of that language?[27]
- What additional staffing levels are desirable and possible?
- Is an ESL coordinator needed for the school?
- Should the school have an across the curriculum language support team?

- How will in-service training in ESL be provided for classroom teachers?
- How will in-service training be provided for ESL teachers?
- How will children with specific learning difficulties and other exceptional pupils be integrated into the programme?[28]
- When and how will the ESL programme be evaluated?
- What organizational arrangements best suit the needs of the students and the school?

ESL teachers are not the only ones responsible for the learning of ESL students in a secondary school. In some places the number of ESL teachers is falling as a few more regular teachers are equipped with ESL training as part of their teacher education.[29] Although this change in policy is still in its early days, the responsibility for ESL work is always shared across the curriculum. The work done by specialist ESL teachers is supported and extended by other teachers who come into contact with the students. While ESL teachers are the experts in this area, with special insights into student strengths and weaknesses that can be shared with other staff, the need for cooperative planning is important; and there are many ways to integrate ESL into the school's organizational patterns.

Types of school organization for ESL

Because of the wide range of ESL needs that students have, schools can choose from a broad range of ESL options. In large language minority communities, schools often provide more than one of these options:

- *Reception units*: placed inside or outside the school offer intensive work for the whole school day mainly for newly arrived students. Their aim is to prepare students as quickly as possible for integration into the school's regular programme. They usually use a variety of teaching methods including language experience activities aimed at academic growth and special purpose English study relevant to subject areas.
- *Integrated and cooperative teaching*: provided across the curriculum with the ESL teachers working in one curriculum area at a time or working alongside class teachers but mainly with ESL students. Both ESL and class teachers are concerned with the full development of the children across the curriculum. Shared responsibility of this kind is very rewarding for ESL students, especially if the ESL teacher is seen as a full and equal colleague by the classroom teacher.
- *Paired teaching*: where ESL teachers team with class teachers to plan, implement and evaluate programmes. Both types of teachers have equal status in the arrangement.
- *Parallel teaching and programming*: where the ESL teacher and the class teacher plan together but teach independently. The ESL teacher takes a

class of mainly ESL students and teaches one or more subjects or topics in a block, while other students study the same subjects or topics. This is common in secondary schools, especially in language arts and social science subjects. It uses time well, is easy to manage, and gives the ESL teacher autonomy and status.

- *Withdrawal teaching*: where ESL students work outside normal classes in special small-group units for intensive immersion work or on blocks of specially prepared material based on their regular curriculum. These group children by age or achieved English proficiency. Where withdrawal is partial, care is needed in selecting the subject area for withdrawal because some ESL students can be disadvantaged by leaving the regular class if they lose touch with regular curricular content or miss an opportunity to excel in some area of proficiency. Withdrawal teaching can also reduce the variety of language situations available to ESL learners.

- *ESL extension*: where students do ESL extension work, perhaps for some special purpose or in some more technical curricular area, while other students take other regular optional units. An alternative is to offer ESL extension as an optional subject for credit in place of English as a school subject.

- *Correspondence school enrolment*: where students are proficient in most contexts but need special purpose development which the school is not equipped to provide.

- *Peer support systems*: where the school employs a 'buddy system' that teams the student with an English-competent peer.

- *Enrolment in ESL evening classes*: where mature students, who are proficient English users in most contexts, get special purpose development which the school is not equipped to provide.

- *First language support*: where schools recognize the children's first language as an important learning tool for gaining ESL proficiency and use content materials prepared in the first language by ESL teachers familiar with that language. First language maintenance seems very desirable for children in their early to middle years of schooling.

- *Development of study skills*: more proficient students concentrate on study skills that are useful across the curriculum. Several of the arrangements already mentioned can be linked with this activity.[30]

- *Familiarization programmes*: where the students have induction programmes, conducted in their first language, aimed at giving them basic knowledge about school itself in the new country including any English language school concepts that may be useful to them.

- *Language support across the curriculum*: where students use special support materials to help match their own language proficiency with the intellectual demands of specialist subjects. ESL teachers prepare these materials after observing the students working in the subject area.

- *Incidental teaching*: where older students get occasional personal tuition at their own request from an ESL teacher available for consultancy work in a private room. Usually the ESL teacher is proficient in the subject area of the student's problem.
- *Rotation teaching*: where the ESL and regular teachers share the total pool of students and rotate them so that every teacher at some time in a school week works with every child, making best use of the teaching strengths and interests that each teacher offers.
- *Special purpose teaching*: where ESL teaching is matched to the specific needs of the learners, usually to meet the technical demands of some curriculum area. In 'studies in work across the curriculum',[31] for example, ESL students can engage with aspects of English used in some special work setting.

ESL teaching approaches and provisions for secondary students

Language learning and conceptual understanding develop when students engage in purposeful talk with others. However, even to get to this stage the task that new ESL students meet in secondary schools is rather daunting. Moreover the size of the difficulty they face is affected by life experiences unique to individual children:

- their length of residence in their new country
- their access to prior education in their homeland, if any[32]
- traumatic life experiences that they lived through before arrival
- length and continuity of their ESL education in elementary school
- level of proficiency that they have in their first language
- all of the other social class related factors discussed in earlier chapters.

These factors often place severe limitations on ESL students. Most immigrant ESL students have to catch up academically, learn to use English, and integrate into a wholly new culture and society all at the same time. But because the usual outcome of secondary ESL education is the full integration of students into regular classrooms, students are managing to do all of this, even in the face of the obstacles. How do high schools help in this?

Learning to use the academic language of English
For most ESL students, it can take five to seven years to acquire a second language to a level of proficiency adequate to begin to deal with ordinary secondary classroom activities.[33] Under ideal conditions, students can do less complex things quite quickly in their second language. But almost all ESL students have some difficulties with most of the curriculum offered in high schools. In fact, just to begin using academic language, ESL students

have to acquire certain competencies, and none of these is easy to master in the language of a new culture:

- *linguistic competence*: to use and interpret the structural elements of English
- *sociolinguistic competence*: to use language appropriately for any given situation
- *discourse competence*: to detect coherence of separate utterances in meaningful patterns
- *social competence*: empathy and the ability to handle social situations using language
- *sociocultural competence*: familiarity with the real-world context where English is used
- *strategic competence*: to use verbal and non-verbal strategies to make up for any gaps in English knowledge.

Even while mastering these difficult competencies to a reasonable level of proficiency, ESL students still have to 'get inside' the academic concepts that are the very stuff of the secondary curriculum. These academic concepts are the meanings of specialist words, expressions, and other abstract signs, whose use allows communication in complex areas.

Learning academic concepts in English as a second language
Interest in the role of words in learning English as a second language is now at the heart of ESL practice. But with only an occasional exception, the early work in linguistic studies gave scant attention to vocabulary, or neglected it entirely (Meara 1982). So the upsurge of interest in vocabulary in the 1980s and 1990s, among ESL and other second language researchers, is a notable shift.[34]

Many immigrant ESL students have special difficulties using English for academic purposes. Chapter 5 discusses the difficulties that the Graeco-Latin vocabulary of English creates for children from some social class backgrounds. This academic vocabulary is different in important ways from the basic vocabulary of English. Apart from conceptual difficulty, academic words tend to be much longer; they tend to be different in shape; they are drawn almost entirely from Latin and Greek, rather than from Anglo-Saxon sources; and they appear rarely or not at all in everyday language use.[35] Students coming from some backgrounds, especially from non-European backgrounds, can have serious problems with this kind of academic vocabulary and related academic concepts.

Academic words appear in certain precise and limited areas of discourse. Their learnability really depends on ESL learners having rich contacts with the specialist areas in which they appear, as well as frequent contacts with the words themselves. Their meanings become clearer by trying them out in talk, by linking them to the students' own intentions and purposes, and by hearing them used in reply. In this way, the conceptual difficulty gradually falls away. This happens more easily when learners can negotiate their own meanings with more experienced users. Indeed, echoing discussion in Chapter 5, it suggests a clear conclusion for any form of education: we improve our grasp of academic concepts through conversations about the subject matter that uses the signs that give a name to those concepts.

Talking about text

Research does suggest an important role for reading experience in promoting vocabulary development, especially for younger children and young adults. But adolescents close to the end of their compulsory schooling have real problems learning and using academic concepts if they meet them only in their reading, because secondary school students meet academic demands that are unlike the more moderate demands placed on younger children. They are also unlike the demands placed on young adult university students, who are well inside specialist meaning systems to a much greater extent. While mastering the background knowledge of a number of complex fields, adolescents are asked to master the rules of use for huge numbers of new words, and these meanings are novel, unusual, and often change in different contexts and across meaning systems. To do this, students need far more than to come across words in print: they need wide opportunities to engage in motivated talk about the texts that they read, or view, or hear read to them.

The increased integration of school-age ESL students into regular classrooms in many places is beginning to give them these wider opportunities to interact in natural language settings with native speakers. In mainstream classes, the motivation to use language with proficient classmates is higher, and wider social contacts and models of proficient usage are more numerous. These natural language conversations with native English speakers, linked to instructional exchanges, seem the best way to stimulate the learning and use of the kind of English needed to succeed in secondary education.[36]

It is clear that second language learners have many more opportunities to use the target language in groupwork than in teacher led activities (Kowal and Swain 1994). But it is also clear that the changes that occur in student–student interactions give more meaning to the input received from the teacher, and the student talk itself is changed by conversational features like requests from others in the group for clarification. It seems that a good way to provide this learning environment is in regular classrooms supported by regular teachers who are ESL specialists themselves. In this setting, students interact with their English-speaking classmates and with a subject teacher skilled in working with ESL students.[37]

Few of the world's regular secondary school teachers are trained in ESL teaching, and many secondary teachers are uncertain about integrating ESL students into their classes. V. Edwards and Redfern (1992) have researched this issue and advocate much more integration of students into regular class-rooms. However, they cannot see it working with the secondary teachers who presently staff most schools. Even ESL teachers, convinced of the benefits of a move to the mainstream, tend to resist full integration. Nor is there much professional development of practising teachers in this area, while in English-speaking countries there is little or no provision in present teacher education courses to give newly graduated teachers this proficiency.

> So with minimal training being provided at preservice level, minimal professional development funds at school level, the reality is that the vast majority of regular teachers are quite unprepared to teach ESL students. Unprepared often in both senses of the term.
>
> (Cummins, personal communication)

Consequently for the foreseeable future at least, the bulk of ESL work will continue to fall on ESL specialists. Fortunately there is already a lot of 'talking about text' in good ESL programmes, but students begin to miss out on this kind of academic talk when they enter regular classes, where subject specialists make less use of interactive teaching approaches. So perhaps ESL teachers have a special modelling role here, as I suggest in a later section.

Studying Romance languages

Another learning experience helpful for academic vocabulary development is studying second languages other than English. There were once pronounced English vocabulary advantages in studying Latin and Ancient Greek, and these are still relevant to learning and using academic words. These advantages are now more widely available elsewhere, however, through the study of Romance languages, and are not just for ESL students.

Students used to receive wide exposure to the history of English words when translating into and out of Latin and Greek, an interesting if minor bonus that went with the teaching of these subjects. This process of looking at the roots, affixes, and other parts of words seems very important: it helps to give students information that is useful for word learning and use. The words and their meanings become more transparent for a language user if their concrete roots in another language are known. Without this, English academic words often remain 'hard' words whose form and meaning seem strange to those coming to them for the first time.

Because this kind of learning is quite rare in natural language settings, courses of second or third language study can give rich benefits for ESL development. As Latin and Greek are less taught, the Romance languages (French, Italian, Spanish, Portuguese, Romanian, etc.) seem more useful. Romance language students seem well placed in learning academic English because of the similarity that many English academic words already have for them. The evidence that students transfer knowledge from one language to another is now strong,[38] especially where the two languages are similar.[39]

ESL adolescents, who are studying one of the major Romance languages as a third language, are often successful students already, probably without having any Romance language study. In addition, Romance language students are only a small minority of students in school systems in English-speaking countries. Therefore if all ESL students are going to have the advantages that come from studying Romance languages, other approaches are needed.

ESL language awareness and critical language awareness

Studies in language awareness are very helpful, not only for learning about academic words and not only for ESL students. There are many other things that language learners need to know about language, so many in fact that they cannot be listed here in detail.[40] But if all the many kinds of language awareness could always be found in the natural language experiences of people, then courses of language awareness would not be needed in formal education. Unfortunately ESL learners rarely get these experiences in natural language settings, so schools need to provide them.

A good language learning environment in schools also develops ESL students' *critical* language awareness.[41] They can learn about things like 'labelling', 'sexist language', 'discursive bias', 'prejudice in language', 'rhetorical language', and 'discourse and discrimination'. ESL students need to know about the use and functions of academic words, because this sort of information is not usually passed on in regular ESL classes.

It is important for second language learners to know that sometimes these English words, borrowed from Latin and Greek, are used in rather negative ways, to show unnecessary formality, or to exercise power. Giving students this critical kind of language awareness helps take some of the unwanted rules of use away from these words: rules of use that exclude some people from interaction, rather than others; rules of use that give the word user a higher status than the one that is needed in the context; and rules of use that suggest a level of language evaluation that is not needed by the subject matter.[42]

All these negative attributes of academic words are concepts that teachers of English and other high school subjects are beginning to give more thought to. In formal teaching situations, it is easy to insist on the use of these academic words, even when they are not really needed in the context: it is easy to place too much value on the academic vocabularies of the school and in so doing devalue the vocabularies of students.[43] However, everyone needs to know that when an academic word suits the meaning of the moment, then its use really does help communicate meaning within one of the academic meaning systems of English.

School policies for collaboration and support from ESL specialists

Because they are skilled in using interactive teaching methods, ESL specialists are a resource in a school that other teachers often draw on, although teachers of students from backgrounds of diversity frequently fill marginal roles in the staff of schools, and their work is not always given the same respect as teachers of mainstream students. Bascia (1996) sees critical connections between how minority teachers interact with and advocate for minority students, and how the same teachers are treated by colleagues and school administrators. Often the advocacy work that these teachers do, helping culturally or linguistically different students to get respect in schools, is not formally recognized in any way. Instead the teachers' role is only to solve other teachers' 'problems'; as a result, the problems cease to be the problems of those other teachers. They get hidden away in the school's structures and have to be solved over and over again.

Teachers of students from backgrounds of diversity often have little influence over their colleagues in practical and normative ways. Because of their lack of influence in changing formal school practices, their schools often go on to re-create the same problems with every new generation of students. Bascia (1996) sees a need for changes in administrative conditions to give more weight to the expertise and insights of these teachers who are presently on the fringes of schools. A school language plan can help build effective collaboration between regular subject teachers and ESL teachers. Various ways of organizing this collaboration are tried with success in many places.[44] Perhaps as a very long term goal, all regular classroom teachers will gradually learn to be ESL teachers themselves, so that a school's teaching body becomes a highly proficient ESL teaching force.

Yet even under these conditions, ESL specialists would still be needed. Certain ESL students always need a programme that gives intensive and partial support outside regular classrooms, because some ESL students are highly traumatized when they arrive in a new country, and they need the close contact they can establish with ESL teachers who are sympathetic to their needs and really know what they are doing. At higher grade levels, the language demands placed on newly arrived students are so great that an ESL support programme of some kind is often necessary. Furthermore specialist provisions for gifted and other exceptional ESL students are essential, because there are just as many exceptional ESL students as there are exceptional mainstream students.

To deal with these complex matters of curriculum, learning, and teaching, schools in many places find it useful to draw up a 'school ESL language policy'. This kind of action plan ensures that all teachers know their role in the ESL students' education; that they are willing to work within that role; or that they can get the support or training they need if they currently lack the expertise. These policies also cover ESL assessment.

ESL assessment, evaluation and guidance

Usually a staff member in each school is responsible for tracking each student's ESL development, and even for passing information about individual proficiency levels to a system record that can be referred to by any school that a student attends within the system. Under these arrangements, assessment and evaluation of ESL language proficiency get rigorous monitoring. Appropriate guidance and counselling is normally available in the students' first languages, especially where their learning is affected by some disability or by some emotional problem that has its roots in traumatic experiences elsewhere.

One area that schools are giving more attention to is communicating directly and regularly with parents in their own first languages. There is much that parents can do to support ESL students in their learning. There is also a lot of information about ESL outcomes, stages of acquisition, and the format of report cards to give to parents. So appropriate translation and interpreting services are an integral part of the regular provisions for ESL.

ESL students still have to cope with the regular English curriculum as they get more proficiency. Sometimes there are special ESL English courses for academic credit that parallel regular English courses, but ESL students will usually spend most of their time in English working alongside regular students. Chapter 5 introduced two core areas of the language programme for a secondary curriculum: critical literacy, and the study of a wide range of literature in English. In this chapter, I add another area: a core course of study introducing secondary students to the media in their country, including ways of using it critically and coping with its seductive and varied messages. This sort of course seems very relevant to the needs of ESL students as well.

Media studies and media literacy

This section addresses activities in language that go beyond the usual four activities:

- *listening*: attending to the oral language of others and giving meaning to it
- *speaking*: expressing meaning to others in oral language
- *reading*: attending to the written language of others and giving meaning to it
- *writing*: expressing meaning to others in written language
- *moving*: using facial expression, gesturing and movement to express meaning
- *watching*: attending and giving meaning to the movements of others
- *representing*: using visual effects to express meaning to others
- *viewing*: attending and giving meaning to visual effects created by others.

This list includes the four activities that everyone sees as part of the core curriculum in English language instruction. However, the last four have really come into their own only in recent decades. For many young people, and in most present-day jobs, these last four now assume an importance that gives them a core place in curriculum planning. These are the basic competencies of media literacy.

Media education is education about technology, but it does not stop at the 'how it works' and 'how to operate it' stage. It asks students to think critically about technology, about its cultural and sociological significance, as well as its place in business and science. Media education asks students to look critically at information, regardless of its source or medium. It asks them to see the media as industries whose owners have agendas of their own. It helps students to distinguish between commercial messages, casual communication, and the messages of propagandists. Above all it suggests students recognize that our commonsense judgements are usually filled with prejudice and error, which colours everything that we come into contact with. Clearly media education has close links with critical language awareness.[45]

To meet its aims, media education looks at all the language activities, especially 'watching', 'viewing', 'representing', 'writing', and 'moving'. But there is an even more pressing need in using computer technology that is almost upon us. This is fully consistent with the idea that 'talking about text' is the practical curriculum foundation of secondary education:

> Talking and listening must form a major focus of interest for the future. It is unlikely that the use of computers in the classroom will ever be the same again once teachers and students start to control a computer with speech, see their words appear on the screen as they dictate or ask the computer to say their words.
>
> (Abbott 1997: 186)

This innovation will produce different kinds of speech control, that will impact on traditional spelling and punctuation. Already we see the 'cyberspeak' of the Internet developing its own ways of mimicking stress or intonation. The nature of the collaborative writing process will change when instant transcriptions of discussion become an everyday matter. Teachers of English and ESL teachers will have a more challenging role as these developments spread, and as students take more advantage of the success of the Internet as a site for publishing:

> Already, it is being used by senior pupils in isolated schools in rural Scotland to 'discuss' their literature projects with distant peers, to exchange notes and ideas on texts in supportive networks.
>
> (McGonigal 1997: 255)

The value of the Internet for getting ESL students to work with one another across cultural and linguistic boundaries, to pursue joint projects, and to resolve common problems, is already well understood by some. Cummins and Sayers (1995) give wonderful portraits of culturally diverse students using the Internet in this way:

- between a refugee camp in Croatia, New York and Catalan schools in Spain
- a partnership between classes in Maine and in Québec City
- students dealing with ethnic prejudice in New York and San Francisco schools
- parent–school collaborative desktop publishing in San Diego
- folklore investigations in California and Connecticut
- community action between students in the United States and Nicaragua
- computer networking between Palestinian and Israeli teachers and students
- a holocaust project linking Israel, Argentina, Australia, Russia and Poland.

Activities like these promote higher order thinking and literacy skills, perhaps to a greater extent than many of the traditional activities that secondary schools give curriculum space to.

> The information superhighway offers unprecedented opportunities for educators to create collaborative learning environments that will stimulate critical thinking skills and academic excellence among *all* students . . .
>
> In short, computer-mediated learning networks can act as a catalyst for collaborative critical inquiry that is fundamental in preparing students to participate actively in a democratic society.
>
> (Cummins and Sayers 1995: 15 and 172)[46]

At the same time, there are problems in all this that need the checks and balances of formal guidelines, set out in a school language plan:[47]

Desktop publishing makes it more possible than ever before to see children becoming authors of their own literature, but computer spelling and grammar checkers seem to undermine traditional aspects of authority and craft.

(McGonigal 1997: 255)

Teachers meet a real dilemma on this point. Can we justify the time and space needed in school for spelling, punctuation, and grammar when the new technology itself teaches many students that complete mastery of those skills is becoming redundant for much of the time? At the same time, most teachers have few doubts about the importance of these basic things.

Making ESL education work at high school level: a case study

One model for the secondary education of language minority students is the International High School at La Guardia Community College in New York (DeFazio 1997). This school offers new learners of English a four year comprehensive programme that allows them to satisfy regular school standards while also learning English. Like effective minority language programmes elsewhere, the school sees the student's first language as a resource to be used in education, not a liability. So the school places high value on the 50 or more languages that are brought into it by students. It tries to use those languages as a central part of its approaches to pedagogy and assessment, and, through its programmes, the school also recognizes that ESL students need to understand English in all its modes, to realize their potential in an English-speaking society. How does it manage to do all this?

The school shares a number of features with other schools (described in earlier chapters) but it is unique in the way that it combines the following features to create a strong language-learning environment.

- The school controls and develops its own staffing procedures, choosing staff according to needs.[48]
- Career education is built into the curriculum, at every point, to motivate student language learning.[49]
- The curriculum is organized into six interdisciplinary teams, each with at least two programmes.
- Each linked programme runs for 13 weeks and caters for about 75 students.
- These make use of language development projects in the students' first languages, for example:
  - a biography project where students write about the life of another student
  - a project interviewing the community itself about language issues and analysing the results

- a linguistics project comparing student languages with English, asking, for example:
  - what do all languages share?
  - how do sounds compare across languages?
  - how does syntax compare across languages?
  - how are questions formed?

Two of these linked interdisciplinary programmes are called Motion and Visibility, which combine physics, mathematics, literature, and physical education. As part of their work, students complete two extensive portfolios in which they comment on their own development and their growing knowledge in areas related to the subjects that they are studying. They write self-evaluations and they evaluate the work of other students using again a mixture of first and second languages. They make the choice of language themselves according to the context and pressures that they are working under. But English remains the class language, because it is the only language many of them have in common and it is the language they all have to master.

The assessment methods used across the different programmes also involve parents and guardians writing in different languages. The students write letters home in their first language about their schoolwork, and the parents respond. Where the letters from parents are not in English, the students write English translations for their teachers' use. In this and other ways, the students are continually using both English and their first language for all phases of learning and assessment:

> Reorganizing the curriculum has necessitated rethinking assessment of students. Students at the International High School undergo portfolio assessment where they demonstrate their academic, linguistic and social proficiencies. Traditional testing is eschewed because it is often unfair and counterproductive to linguistically diverse populations who often know much more than they may be able to articulate in English. Portfolio assessment encourages retention, higher-level cognitive skills, development of internal standards, creativity and variety in solving problems.
>
> (DeFazio 1997: 102)

Changing the education of linguistic minority communities

Chapter 3 discussed the many involuntary aboriginal minorities who live in English-speaking countries. There are other involuntary linguistic minorities who have rather different educational needs from those of the world's aboriginal peoples. The speakers of Gaelic languages in Wales, Ireland, and Scotland, or the francophone minorities in anglophone parts of Canada, or the large Hispanic populations in the south-west of the United States are different from aboriginal people in their needs and interests, because all these minorities are European in their cultural history. Consequently, they seem to share most aspects of the dominant culture with their first language English-speaking neighbours, but this can be very misleading for educators. In fact, the cultures of linguistic minority communities are often very different from the majority culture in ways that are still not carefully studied.

Outsiders often miss the extent of these cultural differences. They wrongly conclude that the different educational needs of these minorities can be met by just giving them first language support, in a school setting that remains part of the dominant culture in all other respects. But often the educational needs of minority language communities extend well beyond simple language issues.

In Britain, the three Gaelic languages are at different stages of revival through education (Baker 1997). The Welsh language is a success story that offers a model for other small European languages to follow. Scots Gaelic is also reviving, although a little less spectacularly than Welsh. The Irish language is in a less happy situation, but like the others it should do better under a united Europe that gives greater recognition to the continent's smaller languages. In all three cases, the cultural differences between Gaelic first language speakers and their neighbours, who speak English as their first language, are not great enough to warrant extensive cultural support in fully separate schools.

Despite the fact that the cultural differences are relatively slight, the need for cultural reproduction is certainly driving the revival of all three Gaelic languages, as Baker confirms. Many of the Gaelic speakers are affected more by factors of social class or region of living than by differences in ethnic identity and cultural allegiance. The Welsh tend to be Welsh, the Scots tend to be Scots, and the Irish tend to be Irish, whichever language they speak. This is not the case so much in North America, where linguistic minorities are less ready to believe that they have 'countries' of their own and have cultural allegiances that are rather different from their English-speaking neighbours. Moreover in North America those neighbours are less proud and sometimes intolerant of the differences.

In the United States, there has been a long history of bilingual education for Spanish-speaking residents. This began in the Cuban immigrant communities in southern Florida and spread to the south-west states that border on Mexico (Faltis 1997). Developments across the country have been frequent, but they have also been intermittent because of strong political opposition to the idea of a bilingual and multicultural United States. New developments are now likely, following a shift in the federal guidelines for bilingual funding in the 1990s. Funding is 'contingent upon a school's ability to demonstrate that it has a plan for making bilingual education a part of a whole school effort to address the needs of non-English proficient children and adolescents'. This means that 'teachers, administrators, and curriculum specialists in schools that serve large numbers of language-minority students have to retool themselves to meet this challenge' (Faltis 1997).

Two-way bilingual education has generated considerable interest in the United States (Lindholm 1997). This approach promotes language development for both linguistic minority and language majority students who work alongside one another in the same classroom.[50] As Lindholm points out, however, the knowledge base in the United States for two-way bilingual programmes does not begin to compare in scope with the research conducted in Canada. So a brief outline of the educational situation for francophone minorities in Canada, especially in Ontario, suggests some of the ways that schools in many places are already meeting the different needs of different linguistic minorities.

Large francophone communities live outside Québec in anglophone parts of Canada. Ontario has about half a million people who use the French language for significant activities in their lives and who describe themselves as franco-ontarian; indeed they see themselves as culturally different from the largest French population in Canada, who live in Québec. But those differences do not impinge on their lives as strongly as the other pressures to conform, in both culture and language, that come from English-speaking Ontario. These pressures are similar to those felt by Hispanics in California and New Mexico, and the communities themselves have to work hard to· create educational systems that will allow them to maintain their cultures and their languages.

According to legislation in Canada, all official language minority education is maintenance bilingual education, and French and English are both 'official languages'. But often, because the population is highly dispersed and because most speech outside of school and beyond the family is in English, there is still a high degree of assimilation towards English and towards 'English' culture. Several factors promote this assimilation:[51]

- inactivity by provincial governments in supporting the minority language
- tendency of immersion programmes to anglicize francophone children
- lack of minority control over education
- francophone parents who are indifferent about supporting their language
- lack of social opportunities to function in French outside schools.

All of these factors can keep students away from native speaker proficiency and studies confirm that minority language schooling without home language maintenance does not provide native speaker proficiency. Linking all this with Cummins' two hypotheses, it is clear why franco-ontarian students are often held back in their education and why they are at a particular disadvantage in developing the academic literacy needed for achieving educational success.

Based on the average educational levels achieved, illiteracy levels among franco-ontarians may be around twice those of the anglophone population of the province.[52] One out of every three students is at risk of becoming illiterate in French. In an effort to explain this, Wagner (1991) sees an 'illiteracy of oppression' and an 'illiteracy of resistance' at work here. The illiteracy of oppression results from the pressures to conform to the majority culture that come from its schooling, which quietly destroys identity and the very means that the minority group has to resist assimilation. The illiteracy of resistance is a kind of minority revolt against the tyranny of majority culture schooling and its threat to French. This revolt leads young people to prefer using the spoken rather than the written word, so skills in the written word decline. These two illiteracies lead to three types of illiteracy among franco-ontarians: some become illiterate in both French and English; some become semi-literate in both; and some become illiterate in French but literate in English.

Another important factor at work here is the non-standard nature of franco-ontarian varieties of French. Instead of studying these local varieties, old and new learners of French in Ontario's schools sometimes encounter a French variety from Québec, and sometimes the more dominant variety from metropolitan France. Rarely if ever does the local variety get preferred treatment. Based on her studies in Ontario, Heller (1995) argues that French-language minority education is justified in the public mind by pointing to Canadian French. But this is really a set of non-standard varieties, and these varieties are not used in schools, so social mobility after school in the wider community almost depends on mastery of a standard variety that many franco-ontarian graduates do not acquire.[53]

Changing practices

The minority language as vehicle of instruction

Children from minority groups generally profit from bilingual programmes in which their first language plays the major role, because this lays a language foundation that cannot otherwise be guaranteed. The research evidence for Canadian linguistic minority students supports these conclusions. In programmes of different kinds, it is clear that a culturally appropriate course of study that teaches all subjects in the minority language gives better results, and it does so without compromising attainments in the majority language.[54] Again it seems important that this kind of programme also values the non-standard variety that franco-ontarian children bring with them to school,[55] and provides its instruction in a context that is thoroughly congruent with the minority culture.

Reducing assimilationary pressures

Rampant assimilation is a problem in many places and lack of home support is often a factor that promotes this assimilation, because schools can only do so much and cannot replace the family and community in promoting language vitality (Churchill *et al.* 1986). Without a dynamic curriculum that promotes belief in the language's value and increases competence and use of the mother tongue in the home, there is no way to stop this kind of assimilation. Building on the additive/subtractive model of bilingual education, Landry and Allard (1987) urge minority families and minority schools to act in concert to offset contact with the majority culture and language.

Where linguistic minorities are not in control of the schooling process, this counterbalance is likely to be missing. So Landry and Allard also argue that complete control of institutions is needed to ensure that a maximum number of contexts is available where mother tongue usage is encouraged. They say that deliberate steps need to be taken to place high value on the minority language, because lack of prestige for a language often leads to assimilation of its speakers to the dominant language. In most Canadian provinces now, francophone minority communities control their own boards of education and direct the operation of their own schools (Corson and Lemay 1996).

Linguistic minority literacy and teaching methods

Students need much more than a grounding in the technical skills of reading and writing. Minority students are unlikely to succeed in the academic culture of literacy if they have a low sense of their own cultural identity. Accordingly successful schools are focusing their intervention on cultural and critical literacies that respond to the sociocultural and sociopolitical situation of learners.[56] Talking about text, not just learning how to read it, is central to all this. These things gradually lead to individual and group empowerment, and these things counteract the 'illiteracies of oppression and resistance' described above.

Others make similar observations. Levasseur-Ouimet (1989) sees the pedagogy in schools for francophone minorities, where they are successful, as culturally liberating. This approach to teaching not only reproduces dominant aspects of the majority culture, but also gives legitimacy to the minority students' culture. Moreover it respects their variety of French, while adding other registers to allow full fluency. In drawing up the curriculum and designing their teaching methods, teachers in these schools draw on a rich dialogic process between the school, the community, and the student. They consult the interests of all those with interests at stake. As a result, teachers in these schools are agents of change and liberation, and the francophone minority community itself is beginning to train them to prepare for this role.

Again maximum control of schools by linguistic minority communities ensures that there are as many contexts as possible where mother tongue usage is encouraged and valued. Indeed successful schools in many places in the English-speaking world are also working to offset the constant contact with the majority culture and language that minority children receive outside schools. They are trying to build this idea into their formally agreed policies, so that it impacts across the school and its provisions. Similarly the pedagogy in these schools is culturally liberating: it becomes empowering when it recognizes the minority students' culture and when it shows unqualified respect for their variety of language. These changes are flowing through into the education of another prominent language minority whose cultural and linguistic rights are only now being widely recognized.

Changing the education of the signing Deaf

The natural sign languages of Deaf communities are fully fledged languages, like any other languages, and these sign languages differ from each other as much as sound-based languages. There are families of sign languages, and they have no necessary relationship to the sound-based languages that surround them. In short, sign languages are unwritten, face-to-face languages (Branson and Miller 1997b).

More often than not, educational policies have reduced the status of these languages by banning their use altogether, or by changing them into signed versions of the dominant spoken language. These restrictions on the use of sign languages in schools allow the hearing establishment to exercise symbolic power over Deaf communities. But recent years have seen changes throughout the English-speaking world, and various Deaf communities, who use their own distinct native sign languages, have begun to challenge more traditional views in this area. These signing Deaf communities now consider themselves distinct minority cultural groups who possess all the solidarity and support structures that go with that sense of identity.

As in other areas of bilingual and bicultural education, Deaf communities are beginning to question why education proceeds only through the dominant language. They are asking why the learning styles of hearing people should dominate classroom practices and why only the cultures of hearing people are valued in schools. In this section, I look at these changes in policy and practice that are returning cultural and educational power to signing Deaf minorities, and also improving the education of Deaf children.

Deaf sign languages and mainstreaming

'Signed English' is a different sign language from the sign languages developed by Deaf communities themselves. Signed versions of national spoken or written languages, like Signed English, are *not* fully fledged, natural languages. They use 'frozen signs' or single unchanging signs for each word, or word part, in the spoken language. As a consequence, they lack the dynamism and creativity of natural sign languages which are changing all the time, like all natural languages (Branson and Miller 1997a).

In contrast, sign languages that develop naturally are community languages, and there are many of these. They include British Sign Language (BSL), which is used by 50,000 people in Britain, making it the fourth most used indigenous language after English, Welsh and Gaelic. American Sign Language (ASL) is used in anglophone parts of North America, and La Langue des Signes Québécoise (LSQ) is used in francophone areas. There are natural sign languages in use in every country, and there are non-standard varieties of major sign languages that differ as much from one another as do the non-standard varieties of spoken languages, making them mutually uninterpretable in some cases. Moreover these sign languages can communicate any of the range of meanings and nuances of other languages:

> ASL is capable of expressing the full dimension of human experience including opinions, theory, history and poetry. We now know that ASL is a language that uses handshapes, palm orientation, location, movement and non-manual signals (body and head shifting, body movement and facial markers) with its own content, grammar and formalized rules for use.
>
> (H. Gibson *et al.* 1997: 235–6)

If given the chance, Deaf children learn and use a sign language whether they come from a family background where signing is the custom or not. In Britain, for example, more than 60 per cent of Deaf children have learned to sign by 7 years (Kyle and Woll 1985). But a sign language is usually learned at school, where other Deaf children and an occasional Deaf adult serve as models. Signing is the favoured form of communication among the Ontario Deaf communities in Canada (Mason 1993) and the two sign languages in use in the province are now acknowledged, along with English and French, as official languages of instruction for schools in the province. Similar statutes, supporting the use of ASL in schools, are in place in Alberta and Manitoba (Gibson *et al.* 1997). Signing also provides the immediate form of communication available to Deaf children. In Ontario, the learning of a sign language supports the acquisition of literacy in English or French (Mason 1994) in ways that many educationists are only beginning to appreciate.

Again the 'interdependence hypothesis' helps explain this process, by highlighting the supportive relationship that exists between the learner's first language and a new second language.[57] Like ESL students who are new to English, Deaf children's first (signing) language can also support the learning of English literacy if the sign language is maintained to a high level of proficiency. This leads to certain conclusions about the education of Deaf signing children. In particular, educational policies that put Deaf signing children into regular classrooms come into question.

The mainstreaming of exceptional children, by placing them in regular classrooms is seen as a universal good in progressive educational settings, and it is a good practice for most exceptional students, but it is not suitable for most signing Deaf students. In fact, research and authoritative opinion increasingly argues against the mainstreaming of signing Deaf students because these students are at risk in regular classrooms:[58]

> What is most apparent generally . . . is that deaf children are unable to interact, do not contribute to class lessons through speech, are sub-jected to distorted and exaggerated mouthings by teachers and pupils in order to convey specific information (i.e. not natural language inter-action) and are unlikely to have secure peer group friendships.
> (Kyle and Woll 1985: 239)

In fact, if placed in regular English-based classrooms, Deaf signing students can be seriously held back in their education. This is because they do not 'speak' English and sometimes only a few are fully proficient in signed Eng-lish. In regular classes, they have no opportunity to communicate in their own favoured language, which is the Deaf signing language of their own community. Instead, they are pressured to acquire oral ways of communi-cating, which keeps them away from the complex academic ideas that a Deaf sign language can be used to express: all this has a very negative effect on Deaf communities themselves.

As Branson and Miller (1995) observe, in the eyes of the hearing estab-lishment mainstreaming reinforces the cultural and linguistic incompetence of the Deaf. It helps to marginalize their communities as effectively as ever and it reinforces their status as 'disabled' people who are in need of 'care'. As one close observer of mainstreaming notes, 'it is the most dangerous move yet against the early development of a Deaf person's character, self-confidence and basic sense of identity' (Ladd 1991: 88). For these and other reasons, mainstreaming seems little more than an 'administrative solution with no real base in clinical practice or educational services' (Rodda *et al.* 1986: 153).

Changing school and classroom practices for Deaf signing students

Developments in this area are recent and still not widely studied, so there is some disagreement about what the best practices might be. The issue is com-plicated by the fact that students have varying degrees of deafness that allow some to communicate more readily in non-signed ways than others, which means that the integration of some Deaf signing students is possible for part of the school day, and that special classrooms for Deaf signing students, sited in regular schools, are still seen as one way of providing for this language minority.

As a result, some expert opinion favours partial integration of some students, for some of the school day, while other students remain highly segregated but still work in the same school setting with hearing students (Mason 1993). Other expert opinion also favours a special class in a regular school, using special teachers for signing Deaf students who are bilingual in English and the sign language of the local community, or perhaps who are members of the Deaf community themselves.

Studies of partial integration in Britain, carried out at various ages, have not been encouraging (MacKinnon and Densham 1989). Instead separate schools for the signing Deaf are seen by many as the most suitable and cost effective measure (St Louis 1993). In many North American settings, for example, schools of this kind are moving towards using American Sign Language (ASL) as a medium of classroom instruction (Cummins and Danesi 1990). Gradually the favoured alternative to mainstreaming in North America is to offer signing Deaf students a form of bilingual immersion education in their two languages: ASL and English. This immersion education is presented in separate classes or schools for the Deaf, by specialist teachers who are bilingual themselves in the two languages and also familiar with the culture of the Deaf signing community.

Judging by the assessments of Deaf community members themselves, these new approaches seem overdue and they are very welcome. Heather Gibson is a Deaf educator whose sister and brother are also Deaf. In fact, ASL was the first language of all three. As children they dreamed of sharing that language with other Deaf people. Gibson says that from an early age using ASL was as important to her as breathing, yet few people then believed that using ASL was the most effective way for Deaf people to communicate. Now Gibson is the first Deaf woman vice-principal in Ontario. She has been honoured for her work establishing a bilingual and bicultural Deaf programme at her school for the Deaf, and she described developments at the school in this way:

> The dream we had has not come to fruition yet, but parts of it are a reality now. We do have more deaf teachers working in the system . . . In the past that didn't exist. We've also seen more deaf organizations and individuals come in and be part of our deaf education system. It's a critical thing for deaf children to see. These individuals aren't just role models but mentors and advocates for the children. Students have full access to the school curriculum and that's because we're using ASL, our first language. That allows open access to an education.
>
> (Gibson, quoted in Black 1997: A5)

This approach is spreading quickly in the English-speaking world, as more people begin to recognize that the signing Deaf are minority language users who have a distinct culture of their own to share and transmit. Certain organizational arrangements seem to suit these schools (Israelite *et al.* 1992):

- they have teachers who are knowledgeable about the linguistic properties of native sign language
- they have teachers who know about cultural issues in the Deaf and hearing communities
- they see Deaf teachers or teaching assistants as essential to their students' successful development
- their curriculums give wide opportunities to share personal experiences in the signed language
- their assessment teams include at least one Deaf professional more proficient than the student
- they guarantee parent education as part of Deaf education: in signing, culture, and interaction modes.

Like other students of English as a second language, the signing Deaf in these schools follow a curriculum that gives them the best of both worlds. They have their first signing language supported, including exposure to the culture of the Deaf community which gives that language its meaning, and they also receive literacy in English, because they will live and work in an English-dominant society. The Canadian Association of the Deaf (1990), for instance, places a higher priority on the acquisition of literacy in English or French than it does on oral language skills in English or French, because of the importance for the Deaf of having literacy for finding work and succeeding in post-secondary education. Accordingly, a core English curriculum remains very important for the signing Deaf, because they need to be highly literate and expert in that language. What would this core curriculum look like, if rewritten for signing Deaf students?

An English curriculum for signing Deaf students, taught in a separate school setting, would address the same sets of core competencies and use similar teaching methods to those used in the regular school. But where the core curriculum stressed 'talk', the Deaf core curriculum would stress 'signing' as follows:

- high proficiency in English literacy, using signing as the medium of instruction
- learning about the English language, using signing as the medium of instruction
- instead of 'talking about text', using signing to discuss text

- instead of 'talking about literature', using signing to discuss literature
- instead of 'talking about media', using signing to discuss media.

Other ways of organizing instruction are also being tried, especially for younger students. A bilingual immersion arrangement allows hearing students to work alongside the Deaf and become naturally bilingual in the signed language and in their first language. In Canada, a day care project integrates signing Deaf students in this way with hearing students in a bilingual/bicultural programme using English and ASL (Evans and Zimmer 1993). All the hearing children have some kind of contact with the Deaf community, like a Deaf parent or sibling. In this immersion setting, half the staff are Deaf and the rest are hearing, while the choice of language for use in any classroom interaction is dictated by person and not by activities. In other words, the students themselves choose the language for any interaction.

This programme helps all the children develop pride in both cultures. The signing Deaf children also develop a more positive self-identity and better language skills. The studies so far indicate that all the children are learning either ASL or English as a second language, according to their background. Only 20 per cent of the signing Deaf children have some type of language delay after completing the programme, compared to 70 per cent who were delayed at the beginning of the programme.[59]

In the United States, several schools for Deaf students were on the road to becoming bilingual/bicultural in their programmes. Among the better known of these are the Learning Center for Deaf Children, Framingham MA, the Indiana School for the Deaf, and the California School for the Deaf in Freemount (H. Gibson *et al.* 1997). Experimental bilingual programmes use storytelling to develop young students use of ASL, and their use of ASL in learning English. Here the curriculum focuses on a series of stories that address separate aspects of language. In one programme, the teacher is a native Deaf signer who is bilingual in English and experienced in the art of storytelling. This programme's early success, with 4 to 7-year-olds, led to its further development. A second programme also used role-playing, storytelling by the students, and story writing. Here the students engaged in lots of code-switching, using English with their teachers, and ASL with other students. Their ASL stories became more elaborated and had clearer transitions (Israelite *et al.* 1992).

In languages other than English, there are more long term developments. Students in France and Switzerland receive bilingual/bicultural primary education where the native sign language is used by all participants, both adults and children, for all non-written communication. In both places, the teaching of French proceeds mainly through written language. Other programmes are developing at more senior levels of education (Israelite *et al.* 1992). In

Scandinavia, the move towards full bilingual/bicultural education is still taking place, but in many respects it is ahead of North American developments. Research from Sweden and Denmark show that the reading, writing and overall academic levels of Deaf students in bilingual programmes are on par with hearing children the same age (H. Gibson *et al.* 1997).

These few developments suggest a little of the range of reforms. Moreover the development of effective sign language curricula for the teaching of sign languages in schools and in universities is part of all this; in fact it is central to increasing educational opportunities for Deaf signing students (Branson and Miller 1997b). Most important is the need to end the cycle of low expectations for Deaf students, in the way that Levin's accelerated school's programme raises expectations for inner urban students: for the signing Deaf 'the participants in the program must subscribe to the belief that Deaf people can be expected to learn as much as hearing children' (Johnson *et al.* 1989: 12).

Conclusion: school level policies and practices

In line with the view of social justice presented in Chapter 1, most decisions about minority languages in pluralist societies are made and implemented at the level of the single school. Every school, even every classroom, is a new setting for working out fair arrangements. To make sure that educational professionals have the information they need, local minority language communities in many places are helping to decide the direction of their children's schools. They are having a say in which languages get valued in their own children's schools, and how the schools themselves organize their language programmes.

This does not mean that minority languages are beginning to appear on every school's curriculum, because many minority parents and communities prefer schools to put their efforts into teaching English. Sometimes community education is needed to convince parents of the value of supporting the first languages of younger children. At a minimum, majority culture schools need to value the languages of minority students. But how can the many different minority languages that are spoken now, in most English-speaking countries, be valued by schools in more than token ways?

I have suggested that the ideal way to do this for young children's first languages is to provide bilingual immersion programmes.[60] However in practice, this sort of provision is beyond the reach of most schools and school systems where many different languages are in use. In these settings, schools are trying to value minority languages in other ways. Here are some suggestions for supporting first language development, even when the school teaches only in English.[61]

Staff and visitors

- recruit people who can tutor minority language students fluently using their first languages
- appoint as many staff as possible who share the children's language and culture
- invite guests from the minority language cultures and show them respect
- employ professionals who understand the influence of home language and culture on children's development
- provide leaders, mentors, and models of culturally sensitive practices
- make wide use of the languages and skills of community members in the school.

Curriculum and teaching

- adopt an anti-bias curriculum
- support teaching with images that represent the different cultures
- provide books in the minority languages in the school library, and include bilingual books
- have books and recorded collections in the minority languages in class-rooms
- learn basic words in the community languages
- provide classroom opportunities for children to communicate with others in their first language (in cooperative learning groups, etc.)
- create units of work that incorporate other languages
- encourage students to write in their first language for school newspapers and magazines.

Parents and communities[62]

- involve parents in daily activities, and collaborate with families
- ask families for culturally relevant information
- find translators for parent meetings and interviews
- respect family cultural beliefs and practices
- have programmes that mediate the cultural discontinuities between the children's homes and the school
- present English courses to parents at the same time as their children are studying their first languages
- involve children and parents together in family literacy programmes.

Professional development

- pursue additional research on which to base culturally sensitive practices

- begin by finding out about the languages and varieties used by pupils in the school
- arrange professional development that shares information in all these areas
- give leadership in professional development to ESL and minority teachers
- draw up a school language policy as a year long exercise in professional development.

School organization

- base management on clear principles that promote culturally sensitive practices
- provide signs that welcome people in the different languages
- have bilingual or multilingual signs wherever signs are needed
- use the minority languages in newsletters and other official school communication
- display pictures and objects from the various cultures around the school
- invite ESL students to use their first language at assemblies, prizegivings, and other official functions
- involve the minority language communities in the school's management
- commit school resources to immigrant language maintenance in the community
- deliberately value minority languages in the administrative discourse of the school
- speak about other languages with respect
- above all, ask teachers to allow the minority languages to be used freely whenever possible.

Discussion starters

1 Why is the maintenance of a young immigrant child's first language important for later language development? How can early childhood education make the learning of a first language more easy? How can it make the learning of a second language easier?
2 Explain Cummins' two hypotheses in your own words. Using them as a starting point, what areas of minority language education would you reform if you could? How would you change your own teaching practices?
3 Many teachers work in schools where there is great student diversity and many different cultures are represented. In these settings, what can teachers reasonably do about differences in students' discourse norms?
4 What are the advantages and disadvantages of bilingual immersion and heritage language programmes? Which approach to maintaining children's

first languages is likely to succeed in your educational system? Why? How could any difficulties be overcome in practice?

5 How does bilingual education differ from ESL education? Review the various approaches to organizing ESL education in this chapter. Which ones are already used by schools in your area? Which of the others could be adopted for your local high school students? How would schools in your system need to be changed to make use of these approaches?

6 Are there ideas in the experiences of franco-ontarian schools that could be reapplied in changing the education of linguistic minority students elsewhere? How would you use those ideas in your own practices?

7 Why has the mainstreaming of signing Deaf students lost much of its support among many signing Deaf communities themselves? Are there other ways of organizing the education of Deaf children that work well in your area? What are these?

8 Many teachers work in schools where there is great student diversity and many different immigrant languages are in use. In these settings, what can teachers reasonably do to give value to immigrant students' first languages? Which of these things would schools in your area be willing to insert into their planning and practices? How could you get more of these things working in schools?

seven

MAKING THE EDUCATIONAL WORLD SAFE FOR STUDENTS FROM DIVERSE BACKGROUNDS

I have argued that teachers and administrators *can* change their practices and respond more to student diversity, while *still* providing high quality education for all students. Throughout the book I have used examples of good practices as models to be learned from rather than copied, because every situation of diversity is a new one for teachers to explore and deal with in a fashion sensitive to the context and the students. Good teachers of students from diverse backgrounds are always applying their ingenuity and imagination to the classroom situation, reflecting, borrowing, reshaping, and inventing practices and policies to suit their students' needs and their school's unique context.

It goes without saying, then, that younger, more flexible, and adaptable teachers have certain advantages over their senior colleagues in working with these new ideas, arrangements, and practices. More experienced teachers often have the routines and attitudes of a professional lifetime to uncover and change. These hidden patterns of routine can make it harder for some more senior educators to recognize the need for change, especially if they have been successful practitioners for many years working with students from the mainstream culture.[1] All this suggests, too, that the responsibility for the important changes that are already upon us rests largely with student teachers about to enter schools and with those who have recently graduated. Consequently this final chapter addresses their concerns more directly, as well as teacher professional development more broadly.

In the future, everything that happens in educational policy, school administration, and classroom practice will be influenced by concern for diversity, because cultural pluralism on a vast scale is now normal in all the urbanized areas of the English-speaking world. In countries large and small, communities different from the mainstream are the youngest and fastest growing sections of the population. They are also among the poorest sections of the population, and the gap between rich and poor people has widened everywhere in recent decades.

To address the needs of students from backgrounds of diversity, educational systems are beginning to change the elitist and hierarchical arrangements that were once the custom in educational management. These old structures brought disempowerment on a grand scale to marginal groups, keeping their voices muffled and their interests in the background. To replace these arrangements, educational systems are developing policies and practices that respond more directly to the voices of peoples of diversity. More than this, they are beginning at last to recognize that the people best placed to design education for diversity are the members of the groups themselves.

Even in the recent past, the culturally different have been faced with a stark and cruel choice in English-speaking countries: a choice between the dominant culture and their own culture. This has been a difficult choice because most communities prefer not to abandon one cultural world in favour of the other. They want the best of both worlds for their children's education: they certainly want admission to the high status and mainstream culture of literacy that is the chief output of regular education, but they also want schools to recognize 'their own things' – their own cultural values, language varieties, traditions, and interests. They want these things to become a relevant and important part of the education that their children receive. Furthermore, involuntary minorities usually place more value on 'their own things' than voluntary minorities do. In response, schools for the children of involuntary minorities are often very different from the norm in their practices and policies, and this is only right.[2] In contrast, schools for the children of voluntary minorities are only as different from the norm as parents, teachers, and students want them to be.

To make the educational world safe for students from backgrounds of diversity, education needs two additional benefits not discussed so far in this book. The first is a regular supply of well trained and widely educated new teachers, who can challenge, change, and reform schools as a direct result of the quality of their teacher education. The second is a critically informed knowledge base: the sort of knowledge that beginning and experienced teachers can draw on to bring about the reform of education for diversity. In this brief chapter, I discuss ways of developing *new teachers* equipped with critical insights into their professional work.

Emancipation and neutrality in educational research and teacher education

Teacher education is a thriving area of study in the social sciences, and there are many reasons why it should be. Not least of these is its potential for helping human beings to emancipate themselves, in straightforward ways, through the schools that its graduates directly affect. But for several historical reasons, teacher education as a field of study seems to have developed and now operates without much awareness of the emancipatory potential that it has. Although there have always been professors of teacher education with well developed emancipatory interests, their influence across the field is still rather spasmodic and muted.

In place of any emancipatory interest, there is often a rather tame 'ideology of neutrality' in teacher education research. This trend came about long ago, I think, because the school teachers who became the early professors of teacher education came from bureaucratic systems that demanded system loyalty and professional neutrality as part of the price of their employment. The idea of teaching as a profession, with all the personal autonomy of any profession, was still well in the future, and for many teachers it still is. But generations ago, this political price was an easier one for teachers to pay, because people tended to see schools as rather closed contexts, elevated above the local context, and cut off from the discourses that we now know always reach into schools from every side.

Within these closed systems, a stance of neutrality in relation to the wider context was an easier one for teachers to take than it is now. More often than not, teachers came from the dominant culture. With only rare exception, they had rather mainstream social values. In fact, many social injustices were outside their notice, because the injustices came from gender or sociocultural interests that teachers were rarely aware of, let alone understood. In turn, when some of these teachers became the early professors, their academic work tended to reproduce that situation in university and college departments. In turn, their successors then took that situation for granted. So what does this kind of 'neutral' academic work ignore?

As earlier chapters in this book show, many possible sets of ethnic, gender, and social class interests exist in society. Moreover these are very different from one another and need to be treated differently. Because of this, activities of teaching, research, and publishing in teacher education, that ignore the voices of marginalized interests, risk doing great harm. As mentioned in Chapter 1, these 'neutral' activities try to work out in advance, from the interests of dominant individuals, what arrangements would be chosen by other people whose interests might not be readily understood by anyone who is not from the relevant class, gender or culture.

By ignoring whole areas of human diversity, this approach to teacher education research and teaching came to be accepted uncritically: not only as 'the way things are', but also as 'the way they should be'. Indeed not only has this 'taken-for-grantedness' in teacher education held back an emancipatory concern for diverse interests, but also for much of the time, wherever it falls, the gaze of academic teacher education tends to accredit a non-democratic, hierarchical, and unequal status quo in educational systems. For a long time too, this status quo was supported by the theory of knowledge that dominated educational research. In other words, the idea of 'impartial researcher control' seemed to match the stance of neutrality that was once required from professors of teacher education. But this theory is now kept in place more by institutional pressures than by any scientific merit. What are these 'institutional pressures'?

Pressures to conform include the discourses arising from closed academic journals, conferences, entry requirements, accreditations, grants, consultancies, departments, and associations. These can too easily create a discursive 'positioning' for influential teacher educators. It makes them participants in a closed reality in which they are cut off from discourses that might promote an interest in change. This is because these critical discourses do not seem to be 'neutral', even though this kind of neutrality has always been a problem in applied academic areas. In other words, to profess neutrality often means little more than approving an unsatisfactory status quo, while tinkering with its established and taken-for-granted mechanisms. At the same time, the status quo may be 'unsatisfactory' just because it is not well interpreted out of unrealistic respect for a belief in neutrality!

Fortunately there is another way of building a more reforming knowledge base that can be passed on to teachers. This approach tries to bring a critical eye to the things that oppress people, especially students caught up in educational systems and schools. Its goal quite simply is to help students, teachers and administrators to emancipate themselves from those oppressive structures.

Critical approaches to education begin with the view that schools are not closed systems and are not cut off from wider influences. Accordingly these approaches show how power relations, ideologies, and systems of oppression found outside schools affect schools and classrooms through the discourses that enter them. As a result, ideas about power and the use of discourse are as central to these approaches as they are to teacher education itself.

Discourse and power in education

Current debates on the nature of power link it directly with the use of discourse. Chapter 1 outlines some of these debates, and their link with the postmodern condition. A welcome aspect of this postmodern condition is that more voices seem to be raised and at least heard in society these days. These include the voices of groups who were once dispossessed. But while more diverse voices are being heard, power forces beyond the local continue to ignore the messages that those voices are conveying, and this is nowhere more the case than in education.

Chapter 1 suggests that a critical realist account of discourse and power is useful for bringing questions of access, equity, and quality of provision into educational debates. It also argues that the organization of education everywhere in English-speaking countries is interwoven with capitalist social relations. As a result, a real dilemma for making changes in education for diversity is that capitalist social relations are the most assimilationary cultural forces that the world has ever seen. Any diversity in provision that the new voices are claiming is lost in the pressure towards assimilation and conformity that capitalism creates. This also happens because capitalist social relations are prospering under the new freedoms and the open message systems that are part of the postmodern condition.

Capitalism is a great stimulus to human productivity, but as an indoctrinatory force it can assimilate even the most contrary forms of diversity and make them seem part of itself.[3] In its modern form, capitalism also tends to satisfy people's 'wants' rather than their needs. In other words, instead of the basic human interests and needs that early capitalism made it its business to meet, present-day capitalism finds its quickest rewards in entertainments, gimmicks, and diversions.[4] The effects of all this on education are already serious. Consider the subtle but enforced immersion in a cleaned up version of capitalism that schools provide for our young. Here even the idea of thinking beyond the theory of capitalism is difficult, because of the pervading influence of the ideology itself in the discourses that surround every one of us.

In the capitalist world of affluence, privilege, and consumerism described by theorists of postmodernity, serious advocates for diversity are often ignored. In this world, people's sociocultural identities and allegiances tend to mean less and less. Fewer people accept responsibility for others, or even acknowledge their collective identity. Any voices for diversity that are raised tend to become part of the background noise, unless their owners have power in the marketplace. In addition, all this is happening in spite of the fact that really important human interests and values can never find a place in the marketplace. Although these are literally priceless, they are treated as things of little value in a marketplace that values lesser things much more highly.

A critical realist approach identifies structures that set limits to human action.[5] It suggests ways to change or remove structures, and by doing so to create conditions in which people can emancipate themselves from some of the structural factors that I have been describing. This is not to say that all structures need changing, because many structures are desired by people for the security and purpose that they provide. Cultural values, for example, are things that people cling to, even at the risk of their own well being. Religious values create similar structures in people's lives which many people cherish. Clearly emancipation does not mean removing all structures, only the ones that people themselves really find oppressive and reveal in the signs and symbols of their discourses.

The link between discourse and power is central to all of this, because any exercise of power by human actors is affected by the discursive nature of power itself.[6] As Foucault (1984: 110) observes, history constantly teaches us 'that discourse is not simply that which translates struggles or systems of domination, but is the thing for which and by which there is struggle: discourse is the power which is to be seized'. What does all this mean for research and for teacher education?

Doing critical research for teacher education and teacher practice

A look at the history of modern schooling suggests some of the possibilities for doing critical teacher education research in regular schools and classrooms, and also some of the limits. A focus on 'control' in schools is still one of the key features of education; this 'control' function of education is affected by much older and more influential discourses than people often realize. Indeed a critical look at schools, as institutions, reveals that they are only partly on the side of the angels.

The stress on control in classrooms reflects this ubiquitous ethos of control in education. Children entering classrooms are quickly indoctrinated, through rather passive student activities, into a world where control is taken for granted. Outside classrooms, too, this control function is really what makes schools able to do what they do.[7] Although the role of schools as powerful agencies of social control is rather disguised in modern societies, we can see this control function in the way schools are organized and run, because in this respect modern schools have not changed very much in their general aim since their beginnings in the middle of the nineteenth century.

The designers of modern universal schooling lived at the same time as the designers of prisons, asylums for insane people, and hospitals for the diseased poor. It is no accident that all four types of institution use the term 'superintendent' to describe their executive officers, and operate through hierarchical and controlling structures. In education, beginning in English-speaking countries in the decades around the Taunton Report in Britain (1864–8), these designers were responding to fears about what many children would become if efforts were not made to change them by controlling their socialization through compulsory schooling.

These designers had strong memories of the democratic revolutions across Europe and North America in 1848 and earlier. They were also aware of the bitter and costly uprisings of subject peoples defending their cultural and language rights, and they were keen to avoid a repeat of these experiences. In response, they saw schooling for the masses as a way of bringing their own lower orders into the technologies and values of the mainstream

culture, and as a way of assimilating the culturally and linguistically different. In other words, these designers saw schooling as a way of making children 'better' and as a way of 'civilizing' them.

Structurally schools remain very much in this mould. Often, in spite of
many teachers' best efforts, classrooms tend to reflect the structures of the
wider institution, which themselves often reflect wider forms of oppression
that continue in modern states. We see this in the role that wider formations
have in shaping bilingual education policies for minority language users:
policies that hold back reforms at national, regional, school and classroom
levels (Cummins 1995). We see it in the way wider structures impact directly
on culturally different children in classrooms, right from their earliest years
of schooling. In this process, wider discourses create an array of spoken and
written texts and other sign systems that position children and their cultures
in ways that mark out cultural difference, at the same time as they silence it
(Luke *et al.* 1995).

So there is a need to focus discussion more on the functions that schools
now have, as distinct from their purposes: in other words, the things that
schools actually do, rather than what they would like to do. We need to
address the way that modern schooling typically positions children so that
they are prepared for uncritical admission into sociocultural conditions
determined well in advance of that admission. What I am saying is that
rather than preparing children for 'initiation into an autonomous and
worthwhile form of life', schools offer them a filtered immersion in the discourses in which schools themselves are positioned. They reflect on to children a cleaned up version of the social formations that surround them. By
doing all this, they present the interests of some sectional groups in society
to children as though they were universal interests.

In the face of this uncomfortable description, I have to say that the real
work of research for teacher education has only just begun. To move in more
promising directions, a major task of critical realist researchers is to un-
tangle the ways in which wider structures and processes filter into educational organizations, and then into classrooms to recreate four things:

- ideology-producing classroom processes (i.e. distortions of reality in children's minds)
- instructional rather than educational action (i.e. confusing 'education'
  with 'instruction')
- supervisory rather than relational forms of interaction (i.e. between
  school administrators and teachers, teachers and students, and students
  and administrators)
- a reproduction of unjust sociocultural arrangements.

In all this, there are clear winners and losers. The fact that the losers are
almost always the same people who start out from behind seems a black

mark against the institution of education itself, and of its management in the broadest sense.

Research by teacher-practitioners

An approach for studying all this would begin with the interests of teacher practitioners and practising school administrators themselves, which involves a focus on real contexts where their students' lives intersect with the work of the school. Teachers usually have little interest in doing research for its own sake. Constraints of time and location mean that teacher research begins with what they have in front of them, and with the pressing issues that they face. In general, the aim of teacher-researchers is to 'cultivate wisdom' that they can use to inform their own 'strategic action' (Nixon 1987: 24).

In fact, most of the research done by teacher-practitioners has some 'action research' orientation. McCarty (1997b) summarizes these methods. She reviews the growth of a world-wide teacher researcher movement which covers individual teacher research, teacher-to-teacher collaboration, indigenous teacher study groups, and teachers as ethnographers. As part of her conclusion, she sees teacher research opening up new possibilities that we have hardly begun to explore:

> Teacher research represents a different way of knowing – through relationships, observation and assessment of practice, dialogue, reflection, engagement, and critique. It is research as social transaction. It can become research as social justice. Through its process and products, teacher research encourages us not only to challenge an unjust system, but to examine, confront, and transform the root causes of those injustices.
>
> (McCarty 1997b: 234–5)

For educating for diversity, this suggests concentrating more on the lives and activities of children themselves, notably the things in their lives that affect their education. But this is much easier said than done, partly because schools are in competition with all the other demands made on children's time, and for many children the serious work of schools lies at the distant margins of their lives. Perhaps the best sort of classroom action research, then, is the kind of work that challenges and questions the routine ways in which students' lives are limited and shaped by those other demands.

Television programmes, for example, offer an indirect way into researching the imagined worlds and life interests of most children. By looking at television programmes critically in classrooms, teachers can use them as a vehicle for enlarging children's awareness of the subtle distortions in message systems that surround them. At the same time, this sort of approach to classroom research needs to be carefully thought out, as an example from North America confirms.

A non-profit group called PEACE currently asks about 100,000 students and parents in hundreds of schools to cast television ballots each year:[8]

> Before they vote, children are shown a video in which young viewers give their opinions on what constitutes toxic and positive TV, along with clips of each nominated program . . . But the approach troubles a York University assistant professor of mass communications. Harris Breslow says that while it's good that PEACE is drawing children's attention to the most glaring examples of violence and sexism, the group may be ignoring offensive subtexts in some of the TV programs. *Fresh Prince of Bel-Air*, he says, is listed as a positive program even though its female characters play secondary, traditional roles and are 'morons'. The show also subtly pushes materialistic values and may be conveying a hidden message that money is what counts.
>
> (Small 1997: C11)

Most television entertainments that are targeted on young people, like this one, offer them a world filled with personal problems, but empty of social and cultural problems. Hardly ever do these programmes ask children to think about the link between their personal problems and other problems in the society that surround them. So without identifying that link, teacher research into the lived worlds of children can easily reinforce the misperceptions that children get about these things from the media. Clearly to avoid working against the aims of education in this way, teachers need a level of critical awareness about the discourses that *they* experience before they can begin to challenge those discourses with good educational effect. This suggests that studies in critical language awareness (see Chapter 5) also have an urgent place in the curriculum of teacher education, as well as in the school curriculum itself.

Researchers and teacher-practitioners as co-researchers

Other research also involves critical practitioners and researchers working as co-participants at every point. This sort of research encourages students of education to reflect critically on the good practices of critical practitioners, and then use the evidence of those good practices as insights to be learned from, not as data to be copied. Above all, it tries to trace the seamless links between the discourses of wider social formations, the discourses of schools, and the discourses of classrooms.

Specifically we need more wideranging critical ethnographies like May's (1994) study of Richmond Road School (see Chapter 2). May describes a successful and innovatory model of critical practice in multicultural education for others to learn from. Also we need more conventional ethnographies that compare community and school discursive practices, like Goldstein's (1988) study of the Hmong refugee girls (see Chapter 4), and like Heath's *Ways With Words* (1983) which linked activities in the homes of low income and culturally different communities with the activities of classrooms that serve children from those homes. But future ethnographies will broaden beyond Goldstein's and Heath's concerns, to connect political, economic, and organizational discourses with the discourses of home, community, and classroom.

Also needed are critical discourse analyses that improve on the many introductory studies already under way.[9] Future studies need to extend into the many areas that Foucault identifies. These include the discourses that arise within the organization itself, like

> the decisions and regulations that are among its constitutive elements, its means of functioning, along with its strategies, its covert discourses and ruses, ruses which are not ultimately played by any particular person, but which are nonetheless lived, and ensure the permanence and functioning of the institution.
>
> (Foucault 1980: 38)

Mixed with the need for quality studies is the need for teacher education research that looks outward in every direction, because discursive practices permeate every 'closed' context and every 'closed' system. While this means looking out beyond schools, it also means looking across academic disciplines and subjects. Among the many approaches to research that seem relevant, two in particular seem very useful for 'reclaiming the reality' of teacher education and teacher practice.

Two approaches for teacher research

Some characteristics and aims of critical discourse analysis
The following is a sketch of the aims of critical discourse analysis:[10]

- to explore 'hidden' relationships between a piece of discourse (a text) and wider social formations
- to show how this text is shaped by relations of power and struggles over power
- to reveal links between discourse, ideology, and power, especially things that are hidden from those who benefit from them.

A critical discourse analysis usually involves most of the following:

- an interest in uncovering inequality, power relationships, injustices, discrimination, bias, etc.

- an investigation of language behaviour in natural language situations of social relevance (public institutions, media, political discourse, etc.)
- interdisciplinary research addressing things too complex to be dealt with in only one field
- inclusion of a historical perspective on the research study
- researchers who 'take sides' in order to improve the lives of 'the subjects' in some way
- research that changes social practices and emancipates people.

In education, almost any kind of text is a good basis for this sort of research: an item of school policy; a fragment of teacher or student talk; a passage from a textbook, etc. For example, a curriculum document, written to guide the practices of teachers, is a good example of a text for doing critical discourse analysis. Usually curriculum documents that are written by people outside schools, strive to 'neutralize' the language and the ideas that the text contains. However in the interests of neutrality they do this to such a degree that instead of becoming politically 'neutral', these documents become highly political in the way that they only support the educational status quo. A critical discourse analysis would explore the ways that this 'neutral' document tries to construct educational practice in ways that do not disturb either the existing power arrangements or those who benefit from them.

Critical discourse analysis can also be used as one research activity among several activities used in other approaches to research. For example, it can work very well as part of a more wideranging critical ethnography.

Some characteristics and aims of critical ethnography
The following is a sketch of the aims of critical ethnography:[11]

- to combine the study of a single school, classroom, or its participants with critical insights into sociocultural reproduction (i.e. into how features of society or culture get reproduced in taken for granted ways)[12]
- to understand how wider structures are mediated in a single setting
- to understand how wider structures produce change within schools and classrooms
- to help individuals and groups free themselves from things that oppress them.

A critical ethnography usually means doing most of the following things:

- using a standard participant observation methodology, but drawing insights from critical sociology and philosophy
- noting the relationship between theory and data, and between external things that affect the school

- focusing critically on structures and political processes outside the s̶ that create situations and processes inside it
- negotiating research outcomes with participants
- doing openly ideological research that puts critical theory into practice
- taking critical practitioners as the objects of study.

As an example, a critical ethnography might look at the impact, on teachers, students and classrooms, of the same curriculum document mentioned above. It might examine the positive and negative effects of the document at many levels. For example, it might reveal the following things:

- the way that the document constructs teacher practices
- the way it brings professionals together or keeps them apart
- the way it celebrates or silences diversity
- the way it shapes classroom environments
- the way it contributes to children's own discourses and world view.

The results of research like this could be shared with beginning and experienced teachers to help inform their own critical use of the same curriculum document, and of curriculum documents in general. It is easy to see how research of this kind, shared with student teachers, could help make the educational world much safer for students from backgrounds of diversity.

Conclusion: teacher education for changing education for diversity

Clearly this is the area where emancipatory change begins. Many readers of this book will be newly trained teachers or teachers in training, and they will know that much of their own teacher education *sidesteps* education for diversity issues.[13] Readers will also know of the mismatch between their own life experiences and the cultural backgrounds of most of their students. In fact, the gap that exists in English-speaking countries between the student population in schools and the teaching force is now more obvious than ever. Almost everywhere an increasingly diverse school population encounters a mainly white teaching force drawn from middle class backgrounds (Grant and Secada 1990).[14]

What can be done to narrow the gap? What can be done to allow the culture of the child to show up more in the mind of the teacher? In every country the effectiveness of teacher education itself is at the heart of the problem. If real change is going to take place in teacher education and in the professional development of teachers, it seems likely that the professionals themselves will have to demand more appropriate training for themselves. In this training, they need more exposure to the real conditions that exist in schools for diverse students, and to the role that present-day education has in perpetuating those conditions. They need to insist on better forms of preparation in teacher education so that they can begin to promote emancipatory practices and help in the design of more humane policies.

As part of all this, student teachers need to grapple with complex theoretical ideas that are clearly presented by teacher educators who are well educated in 'education for diversity' issues themselves. Indeed the anti-intellectualism that often separates theory from practice in teacher education is really to the advantage of neither. Nor does it help young teachers to grapple with the complex issues that this book has raised if teachers continue *to see themselves and their own sociocultural experiences as the main source of their most relevant knowledge as practitioners*. As Britzman points out:

> While covering its own theoretical tracks, the myth that teachers are self-made structures a suspicion of theory, and encourages the stance of anti-intellectualism. A larger consequence concerns the rejection of any concept of theory and the valorization of an essential self as the sole source of knowledge.
>
> (Britzman 1991: 231)

To make teacher education work better, Beynon (1997) recommends a more dialogic and critical approach to teacher training that gives students regular, extended, and frank one-to-one interactions with socially critical teacher educators:

> Dialogic practice moves away from an informative dual conversation about topics in teaching to a discussion of the ideological conditions surrounding the topic. It draws on a multiple set of powerful influences which interact, challenge, and revise original ideas and seems to assist student teachers in negotiating the transformation from student to teacher.
>
> (Beynon 1997: 221)

This seems a very important step towards reform. It might turn things around quickly if a few other things were also included:

- these dialogues might focus on 'generative themes' arising directly from aspects of the students' experience, in schools or in training, that trouble or delight them[15]
- the knowledge and experiences that are a background for the dialogues might be rooted in the practices of critical practitioners whom students have observed at work
- the knowledge and experiences that are a background for the dialogues might be rooted in the results of research that has taken nothing for granted.

Often the content knowledge passed on to teachers in training is quite relevant to the diversity they meet in schools. But because they are not asked to let that knowledge 'bump up against' their own discourses, and fill it with their own intentions and purposes, their readiness to apply the knowledge falls short of changing things very much. Although present-day teachers are better informed about issues of diversity, they are probably not much better prepared to implement change than their predecessors who knew much less in these areas. Creating a favourable disposition in themselves towards reforming oppressive practices is what beginning teachers need to do, if their idealism is to survive long in contact with the realities of schools. To help in this, I end this book by suggesting ways that beginning teachers could change themselves, and so cope better with the diversity that they will likely meet:

- In place of a didactic teaching style for working with students from different backgrounds:
  a flexible and self-directed approach to diverse students rooted in the use of natural language.
- In place of a methods-based approach for handling classroom situations:
  a readiness to meet unusual classroom situations in imaginative and ingenious ways.
- In place of whole-class responses to conflict resolution:
  a person-oriented approach, sensitive to the different values and norms of diverse students.
- In place of a curriculum that binds students to abstract knowledge:
  a curriculum that builds critical thinkers who are in control of their lives.
- In place of a curriculum that takes the rough edges off society and its social problems:
  a curriculum that asks: Who makes decisions? Who benefits? Who suffers? How can change occur?
- In place of assessment methods that highlight students' weaknesses:
  an evaluation system that builds, extends, and challenges students to higher levels of achievement.
- In place of a professional persona of objectivity and detachment:
  a professional engagement with diversity that celebrates difference.
- In place of an approach to accountability that blames students for their failure:
  a willingness to look at the school itself as the source of educational failure.
- In place of a view of the school as an isolated institution:
  a view that sees education in the grip of social formations that can also be changed.

Discussion starters

1 Where did your teacher education place you on the above nine points?

2 The impact of educational research on educational practice has been slight. Do you believe that a link could be built between the knowledge that educational research produces and the important needs of teacher education agencies? As a practitioner, what kind of knowledge would you like to get from the work of educational researchers?

3 Can teachers ever be politically neutral in their professional practices? If you think not, give some concrete examples of practices where teachers deliberately adopt a stance that is not neutral? How can you justify those practices? How can teachers design lessons that deal head-on with controversial topics but do so in ways that do not indoctrinate? What would these lessons look like?

4 'A critical look at schools as institutions reveals that they are only partly on the side of the angels'. Linking discussion in this chapter with Bourdieu's ideas in Chapter 1, do you agree or disagree with this statement of mine? Why? Give examples if possible. Which aspects of classroom management or assessment might give children wrong ideas about what matters in the world? How could classrooms operate differently in these areas?

5 Is the exercise of power always linked to the use of discourse? Can you cite examples where it is not? As a teacher, in what ways could you link the exercise of power more often with the use of discourse in such a way as to empower students?

6 Reread Chapter 1's discussion of the coercive and non-coercive uses of power. Are there differences in the role that discourse plays in the exercise of coercive power on the one hand and in the exercise of non-coercive power on the other? Give some examples of ways to empower your students through using discourse while changing the effects of non-coercive power.

7 Does critical realism ask people to do anything that is not in their own interests?

NOTES

1 Reforming education for diversity: leavening power with social justice

1 My definition of education for diversity could also apply quite directly to groups of students who are exceptional in other ways, to do with intellectual, physical or health differences. The educational needs of these other exceptional groups are outside the range of this book.

2 See Hastings (1997) and Skutnabb-Kangas (1997).

3 See Skeggs (1991) and Hargreaves (1994).

4 For a discussion of this trend, see Chapter 3.

5 These views are sometimes called 'New Right' and they have been very successful in political terms. Their beginnings can be traced from the new government that replaced a government overthrown in a *coup d'état* in Australia in 1975. They were developed further in the Thatcher-style governments in Britain from 1979 to 1997, during the Reagan and Bush eras in the United States, and similar adventures in Canada and New Zealand. The attractiveness and success of these policies can be seen from the way that even governments led by political parties that are traditionally more to the left have since followed similar policies in all the above mentioned countries, beginning again in Australia in the early 1980s, continuing elsewhere in the 1980s and into the late 1990s. The effects of all this on educational policy have been devastating, not least for children from diverse class and cultural groups (Corson 1988b).

6 I am using the idea of 'structure' here to refer to the intractability of the social world. Structures set limits to freedom, often in tacit ways, through a complex interplay of powers within social institutions.

7 See Foucault (1972; 1977; 1980).

8 Erickson (1996: 45) spells this out a little more fully: 'Hegemonic practices are routine actions and unexamined beliefs that are consonant with the cultural

system of meaning and ontology within which it makes sense to take certain actions, entirely without malevolent intent, that nonetheless systematically limit the life chances of members of stigmatized groups. Were it not for the regularity of hegemonic practices, resistance by the stigmatized would not be necessary'.

9 See Bourdieu (1966; 1981; 1984). Another key idea that Bourdieu uses is the notion of 'habitus': people acquire certain dispositions in their upbringing that they use to interpret their world and relate to it. In this book, I use the term 'disposition' rather than 'habitus'.

10 These points are based on Harker's analysis (1990: 89ff).

11 For a fuller discussion of 'differential treatment' see Chapter 4 pp. 85–6.

12 This section and the next are an abbreviated discussion taken from Corson and Lemay (1996).

13 See Corson (1993a).

14 See Corson (1993a).

15 See Corson (1993a).

16 For an example of this process at work in a school, see Chapter 3 p. 38.

17 Aboriginal peoples in many parts of the world built their cultures long ago on these more relational 'new possibilities'. As a European social theorist, Habermas does not seem aware of this. Many aboriginal communities are now working to recapture what was lost through their forced contacts with European colonizers (see Chapter 3).

18 See the discussion of 'life chances' in Chapter 4 pp. 86–8. The 'ligatures' discussed in that chapter are good examples of the human interests that Habermas is getting at here.

19 For a discussion of 'discourse norms', see Chapter 3 pp. 64–6; 79–80.

20 This section is an abbreviated discussion taken from Corson and Lemay (1996).

21 Confusion can arise especially in the North American context because the term 'liberalism' is used there in two rather different senses. Liberalism as a political philosophy originated in Europe in the eighteenth century. It was historically associated with the idea of freedom: civil freedom of the individual; free political institutions; freedom of religion, and from the civil constraints of any single religion; freedom of conscience; free enterprise and free trade. Few of these 'freedoms' were guaranteed or existed in eighteenth-century Europe.

   The traditional focus of liberalism was on the individual rather than on the collectivity. But in North America, the use of the term 'liberal' has taken on some different senses. In political discourse, it now includes the ideas of those who might be termed 'social democrats' or 'democratic socialists' elsewhere, rather than 'liberals'. Nevertheless the use of 'liberalism' in philosophical discussions almost everywhere still reflects the historical origins of the term.

22 Elsewhere I discuss the work of these social theorists and their relevance to research, policy, and practice in education (Corson 1991b; 1993a; 1997a).

23 Chapter 2 illustrates the stages more fully in a school's practices.

24 I am not using the word 'problem' here in any evaluative sense. The neutral sense of the word 'problems' suggests the normal challenges of life that confront us, at every moment of living, to which we pose some tentative solution as a response. Human beings are problem solving animals: our ability to solve problems determines our control over the environment and even our survival itself. Problems in

schools are challenges that can be met by proposing a course of policy action (or inaction) as a solution.

25 The model also seems fully consistent with new directions for programme evaluation now being canvassed (House 1990; Madison 1992).

26 For more on approaches to intercultural communication, see I. Young (1981), Corson (1993a) and R. Young (1996).

27 For an example of this, see Chapter 3 p. 36.

28 In outline, it resembles the evolutionary approach described by Lewis and Miles (1990).

2 Building community-based education through critical policy making

1 See Munoz and Garcia-Blanco (1989; 1990).

2 Freire's usual example of a 'generative theme' is the word FAVELA or 'slum' (in Brazilian Portuguese). By breaking words like this into their parts (FA-, -VE- and -LA) students of adult literacy in the Portuguese language were gradually encouraged to master all of the syllabic parts that make up the language's vocabulary. But they were also talking about these themes at the same time and this is what made the pedagogy both humanistic and revolutionary. Freire's approach was remarkably successful in giving people literacy, and it was also very successful in making them critical of the economic, social, and political environments in which they lived.

3 See the discussion of 'critical literacy' in Chapter 5 pp. 142–3.

4 The earlier study was done in Canada by the Assembly of First Nations (1988).

5 See the discussion of the 1989 national reforms in New Zealand in Chapter 3 pp. 56f.

6 See Cazden (1989), Corson (1993a; 1993b) and May (1994).

7 The importance of having strong, culturally authentic leadership is a basic ingredient that other observers note when reforming education for diversity. For example, in South Africa, Bhekuzulu High School was an exemplary rural school run by Black anti-apartheid activists. Yet its achievements largely hinged on the quality of the school's leader. This was so important a factor that in his absence standards of all kinds were seen to slip at the school (Jacobs 1991).

8 See the discussion of 'kohanga reo' or 'language nests' for Maori children in Chapter 3 p. 58–60.

9 Janitor or custodian.

10 See the discussion of Maori educational values in Chapter 3 pp. 59–60 and the discussion of discourse norms and cultural values on pp. 64–6; 79–80.

11 See Bryk and Driscoll (1988).

12 See the description of 'critical ethnography' in Chapter 7 pp. 212–13. This research method seems very appropriate for critical realist research. May's critical ethnography has several unusual strengths. He presents arguments that go well beyond a social critique divorced from a theory of action. Instead his study takes critical practitioners as its objects of study and offers *their* theory of action

as its own conclusion. Also his study engages in a sustained dialogue with those practitioners and provides an original synthesis of the products of that dialogue.
13 For 'hegemony' see Chapter 1 pp. 6–7.
14 For the policy making approach in outline, see Chapter 1 pp. 12ff.
15 See Corson (1995a) for a school situation where minority community interests were literally 'fobbed off'.
16 See Comer (1984), Cummins (1986; 1996), Garcia and Otheguy (1987), Greenberg (1989), Haynes *et al.* (1989), Rasinski and Fredericks (1989), Corson (1993a; 1996) and Corson and Lemay (1996).
17 See Chapter 1 pp. 12ff.

3 Changing the education of aboriginal peoples

1 In the late twentieth century the Kurdish peoples suffer various forms of linguistic and cultural oppression in the five countries that they inhabit as homelands. These include attempts in Iraq to eliminate the Kurds entirely as a people, even though they speak an official language of the country, and legislation in Turkey forbidding the public use of the Kurdish languages and punishing that use in education (McDowall 1994). Elsewhere tacit language policies that are tantamount to linguistic repression continue. In the Chiapas region of Mexico, the Mayan peoples receive little official support for their languages in education even though more than 80 per cent of the indigenous people speak their traditional languages and many speak nothing else. In South and Central America, the languages and cultures of indigenous peoples sometimes get more supportive treatment in educational policies. Some Quechua-speaking children in the Peruvian Andes, for example, receive bilingual education in Quechua and Spanish. Their classroom opportunities and their behaviour contrasts markedly with other Quechua children who are educated only in Spanish (Hornberger 1988a; 1988b). Also, spanning national boundaries, indigenous children in the Amazon basin receive formal and informal bilingual and bicultural education aimed at meeting the linguistic and cultural rights of people who are largely ignored in the official policies of their respective governments (Trapnell 1996).
2 Also see note 1 of Chapter 4.
3 Other involuntary minorities are francophone Canadians who inhabit their ancestral territories *outside* Québec; or the Gaelic peoples of Wales, Ireland, and Scotland; or the large Hispanic populations in the south-west of the United States (see Chapter 6's discussion of all these groups). However, all these are different from aboriginal people in their needs, because they are all European in cultural history. Black South Africans, living under apartheid, were also involuntary minorities, although when taken together these various peoples were really a large majority of the population.
4 See Skutnabb-Kangas (1981), Baker (1988), Skutnabb-Kangas and Cummins (1988) and Romaine (1989; 1991).
5 See Chapter 6. For summaries see Cummins and Swain (1986), Baker (1988), Skutnabb-Kangas and Cummins (1988), Corson (1993a), and Skutnabb-Kangas (1997).

6 See Durie (1997), S. Harris and Devlin (1997), Heimbecker (1997) and McCarty (1997a).

7 This section is taken from Corson (1995d; 1996).

8 This requirement is likely to change so that even one pupil in a school can ask to be taught through Sámi.

9 In reviewing the effects of the Sámi Language Act in this section, I look mainly at provisions for Sámi-as-a-first-language (Corson 1996). But the new provisions for Sámi-as-a-second-language education (Corson 1995d) are also relevant to aboriginal education elsewhere.

10 This section condenses material from Corson and Lemay (1996).

11 See McCaskill (1987) and Regnier (1987).

12 See Hastings (1988; 1997).

13 See Chapter 2 p. 32.

14 See Fesl (1988).

15 See Brandl (1983) and Christie (1988: 5–19).

16 See S. Harris and Devlin (1997).

17 See Harrison (1986) and McCarty (1997a).

18 See the discussion of Kvernmo's research on p. 50.

19 Au and Kawakami's (1994) review confirms how wideranging this research has been.

20 See Philips (1972; 1975; 1983).

21 For 'life chances', see Chapter 4 pp. 86–8.

22 See Erickson (1975) and Gumperz (1976).

23 See the discussion of kura kaupapa Maori for New Zealand Polynesian children on pp. 58f.

24 See Au (1978) and Philips (1983).

25 See pp. 79–80. For a description of how stereotyping works, see Chapter 5 pp. 114–15; 118–19.

26 Although most of the research cited in this chapter comes from non-aboriginal researchers, the balance is gradually shifting as aboriginal people themselves make their views known more forcefully on this point. Other aboriginal researchers cited in this chapter include Kvernmo, Balto, Todal, Magga, Penetito, Hingangaroa Smith, and Durie. It is interesting and perhaps not surprising that apart from Daigle, all these researchers come from the two countries (Norway and New Zealand) where aboriginal solidarity and indigenous cultural power are at their most robust.

27 For a full discussion of 'differential treatment' see Chapter 4 pp. 85ff.

28 See discussions about the importance of 'talking about text' in Chapter 5 pp. 148–52.

29 For the way that different discourses integrate in this process, see Chapter 5 pp. 147–8.

30 See also the fuller discussion of language assessment in Chapter 6.

31 See Wilgosh and Mulcahy (1986) and Crago (1990).

32 See Wilgosh and Mulcahy (1986) and Senior (1993).

33 See Hamilton *et al.* (1994) and Street (1997).

34 See Corson (1995c; 1997f).

35 See Roberts and Clifton (1988) and Leith and Slentz (1984).

36 'Systemic' here refers to bias and discrimination that may be unintentional. It comes about because of unfair structures and practices that have been in place for so long that people take them for granted. A critical realist approach asks teachers to critique structures and their own taken-for-granted practices, so that bias and discrimination can be removed, or at least softened.

37 See Corenblum and Annis (1987) and Fossey (1991).

38 I remember reading an account of an aboriginal Canadian who became a war hero in the Italian campaign in the Second World War. After accepting his decorations he was asked how his future looked to him. He said that he hoped he would not survive the war, because during the war he was a respected hero, but when he returned to Canada in people's eyes he would once again become 'just a poor bloody Indian'.

39 For a description of how stereotyping works, see Chapter 5 pp. 114–15; 118–19.

40 See discussion on p. 65.

41 See Christie (1988), Ward (1990), Lindsay (1992), Ryan (1992; 1994) and Eriks-Brophy and Crago (1994).

4 Changing the education of girls from immigrant cultures

1 The risk of stereotyping groups and individuals is always present when writing about people in descriptive ways. Even Ogbu's useful distinction between voluntary and involuntary minorities is at risk here. That distinction tends to miss the complexity of sociocultural groups, many of whom would see themselves as less one thing and more the other. Immigrants, for example, are often unwilling refugees from situations that are not of their choosing; so are they voluntary or involuntary minorities? Matters of social class are also factors, with people who move into privileged sectors of their new country describing themselves differently from those who do not. See the discussion of other 'involuntary minorities' in Chapter 6 pp. 187–90.

2 See Leder and Sampson (1989), Wilgosh (1994) and C. Hall and Coles (1997).

3 See AAUW Report (1995). Peculiarities in the North American school system probably make it abnormal when set alongside otherwise comparable systems. The excessive stress on male athletics in US secondary schools, its links with the male professional sporting marketplace, and the individual prestige that goes with it, all tend to marginalize girls. At the same time, the participation of girls in peripheral athletics activities, like cheer-leading, tends to trivialize their role and their function, and to lower their self-perceptions. It would be surprising if the discourses associated with all this had no impact on girls' success rates in American coeducational schooling.

4 Studies of girls' self-esteem in school provided a well-spring for researchers in the 1970s and 1980s (see Kenway and Willis 1990 for an overview). The main criticism of this flood of research is that it concentrates on the individual child, rather than on social structures, so it tends to explain low self-esteem among girls as a personal pathology that needs treatment. In one view, the research has often 'failed to take account of those social forces which along with patriarchy are

responsible for the distribution and redistribution of power and privilege' (Tsolidis 1990: 54).

5 Evidence like this suggests that there are important things that schools need to be doing to make literacy more relevant to the interests of North American boys in particular. More socially critical approaches to literacy, aimed at linking the reading and writing that schools promote with the social empowerment of the learner, would obviously be good for both boys and girls. It would certainly attract the interests of many boys, who are presently distracted by other life pursuits from the forms of literacy made available by schools. See the discussion of critical literacy in Chapter 5 and also see developments in Australia (Alloway and Gilbert 1997a).

6 Dahrendorf's *Life Chances* (1978) speaks of options and ligatures as the two distinguishing kinds of life chances that societies offer to their members. I narrow discussion here from 'societies' to 'education within societies'.

7 A key aim of Egbo's studies (1997; 1998) is to show the value of literacy for increasing the options and ligatures of rural women in Sub-Saharan Africa.

8 See the discussion of Foucault's ideas in Chapter 1 p. 5.

9 See Bjerrum Nielsen and Davies (1997) and Corson (1997b).

10 See discussion on this point in Chapter 7 pp. 207f.

11 See the discussion of Goldstein's study in the United States later in this chapter.

12 For the effect that overly positive stereotypes can have on immigrant children, see Chapter 5 p. 119.

13 See the discussion of 'tracking' or 'streaming' in Chapter 5 pp. 145–8.

14 I return to all these things in Chapters 5 and 6.

15 See Jakubovits and Wolfe (1980), Cummins (1984a), Ogbu (1987), Caplan *et al.* (1992) and Corson (1995b).

16 Laos was devastated by systematic American bombing in an undeclared war at the time of the Vietnam War.

17 Chapter 6 suggests why bilingual programmes may not be suitable for immigrant students of secondary school age.

18 See McAndrew (1986), Dhand (1988) and Chester (1989).

19 See Ray (1984), McDougall (1985) and Dei *et al.* (1995).

20 See Corson (1997b).

21 See Luke *et al.* (1995) and Chapter 3 p. 78.

22 See Feuerverger (1994) and V. Edwards and Walker (1994).

23 After Stones, in Corson (1993a); see also Council on Inter-Racial Books for Children (1994).

24 See Kelly (1988) and Bjerrum Nielsen and Davies (1997).

25 See Clewell *et al.* (1992).

26 See the 'detracking' programme described more fully in Chapter 5 pp. 145–8; this programme offers a similar emphasis.

27 Studies cited in Clewell *et al.* (1992).

28 For specific approaches to this kind of planning in areas of culture, gender and language, see Corson (1990) and May (1997b). Also for school policy making on gender issues, see Rudduck (1994).

29 School planning in this area might also address the fact that young women (in the United States) with poor basic skills are three times more likely to become teenage parents than those with average or better skills.

30 Japan is also multi-ethnic of course, but at official levels there is still reluctance to acknowledge the cultural pluralism of the country. Japan's population includes the Ainu aboriginal people, who number around 50,000; large numbers of Korean and Chinese involuntary minorities; other immigrant groups; and the social class/caste of the buraku.

31 See Corson (1991c).

32 See Clewell *et al.* (1992).

33 For more specific and detailed structural and pedagogical reforms, see Gaskell *et al.* (1989), Blackmore and Kenway (1995) and Corson (1997c).

34 Studies cited in Clewell *et al.* (1992).

35 See Tsolidis (1990).

36 See Chapter 5 p. 119.

37 For teacher research methods, see McCarty (1997b).

38 See the discussion of anti-bias policies and practices in Chapter 5, pp. 128ff.

39 See Chisholm and Holland (1987).

40 See Chapter 3 p. 65.

41 For example, a guide reproduced by Clewell *et al.* (1992) addresses the teacher skill of 'asking girls questions'. This guide's recommendations were used successfully in action-research contexts in the United States. They reflect quite clearly the research evidence discussed in this chapter.

42 For small scale and large scale school research methods, see Corson (1990); for a full survey of research methods in language and education, see Hornberger and Corson (1997); and for more on this subject see Chapter 7.

43 See Heath (1983) and Chilcott (1987).

44 See Spindler (1982).

45 Taken from Corson (1992b).

46 See Luke *et al.* (1995).

47 By sitting down in a student's desk to address the class, for example, or by relaxing the posture.

5 Changing the education of the urban poor

1 More than this, inner-city areas are heavily populated by recognizable ethnic groups who tend to be among the poorest members of society (Wilson 1987).

2 History has left behind the 'disadvantage' model of school reform which used to characterize inner-city residents as people not really capable of coping with their lives without professional support (Tomlinson 1984). Present-day critical studies go well beyond this model. See Glasgow (1980), Wilson (1987), Kozol (1991), Tomlinson (1994) and Rury and Mirel (1997).

3 This happened even though the Anglo-Australian adolescents spoke English as their mother tongue, were matched in non-verbal reasoning ability with the immigrant children, and shared identical educational backgrounds, except for ESL exposure (Corson 1995b).

4 See Corson (1990).

5 See Chapter 3 pp. 45–6.

6 See Ford *et al.* (1994) and Lipman (1997).

7 See Ryan (1998).
8 See Harré and Gillett (1994) for more on this discursive analysis of racism.
9 In J. Thompson (1984).
10 See Dei *et al.* (1995).
11 Bascia (1996) reports a number of studies of schools where teachers tend to be identified with particular groups of students. Those teaching lower stream or culturally different students get less administrative support, less say over the timetable, and less respect from their colleagues.
12 See the 'discursive courtesies' at the end of Chapter 4.
13 See Ford *et al.* (1994).
14 See Au and Kawakami (1994).
15 There are many documented accounts of Jewish people who escaped severe persecution during the Holocaust, even though they were in close daily contact with the worst perpetrators of racist acts who also knew them to be Jewish. They were spared sometimes because they performed services for the perpetrators, but also because their racial appearance did not suggest 'the other'.
16 I use the term 'language variety' to cover any non-standard form of a language, whether a geographical or social dialect, a patois, a creole, or some other code of a language. Most speakers of a language use a variety which differs in recognizable ways from 'the standard' variety; none of these varieties is in any sense inherently inferior to the standard variety in grammar, accent, or phonology (Corson 1994). At the same time, these sociocultural and geographical variations within a language are signalling matters of great importance to those who use them. Varieties serve valuable group identity functions for their speakers; they express interests that are closely linked to matters of self-respect and other psychological attributes. It follows that different language varieties deserve respect and recognition in education.
17 The patois used by many children in Britain of Caribbean origin provides a continuum of codes which the children often range across, switching their code depending on the context (V. Edwards 1986). Examples of code-switching of this kind are to be found to some extent in every community where modern schools operate. They offer a different dimension of language variation. For example, Hewitt (1989) identifies two kinds of 'creole' operating among Londoners of Caribbean descent: the relatively stable community language of the older generations of Caribbean immigrants into Britain; and the 'London-Jamaican' anti-language of the young. The former is a creatively developed community language, serving the normal range of everyday functions that community languages serve; the latter is a strategic and contextually variable use of Creole to mark race in the context of the daily anti-racist struggle that adolescents find themselves in. In fact, this form of Creole is structured to heighten its contrast with other forms of language. All this means that there is greater diversity in language varieties than most people realize, and this kind of language knowledge is highly local and context specific. So sometimes it is not easy to make teachers aware of differences that only they themselves are in a position to discover.
18 'Les enfants bâillonnés'.
19 Labov was a protagonist in a celebrated court case that took place in Ann Arbor, Michigan. As part of its judgment in favour of parents, the court

required teachers of culturally different children to take a course of in-service training in sociolinguistics (Labov 1982). In this case, the parents of African American children had brought an action against a school, alleging that their children were failing because they were wrongly labelled 'educationally disabled' on the basis of their use of an African American non-standard variety. But it was found that the language variety used by the children, in itself, was in no sense an obstacle to their success. Rather, the expectations of pupil success that teachers held, based on their stereotypes about that variety, led the school as a whole to misperceive the children's real potential, thus causing them to fail. The children were deemed to be deficient in educational potential because their language variety was wrongly judged to be deficient in the context of the school. Generalizing on this point, much of the blame for misjudgements of this kind is due to simple ignorance among people about the range and regularity of varieties.

20 'Ebonics' is a name given to the varieties of African American English which retain traces of African languages in their forms and structures. Unfortunately the use of this single name is probably not helpful to the debate, because it suggests that these many varieties are only one single variety. This adds to a related difficulty that people have when thinking about so-called 'standard English', which is also not one but many varieties, probably best represented only by written English.

21 See the discussion on non-standard varieties in Canada in Chapter 6 p. 190.

22 Notice that I am describing the 'standard language' as a 'variety' too. As a first step in ending discrimination against non-standard varieties, it is important to see the so-called standard as exactly that too. Again, the standard variety of most languages is not much more than their written varieties reapplied in speech.

23 Harry *et al.* (1995) and Tomlinson (1984). Also see the discussion of the over-representation of students from backgrounds of diversity in special education classes in Chapter 6 pp. 170f.

24 See Chapter 1 pp. 7–8.

25 See Corson (1993a).

26 See the discussion of this topic in Chapter 3 pp. 64–6 and also the risk of stereotyping children by discourse norms on pp. 79–80.

27 Formal educational settings are rich in 'key situations' like sharing time: see Chapter 3 p. 65.

28 Philips (1983) refers to this classroom event as 'show and tell', which is what it is often called in other English-speaking countries. She reports that this participant structure is one that teachers can rarely use with Warm Springs Indian children, because the children are reluctant to participate fully in the activity, even when they reach the senior years of schooling.

29 See Nielsen and Piché (1981), Graves (1986) and Isaacson (1988).

30 See Purves (1988) and Corson (1995b).

31 By 'senior levels' here, I mean formal education provided for children of 12 years and older.

32 See Hoggart (1958), Klein (1965), Nisbet (1967) and E. P. Thompson (1968).

33 I am not suggesting that all poorer working class children are markedly different from upper middle class children in the life experiences that admit them to aca-

demic meaning systems, only that most are. At the same time, children whose families are on the more economically privileged side of the division of labour, are likely to have very different experiences and contacts. These different things more often reveal the rules of use necessary for academic word learning. And the effects of these privileged experiences on active vocabulary range begin to show up most dramatically in the years of middle adolescence (Corson 1995b).

34 See Mercy and Steelman (1982), W. Hall *et al.* (1984), Wells (1986), West and Stanovich (1991) and Stanovich and Cunningham (1992).

35 See Walberg and Tsai (1983).

36 See Chapter 4 pp. 85–6.

37 See Chapter 1 p. 5.

38 A study of the meaning systems that embed gender typologies is an example here. Holland and Quinn (1987) argue that the words that make up the gender labels used by students relate only obliquely to the meaning system that supports the students' knowledge of gender relations. The words themselves label people who infringe cultural norms about gender relations. But really understanding those words means understanding the relations, not just the words as labels.

39 Elsewhere I say more about the overformality and pseudo-prestige of this Graeco-Latin vocabulary (Corson 1995b).

40 The intricate factors underlying that inequality have recently come more to light through the work of Scollon and Scollon (1981), Scribner and Cole (1981), Gumperz (1982), Heath (1983), Philips (1983), Goody (1987), Gee (1988), Hamilton *et al.* (1994), Agnihotri (1997), Auerbach (1997) and Street (1997) among many others. See the discussion of literacy and cultural diversity in Chapter 3 pp. 74–5.

41 Perhaps an important effect of these more general anti-bias policies would be to counter the 'identity politics' that Giroux (1993) presents as a devastating side-effect of the civil rights and other movements.

42 Like the immigrant girls, who were the subject of Chapter 4.

43 See Corson (1997e).

44 Also see the two strategies suggested by Cazden discussed in Chapter 3 pp. 69–71 and discussion in the next section on bringing youth cultures into the work of the school.

45 For youth cultures in North America, England and Northern Ireland, see studies by Humphries (1981), R. Jenkins (1983), Macpherson (1983) and Fine (1991). Willis (1977) and Corrigan (1979) are the forerunners in this tradition with their powerful descriptions of the alienation of working-class young people from schools.

46 See the discussion of Fairclough's 'rewording' in Chapter 1 pp. 7–8.

47 See Chapter 4 pp. 99ff.

48 See Corson (1991c).

49 See Chapter 4 pp. 103–4.

50 See Bryk *et al.* (1984), Chubb and Moe (1986), Coleman and Hoffer (1987) and Wehlage *et al.* (1989).

51 Especially in many of the fourteen schools examined by Wehlage *et al.* (1989).

52 This approach to reform is different from the so-called 'charter schools'

operating in Alberta, which are different again from the 'charters' that New Zealand schools negotiate with the Ministry of Education there. All three policies have different ideologies, different aims, and different results. *These approaches to schooling should not be confused by the accidental use of the word 'charters' in describing them.*

53 See Dei *et al.* (1995).

54 See Luke *et al.* (1995).

55 See Au and Kawakami (1994).

56 See King (1994).

57 See King (1994).

58 See Ford *et al.* (1994) and Luke *et al.* (1995).

59 See Henry (1992).

60 Elsewhere I write at length about standard and non-standard language varieties, and their valuation in education (Corson 1993a; 1997c; 1997d).

61 For example, new aboriginal varieties of English are appearing as aboriginal peoples try to relate their own languages to English and French in Canada (or to English in Australia: see J. Harris (1991). From a comparative study of 200 teachers in Saskatchewan and in the Australian state of Queensland, Blair (1986) concludes that older teachers with more experience tend to support a deficit model of non-standard language (i.e. they believe that non-standard varieties are in some way deficient in the forms and structures that schools need), while younger teachers tend to support a difference model of non-standard language (i.e. they believe that non-standard varieties are different from the language that is presently valued in schools). In spite of this, Blair reports that neither young nor old teachers are prepared to tolerate non-standard varieties from aboriginal students in their classrooms.

62 See Clark and Ivanic (1997) and Janks (1997). See the next section for a fuller discussion.

63 See Andersson and Trudgill (1990).

64 Conversely, sometimes technically incorrect language usages acquire prestige and become the more accepted form. For example, millions of speakers of English say 'between you and I' when the grammatically correct form is 'between you and me'. Also millions of North Americans say 'off of' when they mean just 'off'.

65 Let me stress the point that children need to be aware of the social and historical factors that make one variety of the language more 'appropriate' in prestigious contexts, and others only in contexts at the margins of polite discourse. But Fairclough (1992) asks teachers and others to think carefully about what they mean when they use the idea of 'appropriateness' to discuss the respective place of standard and non-standard varieties in schools. He sees the idea of 'appropriateness' itself as a compromise that allows a standard variety to maintain its position of prestige, thus confusing sociolinguistic reality with ideology.

66 See Corson (1993a).

67 See Auerbach (1997), Janks (1997) and Wallace (1997).

68 Elsewhere I suggest ways of setting out a formal programme of work under these three themes (Corson 1993a).

69 For example, social class varieties, aboriginal varieties, dialects of immigrant languages, etc.

70 For example, English and the Gaelic languages of Britain; Spanish and English in California and New Mexico; and the two official languages of Canada.

71 See Stein and Potenza (1995).

72 See Janks (1993).

73 See R. Gilbert (1997) and Luke (1997); see too the discussion of Freire's ideas in Chapter 2 pp. 26–7.

74 The ideas here draw especially on Corson (1993a), Bigelow *et al.* (1994), Cummins and Sayers (1995), Street (1997) and Luke (1997).

75 One criticism of this reforming effort is its tendency to conceive of educational success mainly in terms of access to higher education.

76 See the discussion of Bourdieu's ideas in Chapter 1 pp. 9–11.

77 Adapted from Lemke (1990).

78 See Tiede (1996) and Ballenger (1997).

79 Many first language English speakers, from marginal social backgrounds, may be so affected by the traditional norms of discourse required in regular science classrooms that they are left with two choices: either use the formal style, or remain silent. For many students, the idea of relating to science in their colloquial and informal language seems out of the question.

80 See Olson (1997).

81 See Ceci (1990) and Cipielewski and Stanovich (1992).

82 See Corson (1995b).

83 Some of my own work in this area has tried to change initial teacher education so that different oral language practices can begin to enter classrooms (Corson 1984; 1988a).

84 See Wells (1989; 1992), Davies and Corson (1997), V. Edwards (1997), Lyle (1997), Mercer (1997) and Westgate (1997).

85 See Sinclair and Coulthard (1975).

86 See R. Young (1992), Alloway and Gilbert (1997b), R. Gilbert (1997) and Grundy (1997).

87 See A. Edwards and Westgate (1994) and Davies and Corson (1997).

88 See Chapter 6 pp. 179–80.

89 See Johnson *et al.* (1989).

90 See McGonigal (1997).

91 See N. Jenkins and Cheshire (1990) and Cheshire and Jenkins (1991).

92 See Corson (1990) and May (1997b).

93 See the stages of critical policy making described in Chapters 1 and 2.

94 See Chapter 4 pp. 105–7.

95 For example, a British report suggests that schools should designate a senior member of staff who could be responsible for school and community links (Tomlinson 1984). This kind of delegated responsibility is very necessary for dealing with complex interests that can too easily 'fall through the cracks'.

96 Oakes asks schools to dare to be different, because 'the central lesson of the effective-schools research is that, under the right conditions, inner-city poor and minority children can learn' (Oakes 1987: 54). For critical insights into the role that schools can play in communities where class and cultural diversity is commonplace, see Connell *et al.* (1982).

97 See Wang and Gordon (1994).

98 See Murphy (1980), Fargher and Ziersch (1981), Pascal (1987) and Lipman (1997).
99 See the four points from Bourdieu's analysis in Chapter 1 that link schools with parents and pupils as interacting agents in reproducing educational disadvantage.
100 See the discussion of the 1989 national reforms in New Zealand in Chapter 3.
101 See Chapter 2. By the early 1990s a variety of educational systems, separated by distance and ideology, had begun to devolve more and more decision making in important areas to individual schools and their communities. These systems now include England and Wales (*Education Reform Act 1988*, 1989); Sweden; Edmonton, Canada (Education Board 1989; McConaghy 1989); Chicago (Hess 1992; 1994); New South Wales (NSW Department of Education 1989; Sharpe 1993); Western Australia (Ministry of Education 1987); Victoria (Minister of Education 1983/84); and New Zealand. In New Zealand the devolution process moved most swiftly (Lange 1992).
102 Examples include Dade County, Rochester, Boston and others (Forsyth and Tallerico 1993).
103 See Smyth (1993; 1996).
104 See National Coalition of Advocates for Students (1992) and Cummins (1996).

6 Changing the education of minority language groups

1 I use the phrase 'linguistic minority' deliberately to distinguish this category of minorities from the other types of language minorities discussed in this chapter.
2 Throughout this chapter, the word 'immigrants', refers to immigrants and refugees. In some places, there is a distinction between the two categories of new settlers, and of course there are significant differences for the people themselves that often cast them respectively as 'voluntary' or as 'involuntary' minorities.
3 For broad reviews of the literature, see Corson (1988a; 1990).
4 Chapter 5 discusses the unusually high word-learning demands of secondary education and recommends approaches for teaching and curriculum.
5 See the *Report of the Royal Commission on Learning in Ontario* (1995).
6 In US jails, more than 80 per cent of prisoners are high school dropouts. Each one costs the government a minimum of $20,000 a year. In Canada, it costs nearly $70,000 to keep one young offender in secure custody for one year, not including treatment or rehabilitation.
7 See the discussion of the need for 'shared experiences' and how these change across cultures and across student age groups, in Chapter 3 pp. 70–1.
8 For the role of age in acquiring a second language, see Harley (1997).
9 Nemetz Robinson (1978), cited in Corson (1993a: 73).
10 See Cummins (1984b) and Cummins and Swain (1986).
11 See Cummins and Swain (1986) and Carey (1991).
12 Like the work of Sanchez (1934).
13 In other words, this means the sort of proficiency in their first languages that older ESL learners usually have.

14 Comparison studies like these are very difficult to organize, however, because of the huge variations in bilingual practice that exist in schools. Researchers report that many American bilingual classrooms are bilingual in name only, and really are more like regular classrooms (Wong-Fillmore and Valdez 1986). This may help explain the results of a study by Ramirez (1992) that found no significant differences in student achievement between three different 'bilingual' approaches.

15 See Campos and Keatinge (1988) and Gándara (1994).

16 See the later section on linguistic minorities.

17 Later in this chapter there is a longer list of ways to value first languages that can be used even in schools that do not have bilingual education programmes.

18 I turn to these matters again in the conclusion to the chapter.

19 For example, recommendations made by Au and Jordan (1981) and by Heath (1983). Similarly, Cazden (1990) finds that teachers in New Zealand are rather reluctant to apply the findings of research and change their teaching with Maori children.

20 See Cummins (1984a; 1987; 1989).

21 Paradoxically a developing problem in parts of the United States is the *under-representation* of linguistic minority students in special education classes for the learning disabled. This underuse of referral services is thought to be a reaction against the litigation and protests that have accompanied some high profile cases of overrepresentation. Researchers are beginning to document the plight of low achieving minority language students left, with good intentions but unwisely, in regular clasrooms (Gersten and Woodward 1994).

22 Another partial explanation for the overreferral of minority language students to special education services is the pressure that teachers work under, and the very real increase in pressure that minority language students can bring with them into regular classrooms. A factor in overreferral can be a given teacher's sincere belief that he or she is unable to provide adequate instruction for a given child from a diverse background (Gersten and Woodward 1994).

23 See Chapter 3 p. 73.

24 See Cummins and Danesi (1990) and J. Edwards (1993). These heritage programmes have been renamed International Language Programs in Ontario.

25 See Clapham and Corson (1997).

26 See Tucker and Corson (1997).

27 See the concluding section on pp. 198–200.

28 See Hamayan (1997).

29 See Reid (1988) and Clegg (1996).

30 For some guidance on approaches here, see discussion of the 'untracking' programmes in Chapter 5 pp. 145–8.

31 See Chapter 5 pp. 132f.

32 Students from backgrounds where first language literacy levels are low have special needs. They are typically three or more years below their age appropriate grade level and their acquisition of literacy in English is usually slow and difficult. Hamayan (1997) sees problems with the nature of ESL literacy programmes themselves. These programmes are usually based on phonetic approaches that assume mastery of an English sound system that new arrivals

just do not have. She suggests that partially literate students would benefit from programmes that stress meaning-based literacy experiences that match their oral language use quite closely.

33 See Cummins and Swain (1986) and Klesmer (1994).

34 See Carter and McCarthy (1988), P. Nation and Carter (1989), McCarthy (1990), I. Nation (1990), Meara (1993); Harley (1995) and Lawson and Hogben (1996).

35 Academic Graeco-Latin words are mainly literary in their use. Most native speakers begin to encounter these words in quantity in their upper primary school reading and in the formal secondary school setting. So their introduction in literature or textbooks, rather than in conversation, restricts people's access to them. Printed texts provide much more exposure to these words than oral ones. For example, even children's books contain 50 per cent more rare words than either adult prime-time television or the conversations of university graduates, while popular magazines have three times as many rare words as television and informal conversation (Corson 1995b).

36 See Crandall (1997) and Singleton (1997).

37 This approach is developing in some places, notably in Vancouver and in England (Clegg 1996).

38 See Gass and Selinker (1983) and Harley (1995).

39 See Ard and Homburg (1983), Ringbom (1987), Hancin-Bhatt and Nagy (1994), Ellis and Beaton (1995), Harley (1995) and Umbel and Oller (1995). For example, Spanish/English bilingual students find low frequency Latinate words in English less difficult because the cognate words in Spanish are high frequency, everyday words (e.g. INFIRM, ENFERMO [Sp. 'sick']: Hancin-Bhatt and Nagy 1994).

40 See Van Lier and Corson (1997).

41 See Chapter 5 pp. 138–41.

42 See Corson (1995b).

43 See Chapter 5 pp. 122ff.

44 See an earlier section in this chapter: examples of collaborative organization include integrated and cooperative teaching, paired teaching, parallel teaching and programming, and rotation teaching (pp. 175–7).

45 See Chapter 5 pp. 139–41.

46 Their book also offers lots of practical material for curriculum planners: a list of Language Arts Listservs, E-Journals and Newsletters, Usenet Newsgroups, Gophers, World Wide Web, and Telnet sites; a Guide to the Internet for Parents and Teachers; and Selected Annotated Listings of Internet Resources for K-12 Education.

47 See Chapter 5 p. 153: See N. Hall and Robinson (1996).

48 Its personnel procedures are so successful that they have been adopted city-wide in New York and approved for system-wide use (DeFazio 1997).

49 See Chapter 5 pp. 132–3.

50 A problem with this approach, for minority language communities, is that this kind of mixed immersion education has been found in Canadian francophone minority settings, to gradually erode francophone children's use and command of French. Mougeon and Beniak (1988a; 1988b) see more disadvantages than

gains in francophones opening their schools to the children of the anglophone majority in immersion programmes. But elsewhere this is less of a problem. In Britain native speakers of the Gaelic languages often sit alongside students learning these as second languages. Probably the differences can be explained by the high level of general support that the Gaelic languages receive in the wider community, which contrasts with the very low support for minority French in anglophone Canada.

51 See Lapierre (1988) and Lentz (1988a; 1988b).
52 See Churchill *et al.* (1986), Cummins (1991) and Wagner (1991).
53 Drawing on data comparing an advanced level French class of mostly middle class students, with a general level class of mostly working-class students, Heller (1995) argues that the interests of middle class students coincide with those of the school, which is directed towards language standardization. At the same time, the school leaves working-class students on the academic margins, along with their non-standard varieties.
54 See Baril (1986), Landry and Allard (1987; 1991), Levasseur-Ouimet (1989) and Gérin-Lajoie (1997).
55 See Chapter 5's section on 'Bias against non-standard varieties' (pp. 137–9).
56 For critical literacy see Chapter 5 pp. 142–3.
57 See Cummins and Swain on pp. 162–3.
58 See Rodda *et al.* (1986), Stewart and Akamatsu (1988), Ladd (1991), Israelite *et al.* (1992), Stewart (1993) and Mason (1994); Branson and Miller (1997a).
59 'The most important conclusion drawn from the language assessment data is that all children (whether they are hearing, Deaf, of Deaf parents or hearing parents) have the potential to develop effective bilingual/bicultural skills when exposed to the appropriate environment and language models' (Evans and Zimmer 1993: 69).
60 For example by following the successful and relatively inexpensive model offered in Canada's prairie provinces (see earlier in this chapter).
61 This list is based on Corson (1990), Cummins and Danesi (1990), Provost (1990), Houston (1992), Feuerverger (1994), LaGrange *et al.* (1994) and Auerbach (1997).
62 See Cummins (1996) for examples of the successful involvement of parents from marginal backgrounds in their children's education.

7 Making the educational world safe for students from diverse backgrounds

1 See the discussion of Blair's research in note 61 to Chapter 5 for an illustration of this point.
2 See the Conclusion to Chapter 3 pp. 80–1.
3 For example, the entire People's Republic of China has become part of the capitalist world although it is steeped in a system of oppression that is hostile to the very freedoms that allowed capitalism to flourish in the nineteenth century.
4 All this seems very damaging to the long term future of human beings in general.

The rampant individualism typical of the modern capitalist marketplace can carelessly sacrifice the general good for the sake of the wants, not the needs, of well placed individuals.

5   See note 6 of Chapter 1 for a definition of 'structures'.

6   See the outline of Foucault's ideas in Chapter 1 p. 5.

7   There is a bitter irony in the role that schools play: to develop autonomous human beings who value freedom, schools take away that freedom for twelve years or so, and compel children to the constraints of institutions that no adults would allow themselves to be students in. This creates massive contradictions for formal education that most people take for granted.

8   Positive Entertainment Alternatives for Children Everywhere (PEACE) was founded in Québec in the early 1990s. Its work is endorsed by the Ontario Teachers' Federation and the Canadian Teachers' Federation.

9   See the special issue of *Language and Education* guest edited by Sarangi and Baynham: 'Discursive construction of educational identities' (vol. 10: 2 and 3, 1996); see also the many studies in Corson (1995a).

10 See Fairclough (1985), Wodak (1989) and Peirce (1997).

11 See Angus (1986), Anderson (1989), May (1994; 1997a) and Beynon (1997).

12 See Chapter 1 pp. 8–11.

13 This is not to say that teacher education and professional development are over-looked in critical research. They are certainly 'sites' where teachers, who are learning about teaching often resist unwanted pressures to conform (see Ginsburg and Newman 1985; Kanpol 1988; Smyth 1991; Corson 1995a; and Beynon 1997).

14 This was not always the case. A generation ago (in Australia and England at least), teachers mainly came from working class backgrounds, and joined the ranks of the middle classes by becoming teachers. Present-day costs of taking part in higher education, in English-speaking countries, mean that teaching is increasingly reserved for people who come from more affluent backgrounds. As a result, teachers are more and more distant in culture and interests from most of the students that they meet.

15 See discussion of the idea of 'generative theme', that Freire introduced into educational practice, in Chapter 2 pp. 26–7.

REFERENCES

AACLAME (1990) *The National Policy on Languages: Report to the Minister for Employment, Education and Training by the Australian Advisory Council on Languages and Multicultural Education.* Canberra: AACLAME.

AAUW Report (1995) *How Schools Shortchange Girls: A Study of Major Findings on Girls and Education.* New York: Marlowe.

Abbott, C. (1997) Information technology and literacy, in V. Edwards and D. Corson (eds) *Literacy.* Boston, MA: Kluwer.

Abella, R. (1991) Solidarity attacked by exclusion: respecting equality and diversity. *Queen's Quarterly,* 98: 353–62.

Abi-Nader, J. (1993) Meeting the needs of multicultural classrooms: family values and the motivation of minority students, in M. O'Hair and S. Odell (eds) *Diversity and Teaching.* Fort Worth, TX: Harcourt.

Aggleton, P. (1997) *Rebels without a Cause.* London: Falmer.

Agnihotri, R. (1997) Sustaining local literacies, in V. Edwards and D. Corson (eds) *Literacy.* Boston, MA: Kluwer.

Albert, M. and Obler, L. (1979) *The Bilingual Brain.* New York: Academic Press.

Alloway, L. and Gilbert, P. (1997a) Boys and literacy: lessons from Australia. *Gender and Education,* 9: 49–58.

Alloway, L. and Gilbert, P. (1997b) Post-structuralist theory and classroom talk, in B. Davies and D. Corson (eds) *Oral Discourse and Education.* Boston, MA: Kluwer.

Anderson, G. (1989) Critical ethnography in education: origins, current status and new directions. *Review of Educational Research,* 59: 249–70.

Andersson, L. and Trudgill, P. (1990) *Bad Language.* Oxford: Basil Blackwell.

Angus, L. (1986) Developments in ethnographic research in education: from interpretive to critical ethnography. *Journal of Research and Development in Education,* 20: 59–67.

Appel, R. (1988) The language education of immigrant workers' children in the Netherlands, in T. Skutnabb-Kangas and J. Cummins (eds) *Minority Education: From Shame to Struggle.* Clevedon: Multilingual Matters.

Apple, M. (1982) *Education and Power*. London: Routledge.

Applebee, A., Langer, J. and Mullis, I. (1987) *The Nation's Report Card: Learning to be Literate: Reading*. Princeton, NJ: Educational Testing Service.

Ard, J. and Homburg, T. (1983) Verification of language transfer, in S. Gass and L. Selinker (eds) *Language Transfer in Language Learning*. Rowley, MA: Newbury House.

Arnot, M. and Weiner, G. (eds) (1987) *Gender and the Politics of Schooling*. London: Unwin Hyman.

Artiles, A. and Trent, S. (1994) Overrepresentation of minority students in special education: a continuing debate. *Journal of Special Education*, 27: 410–37.

Assembly of First Nations (1988) *Tradition and Education: Towards a Vision of Our Future*. Ottawa: Assembly of First Nations.

Au, K. (1978) Participation structures in a reading lesson with Hawaiian children: analysis of a culturally appropriate instructional event. *Anthropology and Education Quarterly*, 11: 91-115.

Au, K. and Jordan, C. (1981) Teaching reading to Hawaiian children: finding culturally appropriate solutions, in H. Truba, G. Guthrie and K. Au (eds) *Culture and the Bilingual Classroom: Studies in Classroom Ethnography*. Rowley, MA: Newbury House.

Au, K. and Kawakami, A. (1994) Cultural congruence in instruction, in E. Hollins, J. King and W. Hayman (eds) *Teaching Diverse Populations*. Albany, NY: State University of New York Press.

Au, K. and Mason, J. (1983) Cultural congruence in classroom participation structures: achieving a balance of rights. *Discourse Processes*, 6: 145–67.

Auerbach, E. (1997) Family literacy, in V. Edwards and D. Corson (eds) *Literacy*. Boston, MA: Kluwer.

Baffin Divisional Board of Education (1989) *Piniaqtavut: Integrated Program*. Baffin Island: Baffin Divisional Board of Education.

Baker, C. (1988) *Key Issues in Bilingualism and Bilingual Education*. Clevedon: Multilingual Matters.

Baker, C. (1997) Bilingual education in Ireland, Scotland and Wales, in J. Cummins and D. Corson (eds) *Bilingual Education*. Boston, MA: Kluwer.

Bakhtin, M. (1981 [1975]) *The Dialogic Imagination: Four Essays*. Austin, TX: University of Texas Press.

Ballenger, C. (1997) Science talk in a bilingual classroom. *Language and Education*, 11: 1–14.

Balto, A. and Todal, J. (1997) Saami bilingual education, in J. Cummins and D. Corson (eds) *Bilingual Education*. Boston, MA: Kluwer.

Baran, G. (1987) Teaching girls science, in M. McNeil (ed.) *Gender and Expertise*. London: Free Association Books.

Baril, P.-A. (1986) Dominance linguistique et maintien de la langue chez la jeunesse franco-manitobaine. *Centre d'études franco-canadienne de l'ouest*, 24: 14–29.

Bascia, N. (1996) Inside and outside: minority immigrant teachers in Canadian schools. *Qualitative Studies in Education*, 9: 151–65.

Battiste, M. and Barman, J. (1995) *First Nations Education in Canada: The Circle Unfolds*. Vancouver: University of British Columbia Press.

Baugh, J. (1983) *Black Street Speech: Its History, Structure and Survival*. Austin, TX: University of Texas Press.

Baugh, J. (1997) Research on race and social class in language acquisition and use, in N. Hornberger and D. Corson (eds) *Research Methods in Language and Education*. Boston, MA: Kluwer.

Bernstein, B. (1975) On the classification and framing of educational knowledge, in B. Bernstein (ed.) *Class, Codes and Control Volume 3: Towards a Theory of Educational Transmissions*. London: Routledge and Kegan Paul.

Beynon, C. (1997) 'Crossing over from student to teacher', unpublished PhD thesis. University of Toronto.

Bhaskar, R. (1986) *Scientific Realism and Human Emancipation*. London: Verso.

Bigelow, B., Christensen, L., Karp, S., Miner, B. and Peterson, B. (1994) *Rethinking Our Classrooms*. Milwaukee, WI: Rethinking Schools.

Biggs, N. and Edwards, V. (1991) 'I treat them all the same': teacher–pupil talk in multi-ethnic classrooms. *Language and Education*, 5: 161–76.

Bjerrum Nielsen, H. and Davies, B. (1997) The construction of gendered identity through classroom talk, in B. Davies and D. Corson (eds) *Oral Discourse and Education*. Boston, MA: Kluwer.

Black, D. (1997) Educator honored for her work with deaf, *Toronto Star*, 3 May.

Blackmore, J. and Kenway, J. (1995) Changing schools, teachers, and curriculum: but what about the girls?, in D. Corson (ed.) *Discourse and Power in Educational Organizations*. Cresskill, NJ: Hampton Press.

Blair, H. (1986) Teacher's attitudes toward the oral English of indigenous children in Saskatchewan and Queensland, in *Mokakit: Selected Papers from the First Mokakit Conference*, 25–27 July 1984, Vancouver, 22–35.

Bottomley, G. (1977) Women, the family, and social change, in M. Bowen (ed.) *Australia 2000: The Ethnic Impact*. Armidale, NSW: University of New England Publishing Unit.

Bourdieu, P. (1966) L'école conservatrice. *Revue Française de Sociologie*, 7: 225–6; 330-42; 346–7.

Bourdieu, P. (1971) Systems of education and systems of thought, in M. Young (ed.) *Knowledge and Control*. London: Collier Macmillan.

Bourdieu, P. (1981) *Ce que parler veut dire: l'économie des échanges linguistique*. Paris: Fayard.

Bourdieu, P. (1984) *Distinction: A Social Critique of the Judgement of Taste*. Cambridge, MA: Harvard University Press.

Boykin, A. (1994) Harvesting talent and culture: African American children and educational reform, in R. Rossi (ed.) *Schools and Students at Risk*. New York: Teachers College Press.

Brady, P. (1991) An analysis of program delivery services in First Nations, federal, and provincial schools in Northwestern Ontario. *Canadian Journal of Native Education*, 18(1): 65–71.

Brandl, M. (1983) A certain heritage: women and their children in north Australia, in F. Gale (ed.) *We are Bosses Ourselves: The Status and Role of Aboriginal Women Today*. Canberra: Australian Institute of Aboriginal Studies.

Branson, J. (1991) Gender, education and work, in D. Corson (ed.) *Education for Work*. Clevedon: Multilingual Matters.

Branson, J. and Miller, D. (1995) Sign language and the discursive construction of power over the Deaf through education, in D. Corson (ed.) *Discourse and Power in Educational Organizations*. Cresskill, NJ: Hampton Press.

Branson, J. and Miller, D. (1997a) National sign languages and language policies, in R. Wodak and D. Corson (eds) *Language Policies and Political Issues*. Boston, MA: Kluwer.

Branson, J. and Miller, D. (1997b) Research methods for studying the language of the signing Deaf, in N. Hornberger and D. Corson (eds) *Research Methods in Language and Education*. Boston, MA: Kluwer.

Britzman, D. (1991) *Practice Makes Practice*. Albany, NY: State University of New York Press.

Bruck, M. (1984) The suitability of immersion education for children with special needs, in C. Rivera (ed.) *Communicative Competence Approaches to Language Proficiency Assessment*. Clevedon: Multilingual Matters.

Bruner, J. (1972) *The Relevance of Education*. Harmondsworth: Penguin.

Bryk, A. and Driscoll, M. (1988) *The High School as Community: Contextual Influences and Consequences for Students and Teachers*. Madison, WI: National Center on Effective Schools.

Bryk, A., Holland, P., Lee, V. and Carriedo, R. (1984) *Effective Catholic Schools: An Exploration*. Washington, DC: National Center for Research in Total Catholic Education.

Campos, S. and Keatinge, H. (1988) The Carpinteria language minority student experience: from theory, to practice, to success, in T. Skutnabb-Kangas and J. Cummins (eds) *Minority Education: From Shame to Struggle*. Clevedon: Multilingual Matters.

Canadian Association of the Deaf (1990) Vision 2000 Conference a huge success. *The Deaf Canadian Advocate*, 5(12): 1–2.

Caplan, N., Choy, H. and Whitmore, J. (1992) Indochinese refugee families and academic achievement. *Scientific American*, 266(2): 36–42.

Carey, T. (1991) The culture of literacy in majority and minority language schools. *Canadian Modern Language Review*, 47: 950–76.

Carter, R. and McCarthy, M. (1988) *Vocabulary in Language Teaching*. London: Longman.

Cazden, C. (1988) *Classroom Discourse: The Language of Teaching and Learning*. Portsmouth, NH: Heinemann.

Cazden, C. (1989) Richmond Road: a multilingual/multicultural primary school in Auckland, New Zealand. *Language and Education*, 3: 143–66.

Cazden, C. (1990) Differential treatment in New Zealand: reflections on research in minority education. *Teaching and Teacher Education*, 6: 291–303.

Ceci, S. (1990) *On Intelligence . . . More or Less: A Bio-Ecological Treatise on Intellectual Development*. Englewood Cliffs, NJ: Prentice Hall.

Chall, J. (1987) Two vocabularies for reading: recognition and meaning, in M. G. McKeown and M. E. Curtis (eds) *The Nature of Vocabulary Acquisition*. Hillsdale, NJ: Lawrence Erlbaum.

Chamot, A. (1988) Bilingualism in education and bilingual education: the state of the art in the United States. *Journal of Multilingual and Multicultural Development*, 9: 11–35.

Cheshire, J. and Jenkins, N. (1991) Gender differences in the GCSE Oral English Examination: Part 2. *Language and Education*, 5: 19–40.

Chester, R. D. (1989) Picture this: portrayal of visible minorities in basal readers. *Reading Canada Lecture*, 7: 213–17.

Chilcott, J. (1987) Where are you coming from and where are you going? The reporting of ethnographic research. *American Educational Research Journal*, 24: 199–218.

Chisholm, L. and Holland, J. (1987) Anti-sexist action research in school: the Girls and Occupational Choice Project, in G. Weiner and M. Arnot (eds) *Gender under Scrutiny: New Inquiries in Education*. London: Unwin Hyman.

Christie, M. (1988) The invasion of aboriginal education, in Institute of Applied Aboriginal Studies, *Learning My Way (Waikaru 16)*. Perth: Western Australia College of Advanced Education.

Chubb, J. and Moe, T. (1986) *Politics, Markets and the Organization of Schools*. Washington, DC: Brookings Institution.

Churchill, S., Frenette, N. and Quazi, S. (1986) *Éducation et Besoins des Franco-Ontariens: Le Diagnostic d'un Système d'Éducation*. Toronto: Le Conseil de l'Éducation Franco-Ontarienne.

Cipielewski, J. and Stanovich, K. (1992) Predicting growth in reading ability from children's exposure to print. *Journal of Experimental Child Psychology*, 54: 74–89.

Clapham, C. and Corson, D. (1997) *Language Testing and Assessment*. Boston, MA: Kluwer.

Clark, R. and Ivanic, R. (1997) Critical discourse analysis and educational change, in L. van Lier and D. Corson (eds) *Knowledge about Language*. Boston, MA: Kluwer.

Clegg, J. (1996) *Mainstreaming ESL*. Clevedon: Multilingual Matters.

Clewell, B., Anderson, B. and Thorpe, M. (1992) *Breaking the Barriers: Helping Female and Minority Students Succeed in Mathematics and Science*. San Francisco, CA: Jossey-Bass.

Coleman, J. and Hoffer, T. (1987) *Public and Private High Schools: The Impact of Communities*. New York: Basic Books.

Collier, V. (1992) A synthesis of studies examining long-term language-minority student data on academic achievement. *Bilingual Research Journal*, 16: 187–212.

Comer, J. (1984) Home/school relationships as they affect the academic success of children. *Education and Urban Society*, 16: 323–37.

Common, R. and Frost, L. (1988) The implications of the mismeasurement of Native students' intelligence through the use of standardized intelligence tests. *Canadian Journal of Native Education*, 15(1): 18–29.

Commonwealth Schools Commission (1984) *A Review of the Commonwealth English as a Second Language ESL Program*. Canberra: Commonwealth Schools Commission.

Connell, R., Ashenden, D., Kessler, S. and Dowsett, L. (1982) *Making the Difference: Schools, Families and Social Division*. Sydney: Allen and Unwin.

Corenblum, B. and Annis, R. (1987) Racial identity and preference in Native and white Canadian children. *Canadian Journal of Behavioural Sciences*, 19: 224–64.

Corrigan, P. (1979) *Schooling the Smash Street Kids*. London: Macmillan.

Corson, D. (1977) 50,000 Tasmanians? The Adult Literacy Program. *Australian Council for Adult Literacy Occasional Papers*, 1: 3–6.

Corson, D. (1978) Profile of the adult literacy student. *Literacy Work*, 8: 65–8.

Corson, D. (1984) The case for oral language in schooling. *Elementary School Journal*, 84: 458–67.

Corson, D. (1988a) *Oral Language across the Curriculum*. Clevedon: Multilingual Matters.

Corson, D. (1988b) Editorial. *Journal of Education Policy*, 3: 219–22.

Corson, D. (1990) *Language Policy Across the Curriculum*. Clevedon: Multilingual Matters.

Corson, D. (1991a) Educational research and Bhaskar's conception of discovery. *Educational Theory*, 41: 189–98.

Corson, D. (1991b) Bhaskar's critical realism and educational knowledge. *British Journal of Sociology of Education*, 12: 223–41.

Corson, D. (ed.) (1991c) *Education for Work: Background to Policy and Curriculum*. Clevedon: Multilingual Matters.

Corson, D. (1992a) Social justice and minority language policy. *Educational Theory*, 42: 181–200.

Corson, D. (1992b) Language, gender and education: a critical review linking social justice and power. *Gender and Education*, 4: 229–54.

Corson, D. (1993a) *Language, Minority Education and Gender: Linking Social Justice and Power*. Clevedon: Multilingual Matters.

Corson, D. (1993b) Discursive bias and ideology in the administration of minority group interests. *Language in Society*, 22: 165–92.

Corson, D. (1994) Minority social groups and nonstandard discourse: towards a just language policy. *Canadian Modern Language Review*, 50: 271–95.

Corson, D. (ed.) (1995a) *Discourse and Power in Educational Organizations*. Cresskill, NJ: Hampton Press.

Corson, D. (1995b) *Using English Words*. Boston, MA: Kluwer.

Corson, D. (1995c) World view, cultural values and discourse norms: the cycle of cultural reproduction. *International Journal of Intercultural Relations*, 19: 50–66.

Corson, D. (1995d) Norway's 'Sámi Language Act': emancipatory implications for the world's aboriginal peoples. *Language in Society*, 24: 493–514.

Corson, D. (1996) Official-language minority and aboriginal first-language education: implications of Norway's 'Sámi Language Act' for Canada. *Canadian Journal of Education*, 21: 84–104.

Corson, D. (1997a) Awareness of non-standard varieties in the schools, in L. van Lier and D. Corson (eds) *Knowledge about Language*. Boston, MA: Kluwer.

Corson, D. (1997b) Critical realism: an emancipatory philosophy for applied linguistics? *Applied Linguistics*, 18: 166–88.

Corson, D. (1997c) Gender, discourse, and senior education: ligatures for girls, options for boys? in R. Wodak (ed.) *Gender and Discourse*. Thousand Oaks, CA: Sage.

Corson, D. (1997d) Non-standard varieties and educational policy, in R. Wodak and D. Corson (eds) *Language Policy and Political Issues in Education*. Boston, MA: Kluwer.

Corson, D. (1997e) Language policies for indigenous peoples, in R. Wodak and D. Corson (eds) *Language Policy and Political Issues in Education*. Boston, MA: Kluwer.

Corson, D. (1997f) Reclaiming reality: laying the ideology of cultural compatibility. *International Journal of Intercultural Relations*, 21: 105–11.

Corson, D. and Lemay, S. (1996) *Social Justice and Language Policy in Education: The Canadian Research*. Toronto: OISE Press/University of Toronto Press.

Costello, P. and Mitchell, S. (eds) (1995) *Competing and Consensual Voices: The Theory and Practice of Argument*. Clevedon: Multilingual Matters.

Coulombe, P. (1993) Language rights, individual and communal. *Language Problems and Language Planning*, 17: 140–52.

Council on Inter-Racial Books for Children (1994) 10 quick ways to analyze children's books for racism and sexism, in B. Bigelow, L. Christensen, S. Karp, B. Miner and B. Peterson (eds) *Rethinking Our Classrooms*. Milwaukee, WI: Rethinking Schools.

Crago, M. (1990) Development of communicative competence in Inuit children: implications for speech-language pathology assessment. *Journal of Childhood Communication Disorders*, 13: 73–83.

Crago, M. (1992) Communicative interaction and second language acquisition: an Inuit example. *TESOL Quarterly*, 26: 487–505.

Crandall, J. (1997) Language teaching approaches for school-aged learners in second language contexts, in G. Tucker and D. Corson (eds) *Second Language Education*. Boston, MA: Kluwer.

Crystal, D. (1987) *The Cambridge Encyclopedia of Language*. Cambridge: Cambridge University Press.

Cummins, J. (1984a) The minority language child, in S. Shapson and V. D'Oyley (eds) *Bilingual and Multicultural Education: Canadian Perspectives*. Clevedon: Multilingual Matters.

Cummins, J. (1984b) *Bilingualism and Special Education: Issues in Assessment and Pedagogy*. Clevedon: Multilingual Matters.

Cummins, J. (1985) Heritage language education: fact and friction. *Orbit*, 15(1): 3–6.

Cummins, J. (1986) Empowering minority students: a framework for intervention. *Harvard Educational Review*, 56: 18–36.

Cummins, J. (1987) Psychoeducational assessment in multicultural school systems. *Canadian Journal for Exceptional Children*, 3(4): 115–17.

Cummins, J. (1989) A theoretical framework for bilingual special education. *Exceptional Children*, 56: 111–19.

Cummins, J. (1991) 'Literacy and illiteracy: the case of the official language minorities in Canada', unpublished paper presented at the UNESCO seminar on Future Contributions to Literacy in Canada, September.

Cummins, J. (1995) Discursive power in educational policy and practice for culturally diverse students, in D. Corson (ed.) *Discourse and Power in Educational Organizations*. Cresskill, NJ: Hampton Press.

Cummins, J. (1996) *Negotiating Identities: Education for Empowerment in a Diverse Society*. Ontario: California Association for Bilingual Education.

Cummins, J. and Corson, D. (1997) *Bilingual Education*. Amsterdam/Boston, MA: Kluwer.

Cummins, J. and Danesi, M. (1990) *Heritage Languages*. Toronto: Garamond Press.

Cummins, J. and Sayers, D. (1995) *Brave New Schools: Challenging Cultural Illiteracy*. Toronto: OISE Press/University of Toronto Press.

Cummins, J. and Swain, M. (1986) *Bilingualism in Education: Aspects of Theory, Research and Practice*. London: Longman.

Cummins, J., Swain, M., Nakajima, K., Handscombe, J., Green, D. and Tran, C. (1984) Linguistic interdependence among Japanese and Vietnamese immigrant students, in C. Rivera (ed.) *Communicative Competence Approaches to Language Proficiency Assessment*. Philadelphia, PA: Multilingual Matters.

Dahrendorf, R. (1978) *Life Chances*. Chicago: University of Chicago Press.

Daigle, J. (1997) 'An examination of community-based education models in first nations communities', PhD thesis in progress. University of Toronto.

Daniels, H. (1983) *Famous Last Words: The American Language Crisis Reconsidered*. Carbondale, IL: Southern Illinois University Press.

Dannequin, C. (1987) Les enfants bâillonnés: the teaching of French as mother tongue in elementary school. *Language and Education*, 1: 15–31.

Davies, B. and Corson, D. (eds) (1997) *Oral Discourse and Education*. Boston, MA: Kluwer.

DeFazio, A. (1997) Language awareness at the International High School, in L. van Lier and D. Corson (eds) *Knowledge about Language*. Boston, MA: Kluwer.

Dei, G., Holmes, L., Mazzuca, J., McIsaac, E. and Campbell, R. (1995) *Drop Out or Push Out? The Dynamics of Black Students' Disengagement from School*, report for the Ontario Ministry of Education and Training. Ontario Institute for Studies in Education.

Department of Education and Science (1975) *Language for Life (The Bullock Report)*. London: HMSO.

Deyhle, D. and Swisher, K. (1997) Research in American Indian and Alaska Native education: from assimilation to self-determination. *Review of Research in Education*, 22: 113–94.

Dhand, H. (1988) Bias in social studies textbooks: new research findings. *History and Social Science Teacher*, 24: 24–7.

Dixon, R. (1989) The original languages of Australia. *Vox*, 3: 26–33.

Dorais, L.-J. (1992) La situation linguistique dans l'arctique. *Études Inuits Studies*, 16: 237–55.

Durie, A. (1997) Bilingual and immersion education developments in Aotearoa-New Zealand, in J. Cummins and D. Corson (eds) *Bilingual Education*. Boston, MA: Kluwer.

Durkheim, E. (1964 [1893]) *The Division of Labour in Society* (translated by George Simpson). London: Free Press of Glencoe.

Edelman, M. (1984) The political language of the helping professions, in M. Shapiro (ed.) *Language and Politics*. Oxford: Basil Blackwell.

Education Board (1989) *School Budgeting Manual*. Edmonton: Public School Education Board.

Education Reform Act 1988 (1989) London: HMSO.

Edwards, A. (1997) Oral language, culture and class, in B. Davies and D. Corson (eds) *Oral Discourse and Education*. Boston, MA: Kluwer.

Edwards, A. and Westgate, D. (1994) *Investigating Classroom Talk*. Brighton: Falmer.

Edwards, J. (1989) *Language and Disadvantage: Studies in Disorders of Communication*, 2nd edn. London: Cole and Whurr.

Edwards, J. (1993) Identity and language in the Canadian context, in M. Danesi, K. McLeod and S. Morris (eds) *Heritage Languages and Education: The Canadian Experience*. Oakville, Ontario: Mosaic Press.

Edwards, V. (1986) *Language in a Black Community*. Clevedon: Multilingual Matters.

Edwards, V. (1997) Teacher–pupil talk in multi-ethnic classrooms, in B. Davies and D. Corson (eds) *Oral Discourse and Education*. Boston, MA: Kluwer.

Edwards, V. and Redfern, A. (1992) *The World in a Classroom: Language in Education in Britain and Canada*. Clevedon: Multilingual Matters.

Edwards, V. and Walker, S. (1994) Multilingual resources for children. *Language and Education*, 8: 147–56.

Egbo, B. (1997) Female literacy and life chances in rural Nigeria, in V. Edwards and D. Corson (eds) *Literacy*. Boston, MA: Kluwer.

Egbo, B. (1998) *Women, Literacy and Life Chances in Africa*. Clevedon: Multilingual Matters.

Ellis, N. and Beaton, A. (1995) Psycholinguistic determinants of foreign language vocabulary learning, in B. Harley (ed.) *Lexical Issues in Language Learning*. Amsterdam: John Benjamins.

Erickson, F. (1975) Gatekeeping and the melting pot, Harvard Educational Review, 45: 44-70.

Erickson, F. (1996) Transformation and school success: the politics and culture of educational achievement, in E. Jacob and C. Jordan (eds) *Minority Education: Anthropological Perspectives*. Norwood, NJ: Ablex.

Eriks-Brophy, A. and Crago, M. (1994) Transforming classroom discourse: an Inuit example. *Language and Education*, 8: 105–22.

Evans, C. and Zimmer, K. (1993) Sign talk development project, Winnipeg, Manitoba. *ACEHI/ACEDA*, 19: 62–70.

Fairclough, N. (1985) Critical and descriptive goals in discourse analysis. *Journal of Pragmatics*, 9: 739–63.

Fairclough, N. (ed.) (1992) *Critical Language Awareness*. London: Longman.

Fairclough, N. (1995) Critical language awareness and self-identity in education, in D. Corson (ed.) *Discourse and Power in Educational Organizations*. Cresskill, NJ: Hampton Press.

Faltis, C. (1997) Bilingual education in the United States, in J. Cummins and D. Corson (eds) *Bilingual Education*. Boston, MA: Kluwer.

Farah, I. (1997) Ethnography of communication, in N. Hornberger and D. Corson (eds) *Research Methods in Language and Education*. Boston, MA: Kluwer.

Fargher, R. and Ziersch, R. (1981) What happened at Hermansburg?, in *Set*, no. 2. Wellington: NZCER.

Fasold, R. (1984) *The Sociolinguistics of Society*. Oxford: Basil Blackwell.

Fasold, R. (1990) *The Sociolinguistics of Language*. Oxford: Basil Blackwell.

Fesl, E. (1988) 'Language policy formulation and implementation: an historical perspective on Australian languages', unpublished PhD thesis. Monash University.

Feuerverger, G. (1994) A multicultural literacy intervention for minority language students. *Language and Education* 8: 123–46.

Feuerverger, G. (1997) 'On the edges of the map': a study of heritage language teachers in Toronto. *Teaching and Teacher Education*, 13: 39–54.

Feurer, H. (1993) Beyond multilingual education: the Cree of Waskaganish. *Canadian Journal of Native Education*, 20: 87–95.

Fine, M. (1988) Sexuality, schooling, and adolescent females: the missing discourse of desire. *Harvard Educational Review*, 58: 29–53.

Fine, M. (1991) *Framing Dropouts: Notes on the Politics of an Urban Public High School*. Albany, NY: State University of New York Press.

Fine, M. (ed.) (1994) *Chartering Urban School Reform*. New York: Teachers College Press.

Fishman, J. (1980) Minority language maintenance and the ethnic mother tongue school. *Modern Language Journal*, 64: 167–72.

Fishman, J. (1990) What is reversing language shift (RLS) and how can it succeed? *Journal of Multilingual and Multicultural Development*, 11: 5–36.

Fitzpatrick, F. (1987) *The Open Door*. Clevedon: Multilingual Matters.

Ford, D., Harris, J., Webb, K. and Jones, D. (1994) Rejection or confirmation of racial identity: a dilemma for high-achieving Blacks? *Journal of Educational Thought*, 28: 7–33.

Forsyth, P. and Tallerico, M. (eds) (1993) *City Schools: Leading the Way*. Newbury Park, CA: Corwin Press.

Fossey, J. (1991) Native culture. *FWTAO Newsletter*, 10(1): 37–9.

Foucault, M. (1972) *The Archaeology of Knowledge*. London: Tavistock.

Foucault, M. (1977) *Discipline and Punish: The Birth of the Prison*. New York: Pantheon.

Foucault, M. (1980) *Power/Knowledge: Selected Interviews and Other Writings 1971–1977*. New York: Pantheon.

Foucault, M. (1984) The order of discourse, in M. Shapiro (ed.) *Language and Politics*. London: Blackwell.

Freedman, A. and Richardson, P. (1997) Literacy and genre, in L. van Lier and D. Corson (eds) *Knowledge about Language*. Boston, MA: Kluwer.

Freire, P. (1972) *Pedagogy of the Oppressed*. Harmondsworth: Penguin.

Gándara, P. (1994) The impact of the Education Reform Movement on limited English proficient students, in B. McLeod (ed.) *Language and Learning*. Albany, NY: State University of New York Press.

Garcez, P. (1997) Micro-ethnography, in N. Hornberger and D. Corson (eds) *Research Methods in Language and Education*. Boston, MA: Kluwer.

Garcia, G. (1991) Factors influencing the English reading test performance of Spanish-speaking Hispanic students. *Reading Research Quarterly*, 26: 371–92.

Garcia, O. and Otheguy, R. (1987) The bilingual education of Cuban-American children in Dade County's ethnic schools. *Language and Education*, 1: 83–95.

Gardner, E. (1986) Unique features of a band-controlled school: the Seabird Island Community School. *Canadian Journal of Native Education*, 13: 15–32.

Gardner, H. (1983) *Frames of Mind: The Theory of Multiple Intelligences*. New York: Basic Books.

Gaskell, J., McLaren, A. and Novogrodsky, M. (1989) *Claiming an Education: Feminism and Canadian Schools*. Toronto: Our Schools/Our Selves Education Foundation.

Gass, S. and Selinker, L. (eds) (1983) *Language Transfer and Language Learning*. Rowley, MA: Newbury House.

Gee, J. (1988) The legacies of literacy: from Plato, to Freire, through Harvey Graff. *Harvard Educational Review*, 58: 195–212.

Gérin-Lajoie, D. (1997) French language minority education in Canada, in J. Cummins and D. Corson (eds) *Bilingual Education*. Boston, MA: Kluwer.

Gersten, R. and Woodward, J. (1994) The language minority student and special education: issues, trends and paradoxes. *Exceptional Children*, 60: 310–22.

Gibson, H., Small, A. and Mason, D. (1997) Deaf bilingual bicultural education, in J. Cummins and D. Corson (eds) *Bilingual Education*. Boston, MA: Kluwer.

Gibson, R. (1994) Teaching Shakespeare in schools, in S. Brindley (ed.) *Teaching English*. London: Routledge.

Gilbert, A. (1990) *Les Stéréotypes sexistes en milieu scolaire franco-ontariens: un dossier à découvrir*. Ottawa: Action-Éducation Femmes Ontario.

Gilbert, R. (1997) Critical oracy for active citizenship, in B. Davies and D. Corson (eds) *Oral Discourse and Education*. Boston, MA: Kluwer.

Giles, H., Hewstone, M., Ryan, E. and Johnson, P. (1987) Research on language attitudes, in U. Ammon, N. Dittmar, and K. Mattheier (eds) *Sociolinguistics*. Berlin: Walter de Gruyter.

Gillett, J. (1987) Ethnic bilingual education for Canada's minority groups. *Canadian Modern Language Review*, 43: 337–56.

Ginsburg, M. and Newman, K. (1985) Social inequalities, schooling and teacher education. *Journal of Teacher Education*, 36: 49–54.

Giroux, H. (1993) *Living Dangerously: Multiculturalism and the Politics of Difference*. New York: Peter Lang.

Glaser, R. and Chi, M. (1988) Overview, in M. Chi, R. Glaser and M. Farr (eds) *The Nature of Expertise*. Hillsdale, NJ: Erlbaum Associates.

Glasgow, D. (1980) *The Black Underclass: Poverty, Unemployment and Entrapment of Ghetto Youth*. New York: Vintage Books.

Goldstein, B. (1988) In search of survival: the education and integration of Hmong refugee girls. *Journal of Ethnic Studies*, 16: 1–27.

Goody, J. (1987) *The Interface Between the Written and the Oral*. Cambridge: Cambridge University Press.

Gramsci, A. (1966 [1948]) *Opere di Antonio Gramsci (Quaderni Del Carcere XVIII)*, vols I–XI. Turin: Einaudi.

Grant, C. and Secada, W. (1990) Preparing teachers for diversity, in W. Houston (ed.) *Handbook of Research on Teacher Education*. New York: Macmillan.

Graves, M. (1986) Vocabulary learning and instruction. *Review of Research in Education*, 13: 58–89.

Greenberg, P. (1989) Parents as partners in young children's development and education: a new American fad? Why does it matter? *Young Children*, 44: 61–75.

Griffin, C. (1987) Young women and the transition from school to un/employment: a cultural analysis, in G. Weiner and M. Arnot (eds) *Gender Under Scrutiny: New Inquiries in Education*. London: Unwin Hyman.

Grobe, C. (1981) Syntactic maturity, mechanics, and vocabulary as predictors of quality ratings. *Research in the Teaching of English*, 15: 75–85.

Grundy, S. (1997) Challenging and changing: communicative competence and the classroom, in B. Davies and D. Corson (eds) *Oral Discourse and Education*. Boston, MA: Kluwer.

Gudykunst, W. and Schmidt, K. (1987) Language and ethnic identity: an overview and prologue. *Journal of Language and Social Psychology*, 6: 157–70.

Gumperz, J. (1976) Language, communication and public negotiation, in P. Sanday (ed.) *Anthropology and the Public Interest*. New York: Academic Press.

Gumperz, J. (1982) *Discourse Strategies*. Cambridge: Cambridge University Press.

Guskey, T. (1986) Staff development and the process of teacher change. *Educational Researcher*, 15: 5–12.

Habermas, J. (1971) *Knowledge and Human Interests*. Boston, MA: Beacon Press.

Habermas, J. (1979) *Communication and the Evolution of Society* (translated by T. McCarthy). London: Heinemann.

Hagman, T. and Lahdenperä, J. (1988) Nine years of Finnish-medium education in Sweden: what happens afterwards? The education of minority children in Botkyrka, in T. Skutnabb-Kangas and J. Cummins (eds) *Minority Education: From Shame to Struggle*. Clevedon: Multilingual Matters.

Haig-Brown, C. (1988) *Resistance and Renewal: Surviving the Indian Residential School*. Vancouver: Tillacum.

Hall, C. and Coles, M. (1997) Gender readings: helping boys develop as critical readers. *Gender and Education*, 9: 61–8.

Hall, N. and Robinson, A. (1996) *Learning About Punctuation*. Clevedon, Avon: Multilingual Matters.

Hall, W., Nagy, W. and Linn, R. (1984) *Spoken Words: Effects of Situation and Social Group on Oral Word Usage and Frequency*. Hillsdale, NJ: Lawrence Erlbaum.

Hamayan, E. (1997) Teaching exceptional second language learners, in G. R. Tucker and D. Corson (eds) *Second Language Education*. Boston, MA: Kluwer.

Hamers, J. and Blanc, M. (1983) *Bilingualité et bilinguisme*. Brussels: Pierre Mardaga, Éditeur.

Hamilton, M., Barton, D. and Ivanic, R. (1994) *Worlds of Literacy*. Clevedon: Multilingual Matters.

Hancin-Bhatt, B. and Nagy, W. (1994) Lexical transfer and second language morphological development. *Applied Psycholinguistics*, 15: 289–310.

Hargreaves, A. (1994) Development and desire: a postmodern perspective, in T. Guskey and M. Huberman (eds) *New Paradigms and Practices in Professional Development*. New York: Teachers College Press.

Hargreaves, A. (1996) Revisiting voice. *Educational Researcher*, 25: 12–19.

Harker, R. (1990) Bourdieu: education and reproduction, in R. Harker, C. Mahar and C. Wilkes (eds). *An Introduction to the Work of Pierre Bourdieu*. London: Macmillan.

Harley, B. (ed.) (1995) *Lexical Issues in Language Learning*. Amsterdam: John Benjamins.

Harley, B. (1997) Researching age in language acquisition and use, in N. Hornberger and D. Corson (eds) *Research Methods in Language and Education*. Boston, MA: Kluwer.

Harré, R. and Gillett, G. (1994) *The Discursive Mind*. Thousand Oaks, CA: Sage.

Harris, J. (1991) Kriol: the creation of a new language, in S. Romaine (ed.) *Language in Australia*. Sydney: Cambridge University Press.

Harris, S. (1990) *Two-way Aboriginal Schooling: Education and Cultural Survival*. Canberra: Aboriginal Studies Press.

Harris, S. and Devlin, B. (1997) Bilingual programs involving Aboriginal languages in Australia, in J. Cummins and D. Corson (eds) *Bilingual Education*. Boston, MA: Kluwer.

Harrison, B. (1986) Manokotak: study of school adaptation. *Anthropology and Education Quarterly*, 17: 101–10.

Harry, B., Allen, N. and McLaughlin, M. (1995) Communication versus compliance: African-American parents' involvement in special education. *Educational Children*, 61: 364–77.

Hastings, W. (1988) *The Right to an Education in Maori: The Case from International Law*. Wellington: Institute of Policy Studies.

Hastings, W. (1997) International law and language policies in education, in R. Wodak and D. Corson (eds) *Language Policy and Political Issues in Education*. Boston, MA: Kluwer.

Hayes, D. and Grether, J. (1983) The school year and vacations: when do students learn? *Cornell Journal of Social Relations*, 17: 56–71.

Haynes, N., Comer, J. and Hamilton-Lee, M. (1989) School climate enhancement through parental involvement. *Journal of School Psychology*, 27: 87–90.

Heath, S. (1983) *Ways with Words: Ethnography of Communication in Communities and Classrooms*. Cambridge: Cambridge University Press.

Heath, S. (1986a) The functions and uses of literacy, in S. de Castell, A. Luke and K. Egan (eds) *Literacy, Society and Schooling: A Reader*. Cambridge: Cambridge University Press.

Heath, S. (1986b) Critical factors in literacy development, in S. de Castell, A. Luke and K. Egan (eds) *Literacy, Society and Schooling: A Reader*. Cambridge: Cambridge University Press.

Heimbecker, C. (1997) Bilingual education for indigenous groups in Canada, in J. Cummins and D. Corson (eds) *Bilingual Education*. Boston, MA: Kluwer.

Heller, M. (1994) *Crosswords: Language, Education and Ethnicity in French Ontario*. Berlin: Mouton de Gruyter.

Heller, M. (1995) Language choice, social institutions, and symbolic domination. *Language and Society*, 24: 373–405.

Henry, A. (1992) 'Taking back control: toward an Afrocentric womanist standpoint on the education of Black children', unpublished PhD thesis. University of Toronto.

Herodier, D. (1992) *Status Report on Global Education Plan*. Québec City: Cree Programs Education Services Cree School Board.

Herriman, M. and Burnaby, B. (1996) *Language Policies in English-Dominant Countries*. Clevedon: Multilingual Matters.

Hess, G. (1992) Midway through school reform in Chicago. *International Journal of Educational Reform*, 1: 270–84.

Hess, G. (1994) Chicago school reform, in R. Rossi (ed.) *Schools and Students at Risk*. New York: Teachers College Press.

Hewitt, R. (1989) Creole in the classroom: political grammars and educational vocabularies, in R. Grillo (ed.) *Social Anthropology and the Politics of Language*. London: Routledge.

Hewstone, M. and Giles, H. (1986) Social groups and social stereotypes in intergroup communication, in W. Gudykunst (ed.) *Intergroup Communication*. London: Edward Arnold.

Hingangaroa Smith, G. (1995) New formations of whanau as an innovative intervention into Maori cultural and education crises. *He Pukenga Korero*, 1(1): 18–36.

Hirsch, E. (1987) *Cultural Literacy: What Every American Needs to Know*. Boston, MA: Houghton Mifflin.

Hobsbawm, E. (1989) *The Age of Empire: 1875–1914*. New York: Vintage Books.

Hobsbawm, E. (1994) *Age of Extremes: The Short Twentieth Century 1914–1991*. London: Abacus.

Hoggart, R. (1958) *The Uses of Literacy*. Harmondsworth: Pelican.

Holland, D. and Quinn, N. (eds) (1987) *Cultural Models in Language and Thought*. Cambridge: Cambridge University Press.

Holm, A. and Holm, W. (1990) Rock Point, a Navajo way to go to school: a valediction, in C. Cazden and C. Snow (eds) *English Plus: Issues in Bilingual Education*. Newbury Park, CA: Sage.

Holm, A. and Holm, W. (1995) Navajo language education: retrospect and prospects. *Bilingual Research Journal*, 19: 141–67.

Hornberger, N. (1988a) Misbehaviour, punishment and put-down: stress for Quechua children in school. *Language and Education*, 2: 239–53.

Hornberger, N. (1988b) *Bilingual Education and Language Maintenance: A Southern Peruvian Quechua Case*. Dordrecht: Foris.

Hornberger, N. and Corson, D. (eds) (1997) *Research Methods in Language and Education*. Boston, MA: Kluwer.

House, E. (1990) Methodology and justice. *New Directions for Program Evaluation*, 45: 23–36.

Houston, M. (1992) First things first: why early childhood educators must support home language while promoting second language development. *Multiculturalism/Multiculturalisme*, 14: 47–50.

Humphries, S. (1981) *Hooligans or Rebels?* Oxford: Martin Robertson.

Husen, T. and Postlethwaite, T. (eds) (1994) *The International Encyclopedia of Education*. Oxford: Pergamon.

Iglesias, A. (1985) Cultural conflict in the classroom, in D. Ripich and F. Spinelli (eds) *School Discourse Problems*. London: Taylor and Francis.

International Labour Office (ILO) (1990) *ILO Convention Number 169 concerning Indigenous and Tribal Peoples in Independent Countries*. The Hague: ILO.

Isaacson, S. (1988) Assessing the writing product: qualitative and quantitative measures. *Exceptional Children*, 54: 528–34.

Israelite, N., Ewoldt, C. and Hoffmeister, R. (1992) *Bilingual/Bicultural Education for Deaf and Hard of Hearing Students: A Review of the Literature on the Effects of Native Sign Language on Majority-Language Language Acquisition*, report to the Ontario Ministry of Education. Toronto: Queen's Printer for Ontario.

Jacobs, M. (1991) Indigenous technological capability versus apartheid: a case study. *Comparative Education*, 27: 83–99.

Jakubovits, A. and Wolf, E. (1980) *Immigrant Parents and Port Kembla Schools*. Wollongong: Wollongong Centre for Multicultural Studies.

Janks, H. (1993) *Critical Language Awareness Series: Materials for the Classroom*. Johannesburg: Hodder and Stoughton.

Janks, H. (1997) Teaching about language and power, in R. Wodak and D. Corson (eds) *Language Policy and Political Issues in Education*. Boston, MA: Kluwer.

Jenkins, N. and Cheshire, J. (1990) Gender issues in the GCSE Oral English Examination: Part 1. *Language and Education*, 4: 261–92.

Jenkins, R. (1983) *Lads, Citizens and Ordinary Kids: Working Class Youth Life-styles in Belfast*. London: Routledge.

Johnson, R., Liddell, S. and Erting, C. (1989) *Unlocking the Curriculum: Principles for Achieving Access in Deaf Education*, Gallaudet Research Institute working paper. Washington, DC: Gallaudet University.

Jones, A. (1987) Which girls are 'learning to lose'?, in S. Middleton (ed.) *Women and Education in Aotearoa*. Wellington: Allen and Unwin.

Jordan, C. (1985) Translating culture: from ethnographic information to educational program. *Anthropology and Education Quarterly*, 16: 105–23.

Joshee, R. and Bullard, J. (1992) Tensions between homogeneity and diversity: governmental roles in multicultural education. *Canadian Ethnic Studies*, 24(3): 113–26.

Kaestle, C. (1991) *Literacy in the United States*. New Haven, CT: Yale University Press.

Kanpol, B. (1988) Teacher work tasks as forms of resistance and accommodation to structural factors of schooling. *Urban Education*, 23: 173–87.

Kehoe, J. and Echols, F. (1984) Educational approaches for combating prejudice and racism, in S. Shapson. and V. D'Oyley (eds) *Bilingual and Multicultural Education: Canadian Perspectives*. Philadelphia, PA: Multilingual Matters.

Kelly, A. (1988) Gender differences in teacher–pupil interactions: a meta-analytic review. *Research in Education*, 39: 1–23.

Kenway, J. and Willis, S. (1990) *Hearts and Minds: Self-Esteem and the Schooling of Girls*. London: Falmer.

Kessler, S., Ashenden, D., Connell, R. and Dowsett, G. (1985) Gender relations in secondary schooling. *Sociology of Education*, 58: 34–48.

King, J. (1994) The purpose of schooling for African American children: including cultural knowledge, in E. Hollins, J. King and W. Hayman (eds) *Teaching Diverse Populations*. Albany, NY: State University of New York Press.

Kirkness, V. and Bowman Selkirk, S. (1992) *First Nations and Schools: Triumphs and Struggles*. Toronto: Canadian Education Association.

Klein, J. (1965) *Samples from English Cultures, Vols I and II*. London: Routledge and Kegan Paul.

Klesmer, H. (1994) Assessment and teacher perceptions of ESL students' achievement. *English Quarterly*, 26(3): 8–11.

Kowal, M. and Swain, M. (1994) Using collaborative language production tasks to promote students' language awareness. *Language Awareness*, 3: 73–93.

Kozol, J. (1986) *Illiterate America*. New York: Anchor and Doubleday.

Kozol, J. (1991) *Savage Inequalities*. New York: Crown Publishers.

Kvernmo, S. (1993) Sámi youth in the year 1990, in *Rapport fra konferansen og kulturmønstringa i Kautokeino*. Guovdageaidnu: Sámi Allaskuvla.

Kyle, J. and Woll, B. (1985) *Sign Language: The Study of Deaf People and their Language*. Cambridge: Cambridge University Press.

Kymlicka, W. (1989) *Liberalism, Community and Culture*. Oxford: Clarendon Press.

Labov, W. (1966) Finding out about children's language. *Working Papers in Communication*, 1: 1–30.

Labov, W. (1972a) *Language in the Inner City*. Philadelphia, PA: University of Pennsylvania Press.

Labov, W. (1972b) The logic of non-standard English, in P. Giglioli (ed.) *Language and Social Context*. Harmondsworth: Penguin.

Labov, W. (1982) Objectivity and commitment in linguistic science: the case of the Black English trial in Ann Arbor. *Language in Society*, 11: 165–201.

Labov, W. (1987) Are black and white vernaculars diverging? *American Speech*, 65: 5–12.

Ladd, P. (1991) Making plans for Nigel: the erosion of identity by mainstreaming, in G. Taylor and J. Bishop (eds) *Being Deaf: The Experience of Deafness*. London: Pinter.

Ladson-Billings, G. (1995) Towards a theory of culturally relevant pedagogy. *American Educational Research Journal*, 32: 465–91.

LaGrange, A., Clark, D. and Munroe, E. (1994) Culturally sensitive programming: an Alberta study. *Early Childhood Education*, 27: 29–35.

Lambert, W. (1975) Culture and language as factors in learning and education, in A. Wolfgang (ed.) *Education of Immigrant Students: Issues and Answers*. Toronto: OISE Press/University of Toronto Press.

Landry, R. and Allard, R. (1987) Étude du développement bilingue chez les Acadiens des provinces maritimes, in R. Théberge and J. Lafontant (eds) *Demain, la francophonie en milieu minoritaire?* Saint Boniface: Centre de Recherche Collège Saint-Boniface.

Landry, R. and Allard, R. (1991) Can schools promote additive biligualism in minority group children?, in L. Malavé and G. Duquette (eds) *Language, Culture and Cognition: A Collection of Studies in First and Second Language Acquisition*. Clevedon: Multilingual Matters.

Lange, D. (1992) *The Reform of School Administration in New Zealand*, address by the former Prime Minister of New Zealand, David Lange, to the Conference on Restructuring Education. Toronto: Ontario Institute for Studies in Education, March.

Lapierre, É. (1988) Pour un plan de développement de l'éducation française au Canada. *Revue de l'association canadienne d'éducation de langue française*, 16(1): 25–34.

Lawson, M. and Hogben, D. (1996) The vocabulary learning strategies of foreign language students. *Language Learning*, 46: 101–35.

Leder, G. and Sampson, S. (eds) (1989) *Educating Girls: Practice and Research*. Sydney: Allen and Unwin.

Leith, S. and Slentz, K. (1984) Successful teaching strategies in selected Northern Manitoba schools. *Canadian Journal of Native Education*, 12(1): 24–30.

Lemke, J. (1990) *Talking Science: Language, Learning and Values*. Norwood, NJ: Ablex.

Lentz, F. (1988a) L'Enseignement/apprentissage du français langue maternelle en contexte minoritaire: la situation au Manitoba. *Centre d'études franco-canadienne de l'ouest*, 28: 9–21.

Lentz, F. (1988b) Le français langue maternelle en milieu minoritaire: comment bâtir un cadre didactique pour l'enseignement et l'apprentissage du français langue maternelle. *Education Canada*, Winter: 24–7.

Levasseur-Ouimet, F. (1989) Enseigner en milieu minoritaire: réflexions sur la pédagogie. *Éducation et francophonie*, 17(3): 16–22.

Levin, H. (1990) The educationally disadvantaged are still among us, in J. Bain and J. Herman (eds) *Making Schools Work for Underachieving Minority Students*. New York: Greenwood Press.

Levine, D. and Lezotte, L. (1990) *Unusually Effective Schools*. Madison, WI: National Center for Effective Schools Research and Development.

Levine, R. and White, M. (1986) *Human Conditions: The Cultural Basis of Educational Development*. New York: Routledge and Kegan Paul.

Lewis, K. and Miles, M. (1990) *Improving the Urban High School: What Works and Why*. New York: Teachers College Press.

Lindholm, K. (1997) Two-way bilingual education programs in the United States, in J. Cummins and D. Corson (eds) *Bilingual Education*. Boston, MA: Kluwer.

Lindsay, A. (1992) Oral narrative discourse style of First Nations children and the language of schooling. *Reflections on Canadian Literacy*, 10: 205–9.

Lipman, P. (1997) Restructuring in context: a case study of teacher participation and the dynamics of ideology, race and power. *American Educational Research Journal*, 34: 3–37.

Luke, A. (1997) Critical approaches to literacy, in V. Edwards and D. Corson (eds) *Literacy*. Boston, MA: Kluwer.

Luke, A., Kale, J. and Garbutcheon Singh, M. (1995) Talking difference: discourses on aboriginal identity in grade one classrooms, in D. Corson (ed.) *Discourse and Power in Educational Organizations*. Cresskill, NJ: Hampton Press.

Lyle, S. (1997) Children's collaborative talk, in B. Davies and D. Corson (eds) *Oral Discourse and Education*. Boston, MA: Kluwer.

Maccoby, E. and Jacklin, C. (1974) *The Psychology of Sex Differences*. Stanford, CA: Stanford University Press.

Mackay, R. and Myles, L. (1989) *Native Student Dropouts in Ontario Schools*. Toronto: Queen's Printer for Ontario.

MacKinnon, K. and Densham, J. (1989) Ethnolinguistic diversity in Britain: policies and practice in school and society. *Language, Culture and Curriculum*, 2: 75–89.

Maclear, K. (1994) The myth of the 'model minority': rethinking the education of Asian Canadians. *Our Schools/Our Selves*, 5(3): 54–76.

Macpherson, J. (1983) *The Feral Classroom*. London: Routledge.

Madison, A.-M. (1992) Primary inclusion of culturally diverse minority program participants in the evaluation process. *New Directions for Program Evaluation*, 53: 35–43.

Magga, O. (1995) The Sámi Language Act, in T. Skutnabb-Kangas and R. Phillipson (eds) *Linguistic Human Rights*. The Hague: Mouton de Gruyter.

Mallea, J. (1989) *Schooling in a Plural Canada*. Philadelphia, PA: Multilingual Matters.

Mason, D. (1993) Personal communication via Bell Canada Relay Service transcriptionist.

Mason, D. (1994) Bilingual/bicultural deaf education is appropriate, in Association of Canadian Educators of the Hearing Impaired, *Occasional Monograph Series, no. 2*. Toronto: Association of Canadian Educators of the Hearing Impaired.

May, S. (1994) *Making Multicultural Education Work*. Clevedon: Multilingual Matters.

May, S. (1997a) Critical ethnography, in N. Hornberger and D. Corson (eds) *Research Methods in Language and Education*. Boston, MA: Kluwer.

May, S. (1997b) School language policies, in R. Wodak and D. Corson (eds) *Language Policy and Political Issues in Education*. Boston, MA: Kluwer.

Maylath, B. (1994) 'Words make a difference: effects of Greco-Latinate and Anglo-Saxon lexical variation on post-secondary-level writing assessment in English', unpublished PhD thesis. University of Minnesota.

McAndrew, M. (1986) Le traitement du racisme, de l'immigration et de la réalité multi-ethnique dans les manuels scolaires francophones au Québec. *Canadian Ethnic Studies*, 18(2): 130–42.

McCarthy, M. (1990) *Vocabulary*. Oxford: Oxford University Press.

McCarty, T. (1989) School as community: the Rough Rock Demonstration School. *Harvard Educational Review*, 59: 484–503.

McCarty, T. (1997a) American Indian, Alaska Native, and Native Hawaiian bilingual education, in J. Cummins and D. Corson (eds) *Bilingual Education*. Boston, MA: Kluwer.

McCarty, T. (1997b) Teacher research methods in language and education, in N. Hornberger and D. Corson (eds) *Research Methods in Language and Education*. Boston, MA: Kluwer.

McCaskill, D. (1987) Revitalization of Indian culture: Indian cultural survival schools, in J. Barman, Y. Hébert and D. McCaskill (eds) *Indian Education in Canada. Volume 2: The Challenge*. Vancouver: University of British Columbia Press.

McConaghy, T. (1989) The quiet revolution: school-based budgeting, *Phi Delta Kappan*, 70: 486–7.

McDougall, D. (1985) The reduction of prejudice through education: strategies for action in Canada and implications for research. *Canadian Ethnic Studies*, 17(3): 81–90.

McDowall, D. (1994) *A Modern History of the Kurds*. London: I. B. Tauris.

McGonigal, J. (1997) Using oral discourse in literary studies, in B. Davies and D. Corson (eds) *Oral Discourse and Education*. Boston, MA: Kluwer.

McKay, A. and McKay, B. (1987) Education as a total way of life: the Nisga'a experience, in J. Barman, Y. Hébert and D. McCaskill (eds) *Indian Education in Canada. Volume 2: The Challenge*. Vancouver: University of British Columbia Press.

Meara, P. (1982) Vocabulary acquisition: a neglected aspect of language learning, in V. Kinsella (ed.) *Surveys 1: Eight State-of-the-Art Articles on Key Areas in Language Teaching*. Cambridge: Cambridge University Press.

Meara, P. (1993) *Vocabulary in a Second Language: Volume III 1986–1990*. Swansea: Centre for Applied Language Studies.

Mehan, H., Hubbard, L., Lintz, A. and Villanueva, R. (1994) *Tracking Untracking: The Consequences of Placing Low Track Students in High Track Classes*. Santa Cruz, CA: National Center for Research on Cultural Diversity and Second Language Learning, University of California.

Mercer, N. (1997) Effective educational talk, in B. Davies and D. Corson (eds) *Oral Discourse and Education*. Boston, MA: Kluwer.

Mercy, J. and Steelman, L. (1982) Familial influence on the intellectual attainment of children. *American Sociological Review*, 47: 532–42.

Michaels, S. (1981) 'Sharing time': children's narrative styles and differential access to literacy. *Language in Society*, 10: 423–42.

Minister of Education (1983/84) *Ministerial Papers Number 1–6*. Melbourne: Department of Education.

Ministry of Education (1987) *Better Schools in Western Australia: A Program for Schools*. Perth: Ministry of Education.

Ministry of Education and Training (MET) (1995) *The Ontario Grade 9 Reading and Writing Test: The Provincial Report of the 1994–95 Test*. Toronto: Queen's Printer for Ontario.

Moffett, J. (1968) *Teaching the Universe of Discourse*. London: Houghton Mifflin.

Moffett, J. (1989) Censorship and spiritual education. *English Education*, 21: 70–87.

Moore, D. (1992) The case for parent and community involvement, in G. Hess (ed.) *Empowering Teachers and Parents: School Restructuring through the Eyes of Anthropologists*. New York: Bergin and Garvey.

Moorfield, J. (1987) Implications for schools of research findings in bilingual education, in W. Hirsh (ed.) *Living Languages*. Auckland: Heinemann.

Mougeon, R. and Beniak, E. (1988a) Minority language schooling without home language maintenance: impact on language proficiency, in A. Holmen (ed.) *Copenhagen Studies in Bilingualism, Volume 4: Bilingualism and the Individual*. Clevedon: Multilingual Matters.

Mougeon, R. and Beniak, E. (1988b) Should the French-Canadian minorities open their schools to the children of the Anglophone majority?, in J. Jorgensen (ed.) *Copenhagen Studies in Bilingualism, Volume 5: Bilingualism in Society and School*. Clevedon: Multilingual Matters.

Munoz, B. and Garcia-Blanco, A. (1989) Special issue on community based education: part 1. *Harvard Educational Review*, 59(4): *passim*.

Munoz, B. and Garcia-Blanco, A. (1990) Special issue on community based education: part 2. *Harvard Educational Review*, 60(1): *passim*.

Murphy, J. (1980) School administrators besieged: a look at Australian and American education. *American Journal of Education*, 88: 1–26.

Myles, D. and Ratzlaff, H. (1988) Teachers' bias toward visible ethnic minority groups in special education referrals. *B.C. Journal of Special Education*, 12(1) 19–28.

Nation, I. (1990) *Teaching and Learning Vocabulary*. Rowley, MA: Newbury House.

Nation, P. and Carter, R. (1989) *Vocabulary Acquisition (AILA Review 6)*. Amsterdam: Free University Press.

National Coalition of Advocates for Students (1988) *New Voices: Immigrant Voices in US Public Schools*. Boston, MA: National Coalition of Advocates for Students.

National Coalition of Advocates for Students (1992) *The Good Common School: Making the Vision Work for All Children*. Boston, MA: National Coalition of Advocates for Students.

National Indian Brotherhood (1972) *Indian Control of Indian Education*, policy paper presented to Minister of Indian Affairs and Northern Development, Ottawa.

National Languages and Literacy Institute of Australia (NLLIA) (1993) *Workplan '93*. Canberra: NLLIA.

Nemetz Robinson, G. (1978) *Language and Multicultural Education: An Australian Perspective*. Sydney: ANZ.

Nielsen, L. and Piché, G. (1981) The influence of headed nominal complexity and lexical choice on teachers' evaluation of writing. *Research in the Teaching of English*, 15: 65–73.

Nieto, S. (1995) *On the Brink Between Triumph and Disaster*, paper presented at the Annual Meeting of the AERA (American Educational Research Association), San Francisco, CA, April.

Nisbet, R. (1967) *The Sociological Tradition*. London: Heinemann.

Nixon, J. (1987) The teacher as researcher: contradictions and continuities. *Peabody Journal of Education*, 64: 20–32.

Nozick, R. (1974) *Anarchy, State and Utopia*. Oxford: Blackwell.

NSW Department of Education (1989) *The Carrick Report*. Sydney: Department of Education.

Oakes, J. (1987) *Improving Inner-City Schools*. Rutgers, NJ: Rand Corporation.

Oakes, J., Kuartz, K. and Wells, A. (1993) Creating middle schools: technical, normative and political considerations. *Elementary School Journal*, 93: 461–79.

Ogbu, J. (1987) Variability in minority school performance: a problem in search of an explanation. *Anthropology and Education Quarterly*, 18: 312–34.

Okano, K. (1992) *School to Work in Japan: A Bilingual Ethnography*. Philadelphia, PA: Multilingual Matters.

Olson, D. (1997) Talking about text and the culture of literacy, in B. Davies and D. Corson (eds) *Oral Discourse and Education*. Boston, MA: Kluwer.

Osborne, B. (1991) Towards an ethnology of culturally responsive pedagogy in small-scale remote communities: Native American and Torres Strait Islander. *Qualitative Studies in Education*, 4: 1–17.

Pascal, C. (1987) Democratised primary school government: relevant theoretical constructs. *Oxford Review of Education*, 13: 321–30.

Peal, E. and Lambert, W. (1962) The relation of bilingualism to intelligence. *Psychological Monographs*, 76(546): 1–23.

Peirce, B. (1997) Critical discourse research, in N. Hornberger and D. Corson (eds) *Research Methods in Language and Education*. Boston, MA: Kluwer.

Pence, A., Kuehene, V., Greenwood-Church, M., Opehokew, M. and Mulligan, V. (1992) First Nations early childhood care and education: the Meadow Lake tribal council/school of child and youth care curriculum development project. *Multiculturalism/Multiculturalisme*, 14(2/3): 15–17.

Penetito, W. (1986) *Towards Social Justice: Curriculum, Culture and Context*, paper presented to Wellington Institute for Educational Research, Education House, Wellington.

Peters, R. (1967) *The Concept of Education*. London: Routledge and Kegan Paul.

Philips, S. (1972) Participant structures and communicative competence: Warm Springs children in community and classroom, in C. Cazden, V. John and D. Hymes (eds) *Functions of Language in the Classroom*. New York: Teachers College Press.

Philips, S. (1975) Literacy as a mode of communication on the Warm Springs Indian Reservation, in E. H. Lenneberg and E. Lenneberg (eds) *Foundations of*

Language Development: A Multidisciplinary Approach. New York: Academic Press.

Philips, S. (1983) *The Invisible Culture: Communication in Classroom and Community on the Warm Springs Indian Reservation*. New York: Longman.

Philips, S., Steele, S. and Tanz, C. (eds) (1987) *Language, Gender, and Sex in Comparative Perspective*. Cambridge: Cambridge University Press.

Popkewitz, T. (1982) Educational reform as the organization of ritual: stability as change. *Journal of Education*, 164: 5–29.

Provost, M. (1990) La situation en gros plan: acquis et défis réunis. *Vie Pédagogique*, 67(mai-juin): 38–40.

Purves, A. (1988) Commentary – research on written composition: a response to Hillocks' report. *Research in the Teaching of English*, 22: 104–8.

Ramirez, J. (1992) Executive summary. *Bilingual Research Journal*, 16: 1–62.

Randall, G. (1987) Gender differences in pupil–teacher interaction in workshops and laboratories, in G. Weiner and M. Arnot (eds) *Gender under Scrutiny*. London: Hutchinson.

Rasinski, T. and Fredericks, A. (1989) Dimensions of parent involvement. *Reading Teacher*, 43: 180–2.

Ray, D. (1984) Cultural identity and education, in R. Samuda, J. Berry and M. Laferrière (eds) *Multiculturalism in Canada: Social and Educational Perspectives*. Toronto: Allyn and Bacon.

Reay, D. (1991) Intersections of gender, race and class in the primary school. *British Journal of Sociology of Education*, 12: 163–82.

Regnier, R. (1987) Survival schools as emancipatory education. *Canadian Journal of Native Education*, 14(2): 42–53.

Reid, E. (1988) Linguistic minorities and language education: the English experience. *Journal of Multilingual and Multicultural Development*, 9: 181–91; 220–3.

Rezai-Rashti, G. (1994) The dilemma of working with minority female students in Canadian high schools. *Canadian Women's Studies/Les Cahiers de la femme*, 14(2): 76–82.

Rezai-Rashti, G. (1995) Connecting racism and sexism: the dilemma of working with minority female students, in R. Ng, P. Staton, and J. Scane (eds) *Anti-Racism, Feminism and Critical Approaches to Education*. Westport, CT: Bergin and Harvey.

Richards, M. (1991) Heritage language programs in Canada. *Reflections on Canadian Literacy*, 9(3 and 4): 170–4.

Richardson, B. (1994) Improving Native education. *Early Childhood Education*, 27(1): 25–8.

Ringbom, H. (1987) *The Role of the First Language in Foreign Language Learning*. Clevedon: Multilingual Matters.

Roberts, L. and Clifton, R. (1988) Inuit attitudes and cooperative learning. *McGill Journal of Education*, 23: 213–30.

Rodda, M., Grove, C. and Finch, B. (1986) Mainstreaming and the education of Deaf students. *Alberta Journal of Educational Research*, 32: 140–53.

Romaine, S. (1989) *Bilingualism*. Oxford: Basil Blackwell.

Romaine, S. (ed.) (1991) *Language in Australia*. Sydney: Cambridge University Press.

Ross, R. (1996) *Returning to the Teachings: Exploring Aboriginal Justice*. Toronto: Penguin.

Royal Commission on Learning in Ontario (1995) *For the Love of Learning.* Toronto: Queen's Printer for Ontario.

Rudduck, J. (1994) *Developing a Gender Policy in Secondary Schools: Individuals and Institutions.* Philadelphia, PA: Open University Press.

Rumbaut, R. and Ima, K. (1987) *The Adaptation of South-East Asian Refugee Youth.* San Diego, CA: Office of Refugee Resettlement.

Rury, J. and Mirel, J. (1997) The political economy of urban education. *Review of Research in Education,* 22: 49–110.

Ryan, J. (1992) Formal schooling and deculturation: nursing practice and the erosion of Native communication styles. *Alberta Journal of Educational Research,* 38: 91–103.

Ryan, J. (1994) Organizing the facts: Aboriginal education and cultural differences in school discourse and knowledge. *Language and Education,* 8: 251–71.

Ryan, J. (1998) *Teaching and Learning in Culturally Diverse Schools.* Clevedon: Multilingual Matters.

Sanchez, G. (1934) Bilingualism and mental measures: a word of caution. *Journal of Applied Psychology,* 18: 765–72.

Sarangi, S. and Baynham, M. (eds) (1996) Special issue on discursive construction of educational identities. *Language and Education,* 10(2 and 3): *passim.*

Saville-Troike, M. (1984) What really matters in second language learning for academic achievement. *TESOL Quarterly,* 18: 199–219.

Scollon, R. and Scollon, S. (1981) *Narrative Literacy and Face in Inter-Ethnic Communication.* Norwood, NJ: Ablex.

Scollon, R. and Scollon, S. (1984) Cooking it up and boiling it down: abstracts in Athabaskan children's story retellings, in D. Tannen (ed.) *Coherence in Spoken and Written Discourse.* Norwood, NJ: Ablex.

Scribner, S. and Cole, M. (1981) *The Psychology of Literacy.* Cambridge, MA: Harvard University Press.

Senior, S. (1993) Canadian Native intelligence studies: a brief review. *Canadian Journal of Native Education,* 20(1): 148–56.

Sharpe, F. (1993) *Devolution: Where are We Now?',* paper presented to the Annual Conference of the Australian Council for Educational Administration, Adelaide, September.

Sinclair, J. and Coulthard, M. (1975) *Towards an Analysis of Discourse.* Oxford: Oxford University Press.

Singleton, D. (1997) Age and second language learning, in G. R. Tucker and D. Corson (eds) *Second Language Education.* Boston, MA: Kluwer.

Skeggs, B. (1991) Postmodernism: what is all the fuss about? *British Journal of Sociology of Education,* 12: 255–67.

Skutnabb-Kangas, T. (1981) *Bilingualism or Not: The Education of Minorities.* Philadelphia, PA: Multilingual Matters.

Skutnabb-Kangas, T. (1997) Human rights and language policy in education, in R. Wodak and D. Corson (eds) *Language Policy and Political Issues in Education.* Boston, MA: Kluwer.

Skutnabb-Kangas, T. and Cummins, J. (eds) (1988) *Minority Education: From Shame to Struggle.* Clevedon: Multilingual Matters.

Small, P. (1997) Kids in school cast as critics of 'toxic influences' on TV, *Toronto Star,* 17 April.

Smith, D. (1986) The anthropology of literacy acquisition, in B. Schieffelin and P. Gilmore (eds) *The Acquisition of Literacy: Ethnographic Perspectives*. Norwood, NJ: Ablex.

Smith, J. and Tomlinson, S. (1989) *The School Effect: A Study of Racial Comprehensives*. London: London Policy Studies Institute.

Smyth, J. (1991) *Teachers as Collaborative Learners: Challenging Dominant Forms of Supervision*. Buckingham: Open University Press.

Smyth, J. (ed.) (1993) *A Socially Critical View of the Self-Managing School*. London: Falmer.

Smyth, J. (1996) The socially just alternative to the self-managing school, in *International Handbook for Educational Leadership and Administration*. Boston, MA: Kluwer.

Spindler, G. (ed.) (1982) *Doing the Ethnography of Schooling*. New York: CBS Publishing.

St Louis, R. (1993) Personal communication via Bell Canada Relay Service transcriptionist.

Stairs, A. (1985) The developmental context of Native language literacy: Inuit children and Inuktitut education, in B. Burnaby (ed.) *Promoting Native Writing Systems in Canada*. Toronto: OISE Press/University of Toronto Press.

Stairs, A. (1990) Questions behind the question of vernacular education: a study in literacy, Native language, and English. *English Quarterly*, 22: 103–24.

Stairs, A. (1991) Learning processes and teaching roles in Native education: cultural base and cultural brokerage. *Canadian Modern Language Review*, 47: 280–94.

Stairs, A. (1994) Indigenous ways to go to school: exploring many visions. *Journal of Multilingual and Multicultural Development*, 15: 63–76.

Stanovich, K. and Cunningham, A. (1992) Studying the consequences of literacy within a literate society: the cognitive correlates of print exposure. *Memory and Cognition*, 20: 51–68.

Stein, P. and Potenza, E. (1995) *Level Best: An English Course for Secondary Schools*. Cape Town: Maskew Miller Longman.

Stewart, D. (1993) Bi-Bi to MCE? *American Annals of the Deaf*, 138: 331–7.

Stewart, D. and Akamatsu, C. (1988) The coming of age of American Sign Language. *Anthropology and Education Quarterly*, 19: 235–52.

Stones, R. (1983) *'Pour Out the Cocoa, Janet': Sexism in Children's Books*. York: Longman for Schools Council.

Street, B. (1997) Social literacies, in V. Edwards and D. Corson (eds) *Literacy*. Boston, MA: Kluwer Academic.

Sullivan, M., Douglas, A., Mason, J., McAlpine, L., Pittinger, C. and Smith, D. (1991) Reading and writing with the Algonquin, Cree, Micmac and Mohawk: a learning experience for McGill instructors. *McGill Journal of Education*, 26: 209–17.

Suzuki, D. (1995) The hubris of global economics, *Toronto Star*, 29 July.

Sylvester, E. (1996) 'Inside, outside and in-between: identities, literacies and educational policies in the lives of Cambodian women and girls in Philadelphia', unpublished PhD thesis. University of Philadelphia.

Tallerico, M. (1993) Governing urban schools, in P. Forsyth and M. Tallerico (eds) *City Schools: Leading the Way*. Newbury Park, CA: Corwin Press.

Taylor, C. (1992) *Multiculturalism and 'The Politics of Recognition'*. Princeton, NJ: Princeton University Press.

Thompson, E. P. (1968) *The Making of the English Working Class*. Harmondsworth: Pelican.

Thompson, J. (1984) *Studies in the Theory of Ideology*. Cambridge: Polity Press.

Tiede, K. (1996) 'Appropriating the discourse of science: a case study of a grade eight science class', unpublished PhD thesis. University of Toronto.

Tomlinson, S. (1984) *Home and School in Multicultural Britain*. London: Batsford Academic.

Tomlinson, S. (ed.) (1994) *Educational Reform and its Consequences*. London: Rivers Oram Press.

Trapnell, L. (1996) *Brought Together: Informal and Formal Education in an Indigenous Programme in the Amazon Basin*, paper presented at the Sámi Education Council International Jubilee Conference, Guovdageaidnu, Norway.

Tsolidis, G. (1990) Ethnic minority girls and self-esteem, in J. Kenway and S. Willis (eds) *Hearts and Minds: Self-Esteem and the Schooling of Girls*. London: Falmer.

Tucker, G. R. and Corson, D. (eds) (1997) *Second Language Education*. Boston, MA: Kluwer.

Umbel, V. and Oller, D. (1995) Developmental changes in receptive vocabulary in Hispanic bilingual school children, in B. Harley (ed.) *Lexical Issues in Language Learning*. Amsterdam: John Benjamins.

Ungerleider, C. (1992) Immigration, multiculturalism, and citizenship: the development of the Canadian social justice infrastructure. *Canadian Ethnic Studies*, 24(3): 7–21.

Vallen, T. and Stijnen, S. (1987) Language and educational success of indigenous and non-indigenous minority students in the Netherlands. *Language and Education*, 1: 109–24.

Van Lier, L. and Corson, D. (eds) (1997) *Knowledge about Language*. Boston, MA: Kluwer.

Verhoeven, L. (1994) Transfer in bilingual development: the linguistic interdependence hypothesis revisited. *Language Learning*, 44: 381–415.

Vigil, J. (1994) Gangs, social control, and ethnicity: ways to redirect, in S. Heath and M. McLaughlin (eds) *Identity and Inner-City Youth: Beyond Ethnicity and Gender*. New York: Teachers College Press.

Vogt, L., Jordan, C. and Tharp, R. (1987) Explaining school failure, producing school success: two cases. *Anthropology and Education Quarterly*, 19: 276–86.

Wagner, S. (with Pierre Granier) (1991) *Analphabétisme de minorité et alphabétisation d'affirmation nationale à propos de l'Ontario français. Volume 1: Synthèse théorique et historique*. Ottawa: Mutual Press.

Waite, D. (1992) Instructional supervision from a situational perspective. *Teaching and Teacher Education*, 8: 319–32.

Walberg, H. and Tsai, S. (1983) Matthew effects in education. *American Educational Research Journal*, 20: 359–73.

Walker, J. (1988) *Louts and Legends: Male Youth Culture in an Inner-City School*. Sydney: Allen and Unwin.

Walker, J. (1991) Building on youth cultures in the secondary curriculum, in D. Corson (ed.) *Education for Work: Background to Policy and Curriculum*. Clevedon: Multilingual Matters.

Wallace, C. (1997) The role of language awareness in critical pedagogy, in L. van Lier and D. Corson (eds) *Knowledge about Language*. Boston, MA: Kluwer Academic.

Walsh, M. (1991) Overview of indigenous languages of Australia, in S. Romaine (ed.) *Language in Australia*. Sydney: Cambridge University Press.

Wang, M. and Gordon, E. (1994) *Educational Resilience in Inner-City America*. Hillsdale, NJ: Lawrence Erlbaum.

Ward, A. (1990) Communicative inequality: the participation of Native Indian and non-Native children in instructional dialogue in a cross-cultural kindergarten class. *Reflections on Canadian Literacy*, 8(1): 22–8.

Watson-Gegeo, K. (1997) Classroom ethnography, in N. Hornberger and D. Corson (eds) *Research Methods in Language and Education*. Boston, MA: Kluwer.

Wehlage, G., Rutter, R., Smith, G., Lesko, N. and Fernandez, R. (1989) *Reducing the Risk: Schools as Communities of Support*. London: Falmer.

Wells, G. (1986) *The Meaning Makers: Children Learning Language and Using Language to Learn*. Portsmouth, NH: Heinemann.

Wells, G. (1989) Language in the classroom: literacy and collaborative talk. *Language and Education*, 3: 251–74.

Wells, G. (1992) The centrality of talk in education, in K. Norman (ed.) *Thinking Voices*. London: Hodder and Stoughton.

West, R. and Stanovich, K. (1991) The incidental acquisition of information from reading. *Psychological Science*, 2: 325–30.

Westgate, D. (1997) Preconditions for successful small-group talk in the classroom, in B. Davies and D. Corson (eds) *Oral Discourse and Education*. Boston, MA: Kluwer.

Wilgosh, L. (1994) The underachievement of girls: a societal rather than a gender issue. *Education Canada*, spring: 18–23.

Wilgosh, L. and Mulcahy, R. (1986) Assessing intellectual performance of culturally different, Inuit children with the WISC-R. *Canadian Journal of Behavioural Sciences*, 18: 270–7.

Willis, P. (1977) *Learning to Labour*. Farnborough: Saxon House.

Wilson, W. (1987) *The Truly Disadvantaged: The Inner City, the Underclass, and Public Policy*. Chicago: University of Chicago Press.

Wodak, R. (ed.) (1989) *Language, Power and Ideology: Studies in Political Discourse*. Amsterdam: John Benjamins.

Wodak, R. (1995) Power, discourse, and styles of female leadership in school committee meetings, in D. Corson (ed.) *Discourse and Power in Educational Organizations*. Cresskill, NJ: Hampton Press.

Wodak, R. (ed.) (1997) *Discourse and Gender*. Thousand Oaks, CA: Sage.

Wong-Fillmore, L. and Valdez, C. (1986) Teaching bilingual learners, in M. Wittrock (ed.) *Handbook of Research on Teaching*. New York: Macmillan.

Wrong, D. (1979) *Power: Its Forms, Bases and Uses*. Oxford: Basil Blackwell.

Yau, M., Cheng, M. and Ziegler, S. (1993) *The 1991 Every Secondary Student Survey, Part III: Program Level & Student Achievement*. Toronto: Toronto Board of Education.

Young, I. (1981) Towards a critical theory of justice. *Social Theory and Practice*, 7: 279–302.

Young, R. (1987) Critical theory and classroom questioning. *Language and Education*, 1: 125–34.

Young, R. (1992) *Critical Theory and Classroom Talk*. Clevedon: Multilingual Matters.

Young, R. (1996) *Intercultural Communication*. Clevedon: Multilingual Matters.

INDEX